The Battle for Your Heart

God Wins; Satan Loses

Ronald W. Busby

TEACH Services, Inc.
P U B L I S H I N G
www.TEACHServices.com • (800) 367-1844

All rights reserved. No portion of this book may be reproduced, stored in a retrieval system, or transmitted in any form or by any means (electronic, mechanical, photocopy, recording, scanning, or other) except for brief quotations and critical reviews or articles, without prior written permission of Jeannette Johnson.

The author assumes full responsibility for the accuracy of all facts and quotations as cited in this book. The opinions expressed in this book are the author's personal views and interpretations, and do not necessarily reflect those of the publisher.

This book is provided with the understanding that the publisher is not engaged in giving spiritual, legal, medical, or other professional advice. If authoritative advice is needed, the reader should seek the counsel of a competent professional.

Copyright © 2022 Ronald W. Busby
Copyright © 2022 TEACH Services, Inc.
ISBN-13: 978-1-4796-1309-0 (Paperback)
ISBN-13: 978-1-4796-1310-6 (ePub)
Library of Congress Control Number: 2021915166

All Scripture quotations, unless otherwise indicated, are taken from the King James Version®. Public domain.

Scripture quotations marked NIV are taken from the New International Version. Copyright © 1973, 1978, 1984, 2011 by Biblica, Inc®. Used by permission. All rights reserved worldwide.

Scripture quotations marked NASB are taken from the New American Standard Bible. Copyright © 1960, 1962, 1963, 1968, 1971, 1972, 1973, 1975, 1977, 1995 by The Lockman Foundation. Used by permission.

Scripture quotations marked ESV are taken from the English Standard Version. Copyright © 2001 by Crossway, a publishing ministry of Good News Publishers. Used by permission. All rights reserved.

Scripture quotations marked CSB are taken from the Christian Standard Bible. Copyright © 2017 by Holman Bible Publishers. Used by permission. Christian Standard Bible® and CSB® are federally registered trademarks of Holman Bible Publishers. All rights reserved.

Scripture quotations marked Comparative Study Bible, AMP are taken from the Comparative Study Bible, Amplified Bible. Copyright © 1984 by The Zondervan Corporation, Grand Rapids, Michigan, 49530, U.S.A. Library of Congress Catalog Card Number: 84-51724. All rights reserved. The Amplified Bible, Copyright © 1965.

Scripture quotations marked RSV are taken from the Revised Standard Version. Copyright © 1946, 1952, and 1971 the Division of Christian Education of the National Council of the Churches of Christ in the United States of America. Used by permission. All rights reserved.

Scripture quotations marked NEB are taken from the New English Bible. Copyright© 1961, 1970 by Cambridge University Press, Oxford University Press. All rights reserved.

Scripture quotations marked HCSB are taken from the Holman Christian Standard Bible®. Copyright © 1999, 2000, 2002, 2003, 2009 by Holman Bible Publishers. Used with permission by Holman Bible Publishers, Nashville, Tennessee. All rights reserved.

Scripture quotations marked TLB are taken from The Living Bible. Copyright © 1971 by Tyndale House Foundation. Used by permission.

Scripture quotations marked LASB are taken from the Life Application Study Bible, Personal Size Edition, New Living Translation (Second Edition), pp. 2171–2172, Tyndale House Publishers, Inc., Carol Stream, Illinois, 2004.

Scripture quotations marked CJB are taken from the Complete Jewish Bible by David H. Stern. Copyright © 1998. All rights reserved. Used by permission of Messianic Jewish Publishers, 6120 Day Long Lane, Clarksville, MD 21029. www.messianicjewish.net.

Scripture quotations marked GNT are from the Good News Translation in Today's English Version—Second Edition Copyright © 1992 by American Bible Society. Used by Permission.

Scripture quotations marked NIRV are taken from the Holy Bible, NEW INTERNATIONAL READER'S VERSION®. Copyright © 1996, 1998 Biblica. All rights reserved throughout the world. Used by permission of Biblica.

Scripture quotations marked NKJV, New Millennium Edition, are taken from The Holy Bible, New King James Version. Copyright © 1982 by Thomas Nelson, Inc.

Dedication

To Neil V. Busby ...

My brother Neil was always there. Praying. Encouraging. Supporting.

Sharing my belief

in the eternal, present-truth importance of the Revelation message.

His has been a God-given and Holy Spirit-enabling ministry

that has blessed me more than I can ever express.

To Chester Jarrett ...

A scholar of extraordinary stripe whose fluency in unraveling

the intricacies of the book of

Revelation inspired my own understanding with a sense and

order that many Revelation studies

have lacked heretofore.

* * * * * * * * * * * * *

The history which the great I AM has marked out in His word,

uniting link after link in the prophetic chain,

from eternity in the past to eternity in the future,

tells us where we are today in the procession of the ages,

and what may be expected in the time to come.

All that prophecy has foretold as coming to pass,

until the present time,

has been traced on the pages of history,

and we may be assured that all which is yet to come

will be fulfilled in its order.[1]

---

1   Ellen G. White, *Education* (Mountain View, CA: Pacific Press, 1903), p. 178.

Resources

Books/Materials by Ellen G. White
Acts of the Apostles, The
Christ's Object Lessons
Christian Experience and Teachings of Ellen G. White
Christian Service
Christ Triumphant
Confrontation
Counsels to Writers and Editors
Desire of Ages, The
Early Writings
Education
Ellen G. White 1888 Materials, The
Faith I Live By, The
Fundamentals of Christian Education
Great Controversy, The
Home Missionary, The
Last Day Events
Letters & Manuscripts
Maranatha
Manuscript Release
Patriarchs and Prophets
Prophets and Kings
Publishing Ministry
Review and Herald, The
Selected Messages, book 1
Selected Messages, book 2
Selected Messages, book 3

SDA Bible Commentary (Ellen G. White Comments in)

Testimonies for the Church, vols. 1, 2, 5, 6, 8, 9

Testimonies to Ministers and Gospel Workers

A Word to the Little Flock

Books/Materials by Other Authors/Sources

Abundant Life Bible Amplifier, The. Daniel 7–12 (William H. Shea)

Adult Sabbath School Bible Study Guide, 3rd Quarter 2006. July Lesson 1 (Alden Thompsen)

Adult Sabbath School Bible Study Guide, 1st Quarter 2020. Feb. Lesson 8, (Elias Brasil de Souza)

Adult Sabbath School Lessons, October 25, 1981 (Seaton, Bernard E.)

Catholic Moment, The (Neuhaus, Richard)

Daniel and the Revelation (Uriah Smith)

Encyclopedia of Religion, The (Robert A. Morey)

God Cares (C. Mervyn Maxwell)

Islam Unveiled: The True Desert Storm (Robert A. Morey)

New World Order (Russell Burrill)

Roman Catholicism (Loraine Boettner)

SDA Bible Commentary, The, vols. 4, 5, 6, 7, 7a, 8

Signs of the Times, The

Strong's Concordance

Various websites

Wikipedia

World Religions: From Ancient History to the Present

Charts

To view the charts included in this book at a higher resolution, go to: www.tsibooks.com/pdf/BusbyCharts.pdf

Table of Contents

A Word to the Reader 11
1. The Book of Revelation. 15
2. Revelation 1–3: Introduction to Revelation and the Seven Churches 25
3. Revelation 4–6: Setting Up the Judgment and the Seven Seals 52
4. Revelation 6 and 7: Seals Number 5, 6, and 7 and the 144,000. 73
5. Revelation 8, 9, and 16: The Trumpets and Vials, Numbers 1–4 87
6. Revelation 9 and 16: The Trumpets and Vials, Numbers 5–7 101
7. Revelation 10 and 11: The Rise of Protestantism, Communism, and Atheism: Daniel 12 and the Seven Thunders of Revelation 10. 121
8. Revelation 12 and 13: Three Allegories—The "7/10s" of Prophecy 137
9. Revelation 17: The Third "7/10" of Revelation 17 151
10. Revelation 14 and 15: The Three Angels' Messages and Two Consequences 164
11. Revelation 18 and 19: The End—Last Call, Last Reward, Last Battle. 179
Chart 1: A Frameworks System for Understanding the Bible 23
Chart 2: Apostasy and Reformation 41
Chart 3: The Wilderness Tabernacle 53
Chart 4: 7 Seals: Scenes of the Judgment 61
Chart 5: Believer Tree of Origins. 65
Chart 6: The Seven Heads/10 Horns of Revelation 12 143
Chart 7: Seven Thunders: Revelation 10/Daniel 12. 98
Chart 8: Prophetic Scene Sequence 120

Appendix 1: Daniel 1–12: The Book of Daniel 190
Appendix 2: Daniel 2: The Mystery Stone of Daniel 2 212
Appendix 3: Ezekiel 9: Countdown to Harvest—The Sealing of
  the 144,000. 222
Appendix 4: Daniel 11: The King of the North vs. the King of
  the South 238
Appendix 5: From Laodicea to the 144,000 244
Bibliography 254

A Word to the Reader

This work flows from ten spiritual principles and axiomatic understandings gleaned from a study of the Bible, the Spirit of Prophecy, and reasoning (especially items seven, eight, and ten below). They are as follows:

1. Revelation "unseals" the book of Daniel.[2]
2. The scenes (visions) of Revelation *appear in their order*.[3]
3. Prophecy is to be understood (applied) in the context of those living during its fulfillment—*not* in the context of the prophet.[4]
4. The Bible and the Spirit of Prophecy must agree and must be applied strictly in context (Isa. 8:20).
5. Neither *add to* nor *take away from* the words of prophecy (Rev. 22:18–19).[5]
6. No prophecy of Scripture is of private interpretation (2 Peter 1:20).
7. Many Bible passages are reasoned from *effect* to *cause*, e.g., chiasm, which is a literary device in which a sequence of ideas is presented and then repeated in *reverse order*. The result is a "mirror" effect as the ideas are "reflected" back in the passage.
8. Spiritual messages must not be confused with the messenger.

---

[2] Ellen G. White, *Testimonies to Ministers and Gospel Workers* (Mountain View, CA: Pacific Press, 1923), p. 115 and Ellen G. White, *The Acts of the Apostles* (Mountain View, CA: Pacific Press, 1911), p. 585.

[3] Ellen G. White, *Testimonies for the Church*, vol. 8 (Mountain View, CA: Pacific Press, 1904), p. 302.

[4] Ellen G. White, *Selected Messages*, book 2 (Washington, DC: Review and Herald, 1958), p. 114.

[5] Ellen G. White, *The Great Controversy* (Mountain View, CA: Pacific Press, 1911), p. 268.

9. Spiritual theses are supported by "snippets" of Scripture taken in context (Isa. 28:10, 13).

10. Always move beyond the metaphor (Matt. 16:2–3).

From these statements, scenes of end-time revelation are clearly discernible. Charts have been prepared to illustrate the flow of ideas presented in Daniel's book and in John's Revelation and are indispensable to their understanding.[6] Understanding of last-day events has increased greatly in the past twenty years and will continue to unfold rapidly. An understanding of what God has prepared for His servants during these days will not be exhaustive, and our Laodicean debt is prophesied to be troublesome even to the very elect[7].

I am satisfied that this approach to understanding end-time prophecy is unimpeachable. There remain many things that are yet inexplicable—only advancing events will make them plain. But Revelation IS *present truth* for this time, especially the fourteenth chapter.

It is the primary purpose of this book to trace prophecy and history through the inspired writings available to God's people and to identify those places where they merge. Most emergent are the incarnation of Christ and the events of judgment that close out time. The target audience consists of those whose names are written on the membership rolls of the Seventh-day Adventist Church. By profession of faith they should be the most interested, the most informed, and are certainly the most culpable. The principle sources used are the King James Version of the Bible[8] and the complete library of the Spirit of Prophecy (SOP) which, we believe, was given under inspiration to *direct the study, the mind, the focus **back to Scripture!**[9]* This study proceeds *from* principles discovered in SOP *to* Scripture. A phrase recurring twenty times in SOP is quoted below, in its major context:

"It is a solemn statement that I make to the church, that *not one in twenty* whose names are registered upon the church books are prepared to close their earthly history, and would be as verily without God and without hope in the world as the common sinner."[10]

---

6 See Table of Contents for the list and location of all charts and appendices referenced in this book.
7 See Appendix 5, p. 244 "From Laodicea to 144,000."
8 God has seen fit to provide many versions, study Bibles, and paraphrases. These Bibles, in addition to the King James Version, will bring clarity to the discussion.
9 Ellen G. White, *Testimonies to Ministers and Gospel Workers* (Mountain View, CA: Pacific Press, 1923), p. 114.
10 Ellen G. White, *Last Day Events* (Boise, ID: Pacific Press, 1992), p. 172, emphasis mine.

A Word to the Reader

This is an urgent—*even a final*—call to every Seventh-day Adventist hoping for Christ's second appearing. Further thoughts germane to our current circumstances declare a need for quotation.

"This is the great day of atonement, and our Advocate is standing before the Father, pleading as our intercessor .... Unless we enter the sanctuary above, and unite with Christ in working out our own salvation with fear and trembling, we shall be weighed in the balances of the sanctuary, and shall be pronounced wanting."[11]

It is neither the purpose nor premise of this book that calendar time can or need be fixed with respect to last day events. The principle assumed here is as follows: divine prediction, promise, and sequence are given primarily for encouragement and reassurance. When the days of uncertainty are ushered in full bloom and persecution threatens life itself; when faith trembles even in the most secure, a knowledge of what God has been pleased to reveal with respect to these things will be of utmost encouragement for the faithful. Look up! Lift up your heads, for your redemption draweth nigh! (Luke 21:28).

"Is there a Christian whose pulse does not beat with quickened action as he anticipates the great events already opening before us? The Lord is coming. We hear the footsteps of an approaching God, as he comes to punish the world for their iniquity. We are to prepare the way for him by acting our part to get a people ready for that great day; and to sleep now is a fearful crime."[12]

—Ronald W. Busby

---

[11] Ellen G. White, *SDA Bible Commentary*, vol. 7 (Washington, DC: Review and Herald, 1957), pp. 933–934.

[12] Ellen G. White, "Personal Responsibility and Work," *The Home Missionary*, November 1, 1897.

Chapter 1
The Book of Revelation

"As we near the close of this world's history, the prophecies relating to the last days especially demand our [careful] study. The last book of the New Testament is *full* of truth that we need to understand," Ellen White declares, "[because] Satan has blinded the minds of many, so that they have been glad of any excuse for not making the Revelation their study."[13]

> Let every God-fearing teacher consider how most clearly to comprehend and present the Gospel that our Saviour came in person to make known to His servant John .... None should become discouraged in their study of Revelation because of its apparently mystical symbols. "If any of you lack wisdom, let him ask of God, that giveth to all men liberally, and upbraideth not." [James 1:5] ... We are to proclaim to the world the great and solemn truths contained in the book of Revelation. Into the very designs and principles of the church of God these truths are to enter. There should be a closer and more diligent study of this book, a more earnest presentation of the truths it contains, truths which concern all who are living in these last days. All who are preparing to meet their Lord should make this book the subject of earnest study and prayer. *It is just what its name signifies,—a revelation of the most important events that are to take place in the last days of this earth's history* .... Soon we shall enter upon the fulfilment of the events which Christ showed John were to take place. As

---

13   Ellen G. White, "Our Great Treasure-House," *The Signs of the Times*, July 4, 1906, emphasis mine.

the messengers of the Lord present these solemn truths, they must realize that they are handling subjects of eternal interest, and they should seek for the baptism of the Holy Spirit, that they may speak, not their own words, but the words given them by God.

The book of Revelation must be opened to the people. Many have been taught that it is a sealed book, but it is sealed to those only who reject truth and light. The truths that it contains must be proclaimed, that people may have an opportunity to prepare for the events which are so soon to take place. *The Third Angel's Message must be presented as the only hope for the salvation of a perishing world ....* Let not the solemn scenes that prophecy has revealed are soon to take place be left untouched. We are God's messengers, and we have no time to lose. Those who would be co-workers with our Lord Jesus Christ will show a deep interest in the truths found in this book. With pen and voice they will strive to make plain the wonderful things that Christ came from heaven to reveal.[14]

The Fall of Lucifer

Lucifer, a created being, was the highest and most exalted of all the angels in heaven. "God made him good and beautiful, *as near as possible like Himself.*"[15] Evil originated with Lucifer who rebelled against the government of God. Before his fall he was a covering cherub distinguished by his excellence (Ezek. 28:16). Next in honor to Jesus Christ, God's own Son, he grew envious and gradually assumed a command that belonged to Christ alone. God the Father saw that it was necessary to reaffirm the divinity of His Son. In the presence of the angelic host, He made known that His Son was equal with Himself and should be as readily obeyed as God Himself. Especially was Christ to be primary in the anticipated Creation of the earth. He made plain that He, the Father, would do nothing of Himself alone, but would carry out all His purposes and will through His Son.

---

14 Ibid., emphasis mine.
15 Ellen G. White, *The Faith I Live By* (Washington, DC: Review and Herald, 1958), p. 66, emphasis mine.

After Jesus was reaffirmed as Sovereign of heaven and earth and had emerged unique and beautiful, Lucifer grew even more jealous of Christ and aspired to exalt himself to be equal with the Father. In an attempt to reform the government of God he contended with the angels until open rebellion culminated in war (Rev. 12:7). Defeated, cast out of heaven, Lucifer and his sympathizers sought to establish *a kingdom of their own* upon the newly created earth. Causing the fall of Adam and Eve, he usurped their dominion and prospered until Jesus came and redeemed man from the clutches of the despot.

> *In the presence of the angelic host, He made known that His Son was equal with Himself and should be as readily obeyed as God Himself. Especially was Christ to be primary in the anticipated Creation of the earth.*

Since that dark chapter in earth's history, Lucifer has been identified as Satan, the old serpent, the devil, the great deceiver, the father of lies, that wicked one, the one fallen from heaven and given the keys of the bottomless pit (Rev. 20:2; John 8:44; Matt. 13:19; Rev. 9:1). Near the end of his 6,000-year reign on earth, Scripture further identifies him as "[t]he beast that ... was, and is not, and will ascend ... and go to perdition" (Rev. 17:8, NKJV). But prior to that mysterious ending, he is identified as the great red dragon, the leopard-like beast, the antichrist, the angel of the bottomless pit, and the scarlet-colored beast (Rev. 12:3; 13:2; 1 John 2:22; Rev. 9:11; 17:3). As this study proceeds, we will see how and when the enemy of all righteousness identifies with these symbols.

Satan's strategies will be unveiled in chapters, 5, 7, and 8, where we will study Revelation chapters 9, 16, 12, 13, and 17. These chapters will show the complete destruction of his forces as our Lord Jesus Christ becomes the King of kings and Lord of lords. In the last great struggle, beginning with the Battle of Armageddon and ending 1,000 years later, the entire universe will be forever cleansed from the curse of sin.

Understanding Present Truth in the Twenty-First Century

The seven trumpets and the seven seals of Revelation have had many reapplications. Expositors of these variations have been strongly influenced by appropriate applications of past generations, as well as by popular conjecture.[16] Truth, however, is *present* as well as *eternal*, and it is the Holy Spirit that leads into all truth, keeping us up to date. "Faithful men, who were obedient to the promptings of God's Spirit and the teachings of His word, were to proclaim this warning to the world."[17] The first interpretations respecting the seals, trumpets, and beasts were developed *well before* the eighteenth century (1627), and *long before* the appointed time for their apocalyptic unsealing (1798); and it must be kept in mind that John was instructed to "write" and publish *immediately* for the benefit of those living in his time, as well as for those who would live and work until the final generation.[18]

Therefore, *our* task is how to understand these prophecies *now*, in the twenty-first century. It is not possible for humans to comprehend such revealing unaided. *All* must be laid at the feet of Jesus, and all interpretation must come from the Holy Spirit. "[The Holy Spirit] would not have any man receive the idea that God will teach him only, and that all must come to his light."[19]

Satan lays the track of error so close to the track of truth as to confuse even the most sincere. "So closely will the counterfeit resemble the true that it will be impossible to distinguish between them except by the Holy Scriptures."[20] Thus, anyone

---

16   Ellen G. White, *SDA Bible Commentary*, vol. 7 (Washington, DC: Review and Herald, 1957), pp. 108–111.
17   Ellen G. White, *Maranatha* (Washington, DC: Review and Herald, 1976), p. 17.
18   Ellen G. White, *SDA Bible Commentary*, vol. 7 (Washington, DC: Review and Herald, 1957), pp. 108–111.
19   Ellen G. White, "A Missionary Appeal," *The Review and Herald*, December 15, 1885.
20   Ellen G. White, *The Great Controversy* (Mountain View, CA: Pacific Press, 1911), p. 593.

The Book of Revelation

relying on authorities or sources not directed by the Holy Spirit will be subject to the influence of a false prophet.

As a prelude to this study it must be emphasized that:

- No *human*, of themselves, can interpret divine messages.
- The trumpets and vials have a future application.
- The trumpets sound *after* the close of probation.
- Historical reviews serve to provide context for subsequent reapplication of prophecy, for justifying divine punishment, or for clarifying the application of prophecy to history.

All our understandings should be in harmony with Scripture, as well as with the Spirit of Prophecy. As will be shown, the trumpets do not sound *until the judgment is over.* Spirit of Prophecy states clearly:

"Solemn events before us are yet to transpire. *Trumpet after trumpet is to be sounded; vial after vial poured out one after another upon inhabitants of the earth. Scenes of stupendous interest are right upon us.*"[21]

The trumpets are a divine demonstration to the universe that even after such a devastating experience as the trumpet/vial plagues have inflicted, the lost, who are insensitive to eternal values, are incapable of repentance. Concurrent with the experience of the wicked is the experience of the righteous who will endure a time of trouble such as never was, *yet without sin*.

Following Satan's success in establishing the little horn power (the papacy, the pseudo-King of the North) within the Christian community, he installed *another* religious power (the King of the South) opposed to truth, this time from without. In Mohammed (c. AD 570; died AD 632), born to Arabian princess, Aminah, and posthumously to Abdullah bin Abdul-Muttalib of the tribe of Quraysh, Satan found an easy target. Abdullah claimed to be directly descended from Ishmael, firstborn of Abraham, son of Hagar, the Egyptian.[22]

Mohammed met a lady named Khadija when he was in his early twenties and she was in her late thirties. Her cousin, Waraquah, was a Roman Catholic, and Khadija herself came from a Roman Catholic

---

21 Ellen G. White, *Selected Messages*, book 3 (Washington, DC: Review and Herald, 1980), p. 114, emphasis mine.

22 Robert A. Morey, *Islam Unveiled: The True Desert Storm* (Shermans Dale, PA: The Scholars Press, 1991), pp. 22, 49, 65–66, 71–72, 85 and *World Religions From Ancient History to the Present*, ed. Geoffrey Parrinder (New York, NY: Facts on File Publications, 1983), pp. 466, 474–475, 488–491.

convent. Quite wealthy, she maintained control of the local economy. She employed the young man, Mohammed, and eventually married him when she was forty and he was twenty-five.[23]

Mohammed was serious-minded; he associated with Jews, Christians, and Sun-worshipers of Persia, going often to a cave near Mecca to fast and pray. (Ancient deities communicated from caves.) Upon emerging from his cave on one occasion, he announced, "Allah is the only true god, and Mohammed is his prophet."[24] Allah, a pre-Islamic name corresponding to the Babylonian Bel,[25] was the moon god who married the sun goddess. "Together they produced three goddesses who were called the daughters of Allah."[26]

Mohammedanism is a religion of *works*, reflecting the original effort of Abraham and Sarah, through the handmaid Hagar, to fulfill God's promise of a son. Two quotations from Geoffrey Parrinder's work, *World Religions: From Ancient History to the Present*, will suffice to illustrate this point:

> Islam, it is often said, is a religion of law. Among all the expressions of Islamic piety, law is the most characteristic. The central place of the law in Islamic thought and religious life stems from the fundamental nature of the Islamic experience itself. Perhaps the most important word in the entire religious vocabulary of Muslims is *guidance*.[27] It was guidance which the Koran brought from on high, and guidance which the prophet's example and the tradition of the community elaborated and established. Guidance is above all what the Muslim expects from religion, a series of specific directions for the conduct of life so that in no situation will there be doubt about the right way to act ....[28]

---

23 Ibid.
24 Ibid.
25 Robert A. Morey, *The Encyclopedia of Religion*, ed. Paul Meagher and Robert A. Morey, *Islam Unveiled: The True Desert Storm* (Shermans Dale, PA: The Scholars Press, 1991), pp. 22, 49, 65–66, 71–72, 85.
26 Robert A. Morey, *Islam Unveiled: The True Desert Storm* (Shermans Dale, PA: The Scholars Press, 1991), pp. 22, 49, 65–66, 71–72, 85 and *World Religions From Ancient History to the Present*, ed. Geoffrey Parrinder (New York, NY: Facts on File Publications, 1983), pp. 466, 474–475, 488–491.
27 Guidance by fiat or guidance by principle? One requires blind obedience, the other thoughtful response.
28 *World Religions From Ancient History to the Present*, ed. Geoffrey Parrinder (New York, NY: Facts on File Publications, 1983), pp. 488–491.

The *shariah* [Islamic moral law], therefore, includes a great deal that for the modern world has nothing to do with law. For instance, it regulates everything respecting religion, both belief and ritual. Theology, thus, is technically a part of the *shariah* though it has developed into a semi-independent religious science. Theology is simply the moral aspect of belief. The law also tells a Muslim when and how to perform his prayers, how to observe the fast of Ramadan, how much to pay in the way of alms, and how to perform other religious duties. In the realm of more mundane affairs, the *shariah* prescribes the food permissible for a Muslim to eat, the manner of acceptable dress, and even the forms of courtesy that lubricate social relations.[29]

The beast from the bottomless pit has been thus successful in establishing two parallel religious systems extending to the end of time and embracing more than 2 billion humans. But one (Muslim) was used of God to curb the persecution of the other (papacy), else there would have been left no righteousness in the earth.

The Use of Symbolism

The extensive use of figurative language in Revelation presents, for the average reader, a tremendous barrier to understanding. Why *did* God use figurative language in a book He has chosen to identify as *Revelation*? Certainly, the Holy Spirit and the final generation upon whom these things devolve must be in perfect harmony as to both meaning and application. God's purpose for such strategy might include the following:

- **BREVITY**—Similes, metaphors, and symbols get to the point quicker. They are brief, and pack a lot of meaning in a few words. Explanations in literal language take longer, whereas a picture in the mind is worth 1,000 words.

- **INTEREST**—Similes, metaphors, and symbols create vivid images in the mind, engage our curiosity, and help us remember the main points.

- **CONSISTENCY**—The same colorful, vivid imagery used in telling the Revelation story is also used in the Old Testament book of Daniel to point to future events that are coming down the pike.

---
29   Ibid., p. 491.

- **IMAGERY**—This means pictures created in the mind by colorful, symbolic descriptions that appeal to people in all generations and cultures.

- **TIMING**—By inspiring such vivid, symbolic pictures in the mind, the Holy Spirit could match events to specific times when God was ready to address the needs of a particular generation, including ours.

- **INHIBITING**—God's figurative language requires *help* from His Holy Spirit to figure out the main points of His story so the enemies of God would be inhibited, or prevented, from twisting the true meanings or applying the prophecies falsely.

- **SYMBOLIC FORMAT**—*This is perhaps the most practical* because the language God chooses to tell His story helps Him address the needs of all the people who lived between John's time and our time. Because history repeats itself, God's story can apply to all the generations.

- **ASSURANCE**—Prophecy is intended to give God's end-time people light so that they will recognize these events and know *exactly* where they are in the stream of time—with respect to the issues.

Quite unlike the Koran, the Bible does not—and cannot—micromanage the principles of its message. Careful application is required to move beyond equivocation in apocalyptic prophecy.[30]

The purpose of these studies is to "arouse to comprehend the situation and view the contest before us in *its true bearings* .... to show the people *where we are in prophetic history.*"[31] We should know the time of night. The prophecies have opened to us "the events about to take place,"[32] and we should walk while we have the light, lest darkness come upon us (John 12:35). Jesus Himself warned, "Now I tell you before it come, that, when it is come to pass, ye may believe that I am *He*" (John 13:19, emphasis mine).

---

30 See Chart 1, page 23, "A Frameworks System for Understanding the Bible."
31 Ellen G. White, *Testimonies for the Church*, vol. 5 (Mountain View, CA: Pacific Press, 1889), p. 716, emphasis mine.
32 Ellen G. White, *The Great Controversy* (Mountain View, CA: Pacific Press, 1911), p. 312.

The Book of Revelation

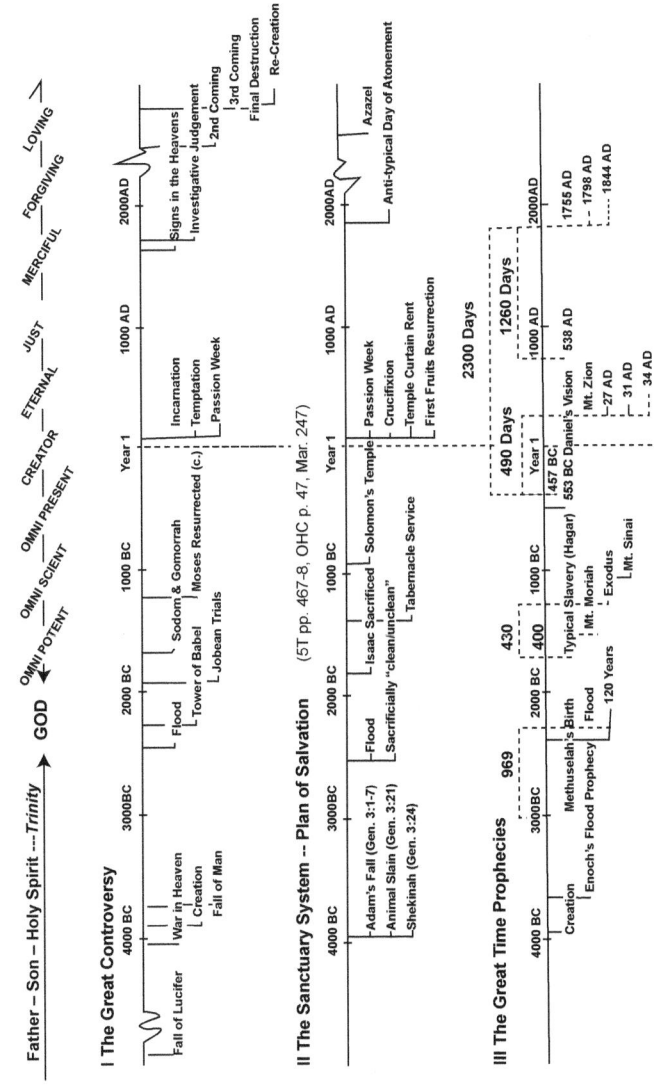

Chart 1: A Framework System for Understanding the Bible

"The coming of Christ is nearer than when we first believed. *The great controversy is nearing its end*. The judgments of God are in the land. They speak in solemn warning, saying: "Be ye also ready: for in such an hour as ye think not the Son of man cometh." Matthew 24:44."[33]

Yet, on the brighter side:

"Language is altogether too feeble to attempt a description of heaven. As the scene rises before me, I am lost in amazement. Carried away with the surpassing splendor and excellent glory, I lay down the pen, and exclaim, *"Oh, what love! what wondrous love!" The most exalted language fails to describe the glory of heaven or the matchless depths of a Saviour's love.*[34]

---

[33] Ellen G. White, *Maranatha* (Washington, DC: Review and Herald, 1976), p. 310, emphasis mine.
[34] Ibid., p. 310.

Chapter 2
Revelation 1–3: Introduction to Revelation and the Seven Churches

The July 2005 *Union Bulletin* (Walla Walla, Washington's only newspaper) published an article headlined, "Terror Experts See a New Kind of War." Two questions were asked: "Where will it all lead? And when will it end?" One of the pundits cited in the article replied, "I don't think it has even started yet! The world has entered a long siege in a *new kind of war*."[35] Certainly, events that have transpired since then have supported that premise.

One resolution in the article suggested that the world's richer powers must address *underlying causes*. Without explicitly identifying underlying causes, some strategies mentioned to accomplish this were to (1) improve economies, (2) establish political rights, (3) improve education for the poorer nations, and (4) provide a *different way out* through U.S. foreign policy. The world is beginning to sense that something stupendous is on the horizon—it knows not what. These suggestions prepare for a congealing mentality anticipated by Richard Neuhaus, author of *The Catholic Moment,* when he declared, "This can and should ... be the moment in which the Roman Catholic Church in the United States assumes its rightful role in the culture-forming task of constructing a religiously informed public philosophy for the American experiment in ordered liberty."[36] Ellen White responds in *The Great Controversy*:

---

35 "Terror experts see a new kind of war on the horizon," Walla Walla Union Bulletin, July 10, 2005.
36 Richard Neuhaus, *The Catholic Moment* (San Francisco, CA: Harper & Row Publishers, 1987), p. 283.

> The Roman Church is .... employing every device to extend her influence and increase her power in preparation for a fierce and determined conflict to regain control of the world, to re-establish persecution, and to undo all that Protestantism has done. Catholicism is gaining ground on every side .... These things should awaken the anxiety of all who prize the pure principles of the gospel![37]

Referring to warnings in the book of Revelation, as well as in Daniel, *The Great Controversy* asks, "Why ... this widespread ignorance concerning an important part of Holy Writ? Why this general reluctance to investigate its teachings?"[38] The answer is supplied in the same paragraph: "It is the result of a *studied* effort of the prince of darkness to conceal from men that which reveals his deceptions."[39] This notion carried to its logical conclusion could validate many of the long-held conspiracy theories.

Another answer is found in *Counsels to Writers and Editors*: "There is no excuse for anyone in taking the position that there is no more truth to be revealed, and that all our expositions of Scripture are without an error. The fact that certain doctrines have been held as truth for many years by our people, is not a proof that our ideas are infallible."[40] I would like to explore that caveat a bit. Certain wide-ranging discrepancies have persisted with respect to understanding prophecy because the Holy Spirit is not permitted to interpret Scripture *for these times*. This notion will be expanded on later, but God has had a loving concern for every generation, from the apostle's time down through the centuries to the present. He wrote the letters of Revelation to minister to the interests and needs of those times as well, so for us to take the ministry that was *adapted* to an earlier Christian period and assume that it either applies to us who live in the last days *in precisely the same way,* or doesn't apply to us at all, is potentially misleading. We must allow the Holy Spirit to respond to *history as it repeats*. Ellen White has told us that "[h]istory will repeat itself."[41] The prophecies of God are—and have always been—dynamic (conditional).

---

37 Ellen G. White, *The Great Controversy* (Mountain View, CA: Pacific Press, 1911), p. 565–566.
38 Ibid., p. 342.
39 Ibid., emphasis mine.
40 Ellen G. White, *Counsels to Writers and Editors* (Nashville, TN: Southern Publishing Association, 1946), p. 35.
41 Ellen G. White, *Christ Triumphant* (Hagerstown, MD: Review and Herald, 1999), p. 256.

The angels of God in their messages to men represent time as very short. Thus it has always been presented to me. It is true that time has continued longer than we expected in the early days of this message. Our Saviour did not appear as soon as we hoped. But has the word of the Lord failed? Never! *It should be remembered that the promises and threatenings of God are alike conditional.*[42]

Past Experiences Prepare for Future—Again and again I have been shown that the past experiences of God's people are not to be counted as dead facts. We are not to treat the record of these experiences as we would treat a last year's almanac. The record is to be kept in mind, for *history will repeat itself*. The darkness of the mysteries of the night is to be illuminated with the light of heaven.[43]

Interjected within this context is a notion applicable to all biblical studies: *applied historicism.* Alden Thompsen, professor emeritus of religious studies at Walla Walla University, coined the term in order to clarify the Seventh-day Adventists' prophetic position. He had this to say:

> It occurred to me that perhaps we could coin a new phrase to identify the Adventist position: *"applied historicism."* That would leave the historical identifications in place, but allow the principles illustrated by the prophecy to be applied to *different times and places,* as the writers of Scripture were so adept at doing. The book of Revelation, for example, speaks of Babylon, not the real Babylon, but the one representing the final persecuting power. In the same way, the classical Protestant interpretation of the fourth beast, Rome, illustrates ways of thinking and acting that find parallels elsewhere in our world. The primary identification (Rome) remains in place, but *other applications are possible.*[44]

In 1896 Ellen White herself wrote: "We may have less to say in some lines, in regard to the Roman power and the papacy."[45] She

---

42   Ellen G. White, *Maranatha* (Washington, DC: Review and Herald, 1976), p. 61, emphasis mine.
43   Ellen G. White, *The Publishing Ministry* (Hagerstown, MD: Review and Herald, 1983), p. 175, emphasis mine.
44   Alden Thompsen, *Probe Study Guide*, Lesson 1, July 1, 2006, p. 12.
45   Ellen G. White, *Testimonies to Ministers and Gospel Workers* (Mountain View, CA: Pacific

was not denying the application to Rome but was suggesting a shift of emphasis. This allows greater freedom for the Holy Spirit to bring clarity to study and is consistent with the way in which New Testament writers—and even Christ Himself—applied inspired utterances.

To a great degree the book of Daniel is to the Old Testament what the book of Revelation is to the New Testament. It drew a prophetic line through the Diaspora to the Messianic period, allowing ancient scholars to trace with precision the first advent of Christ. But it also took its readers beyond that significant event to the very end of time.[46]

"The book of Daniel is unsealed in the *Revelation* to John, and *carries us forward* to the last scenes of earth's history."[47] Notice the bridge directing us to the inspired writings of John:

> In the Revelation are portrayed the *deep things of God.* The very name given to its inspired pages, *"The Revelation,"* contradicts the statement that this is a sealed book. A *revelation* is something revealed. The Lord Himself ... designs that they shall be open to the study of all. Its truths are addressed to those living in the last days of this earth's history, *as well as to those living in the days of John.*[48]

During the month of May 2005 my firstborn, Rhonda, and I toured Italy, Greece, and western Turkey. Flying from Athens to Samos, I then took a hydroplane to the Isle of Patmos and visited the cave where the apostle John lived while exiled there, and where he wrote the book we are now studying. It was a thrilling experience for me to be where John wrote:

"The Revelation of Jesus Christ, which God gave unto *him,* to shew unto *his* servants things which must shortly come to pass; and *he* sent and signified it by *his* angel unto *his* servant John" (Rev. 1:1, emphasis mine).

The revelation *of* Jesus Christ, given *by* God, and *signified* (authenticated, validated, or made known) **by** His angel (Gabriel), **unto** John, His servant. What is to be made known? Something heretofore

---

Press, 1923), p. 112.
46 The book of Daniel sometimes has been called the "primer," or elementary textbook, that is important as an introduction to the book of Revelation. See Appendix 1, "Daniel 1–12: The Book of Daniel," p. 190.
47 Ibid., p. 115, emphasis mine.
48 Ellen G. White, *The Acts of the Apostles* (Mountain View, CA: Pacific Press, 1911), p. 584, emphasis mine.

Revelation 1–3: Introduction to Revelation and the Seven Churches

obscured about Jesus: His unique positioning in the Godhead that has been hidden to our understanding and not made plain, as well as *things which must **shortly** come to pass!*

John's visitation on the Isle of Patmos occurred near the end of his life (he was c. 90 years old).[49] The Christian church, begun seventy years earlier, was in crisis. It was widely believed then that before the original generation had passed, *Jesus would appear the second time*; and now John, the last of the apostles, was an ancient man. What was to become of the church? What now was its mission? Who were to lead, and how? Anxiety over this issue intruded into the work of the church and threatened to derail its purpose. Jesus came to John in his exile to give him detailed information of the future, keeping alive the flame of hope and mission.

> *Jesus came to John in his exile to give him detailed information of the future, keeping alive the flame of hope and mission.*

"[John] bare record of the word of God, and of the testimony of Jesus Christ, and of all things that he saw" (Rev. 1:2).

That is a projection of the *Gospel* of John, written *after* the Revelation, wherein he bore explicit record of the Word, His authority, and His purpose.

"Blessed is he that readeth, and [also] they that hear the words of this prophecy, and *keep* those things which are written therein: for *the time is at hand*" (Rev. 1:3, emphasis mine).

To be "blessed" is to be given advantage and opportunity, enabled, empowered to accomplish a good to someone, to restore harmony. In this case the blessing is doubled: to the one who reads as well as to the ones who hear. In the days before Gutenberg's movable press, those who had manuscripts made them available to readers, who then called for an audience and would read aloud the written word.

But the conditional cautions both the reader and the hearer to "*keep* those things written"; that is, to incorporate into the soul the lifestyle that is presented. And an emergency is appended: "For the time is at hand." That is, *the prophecy commences immediately*. First, John introduces his *authority*, then he introduces himself.

"[T]o the seven churches which are in Asia: Grace be unto you, and peace, from him *which is, and which was, and which is to come*;

---

[49] "John the Apostle," Wikipedia, https://1ref.us/1jd (accessed February 8, 2021) and Ellen G. White, *The Acts of the Apostles* (Mountain View, CA: Pacific Press, 1911), p. 569.

and from the *seven* Spirits which are before *his* throne" (Rev. 1:4, emphasis mine).

From Him *which is,* and *which was,* and *which is to come*: a trinity within the Trinity. (1) *Which is*—the resurrected One. (2) *Which was*—the preexistent One as God incarnate. (3) *Which is to come*—the One who *will* return for His faithful. Included in the holy greeting is recognition of Jesus' Partner in salvation—the seven Spirits, the promised Comforter. This identification will recur several times in John's book and will be counterfeited by Satan in an effort to distract attention from God. To the seven churches, or to *seven of the* churches in Asia, these are to be repository of a great temporal truth significant to the body of Christ to the end of time. To them He extends *grace*, the companion of blessing. Dr. Leslie Hardinge, professor emeritus of religion at Pacific Union University, had a gift for clarifying deep spiritual concepts for his students by using apt illustrations. "Blessing," he told us, "is the power to do that which is *intrinsic* to man." Being endowed with certain capabilities, it remains only to exercise them to God's glory. If there is money in your pocket or water in your flask, it is to be dispensed to those in need. The opportunity thereby supplies you an empowerment that enables another to recognize God in you.

Grace is the power to do that which is *extrinsic* to man, the power to carry out God's *impossible will,* to fulfill opportunities beyond human capacity to accomplish. And He offers peace in the midst of chaos and the tumult of opposition. All this from Him who has oversight of that which was past, of that which is present, and of that which is yet to come. By way of illustration, Dr. Hardinge would say, take a crow and a canary. Ask them both to sing. The canary needs but a blessing. The crow needs grace.

In this passage the seven Spirits which are before His throne is singular, yet sevenfold. Seven is the metaphor of *complete revelation*, of complete resolution. It is the *denouement*, the finishing of all mystery. The Holy Spirit is He whose office empowers the outworking of God's will in the gospel enterprise.

"And from Jesus Christ, who is the faithful *witness*, and the *first begotten* of the dead, and the *prince* of the kings of the earth. Unto *him* that loved us, and washed us from our sins in *his* own blood" (Rev. 1:5, emphasis mine).

That is to say, "Greetings from Jesus Christ." This is followed by a list of qualities endorsing the Person who will figure prominently in the document. The faithful Witness is Someone who has seen a significant event personally and is thus a reliable testifier of that experience. *He is not relating something that someone else saw or heard.* That would be *hearsay,* which in a court of law is not admissible as evidence. Jesus is testifying to what He personally experienced during His incarnation on earth; and it is a comfort for us to know that He is one of us. The first begotten of the dead. NOT the first to die—which is Abel's dubious distinction—but first among *all* who will experience death.

> *In this passage the seven Spirits which are before His throne is singular, yet sevenfold. Seven is the metaphor of complete revelation, of complete resolution. It is the denouement, the finishing of all mystery. The Holy Spirit is He whose office empowers the outworking of God's will in the gospel enterprise.*

"[A]nd has made us to be a kingdom and priests to serve his God and Father—to him be glory and power for ever and ever! Amen" (Rev.1:6, NIV).

Prince of the Kings of Earth

A prince is heir apparent, one who is first in line for kingship (e.g., William Tudor of England), not yet enthroned or crowned, but preordained to power. In verse 6 John extends Jesus' authority by informing his audience that we are now, and in promise, kings and priests, having authority over both temporal and spiritual domains. He calls on us to recognize *His* glory, *His* authority and the scope of such—*His* dominion. Whenever the word *glory* is encountered in Scripture, it is more effactually understood as *authority.*

What *was* the pressing question of the day? In verse 7 John responds to the troubling issue: *when will He come?* We expected Him to come before the apostles died. They have all died but John, and John is old. He, too, will soon pass away! Then what? It was a point of terrible distraction among the faithful. So John is now responding:

"Behold, *he* cometh with clouds; and every eye shall see *him*, and they also which pierced *him*: and all kindreds of the earth shall wail because of *him*. Even so, Amen" (Rev. 1:7).

He *is* coming with the full force of angels in such a manner that all inhabitants of earth will see him: *every eye shall see Him!* Here John adds a peculiar scrap of data "They also, even those who pierced him," will witness His return—even though they, too, are *now* dead. Then Jesus interjects His own endorsement:

"I am Alpha and Omega, the beginning and the ending" (Rev. 1:8).

That's the "A" and the "Z" of the Greek alphabet. Jesus is both *first cause* and *final determiner.* He takes responsibility for allowing all that happens to happen. Finally, John presents personal credentials: he is their companion in tribulation, in the kingdom, and patience of Jesus. That is to say that he sympathizes with their trepidation, with their state of affairs. "I, too, am concerned," he says.

"I ... was in the isle that is called Patmos, for the word of God, and for the testimony of Jesus Christ [That was his crime]" (Rev. 1:9).

Tradition has recorded John's arrest, trial, and sentence to death by boiling in oil. But John was exiled by Domitian, the Roman Emperor, because execution had failed them. Like the three Hebrew worthies before him, John had stood up in the heat of his destruction, free of bonds, and under inspiration had delivered a sermon compared to that of Stephen.[50]

Exile was a legal recourse to isolate a troublemaker. John represented a large Christian following that threatened the worship of demi-gods—Caesars, as well as the pantheon of pagan deities. John was not engaged in labor while on Patmos. He was banned, isolated there. He chose to live in a shallow cave with his disciple and amanuensis, Prochoros. It is not certain that Prochoros was indeed John's disciple; but that he lived with and wrote of John while there at that time is reasonably affirmed.[51] Domition's power ended a year and a half into John's sentence, and it was during that time that John received the visions of Revelation.

---

50 Ellen G. White, *The Acts of the Apostles* (Mountain View, CA: Pacific Press, 1911), pp. 569–570.
51 "Patmos the Island of the Apocalypse (Revelation)," Patmos Island, https://1ref.us/1je (accessed February 8, 2021).

Revelation 1–3: Introduction to Revelation and the Seven Churches

I was in the Spirit on the Lord's day, and heard behind me a great voice, as of a trumpet, Saying, I am Alpha and Omega, the first and the last: and, What thou seest, write in a book, and send it unto the seven churches which are in Asia; unto Ephesus, and unto Smyrna, and unto Pergamos, and unto Thyatira, and unto Sardis, and unto Philadelphia, and unto Laodicea. (Rev. 1:10–11)

Verse 10: On the Lord's day he was taken in the Spirit and was commanded to write on a scroll what he was about to see, and then send copies to *seven* churches identified by Christ Himself. The setting for this magnificent Person included *seven* golden lamp stands, *seven* stars in His hand, and a sharp, double-edged sword in His mouth. When John saw Him, he was overcome, as many of his fellow prophets had been. Jesus now speaks for the next fifty-four verses.

> *The sevens within these verses introduce a phenomenon that dominates the book of Revelation. The number seven is one of seven numeric metaphors, all of which represent some variation of completion. The denouement of a story or play is that part near the end that resolves the issues of plot and character. The book of Revelation is the denouement of the Bible, even of the great controversy.*

The *sevens* within these verses introduce a phenomenon that dominates the book of Revelation. The number seven is one of seven numeric metaphors, all of which represent some variation of *completion*. The *denouement* of a story or play is that part near the end that resolves the issues of plot and character. The book of Revelation is the denouement of the Bible, even of the great controversy. And within the recounting of sin's resolution are many issues and characters that have puzzled intelligences throughout history and the universe. These issues are indicated by the number seven. First mentioned are the *seven churches* in verse 4:

"John, to the *seven churches* in the province of Asia" (Rev. 1:4, NIV, emphasis mine).

These seven churches are seven *of* the churches located in Asia Minor and are to be models of God's organized people throughout the Christian era. "Evil originated with Lucifer, who rebelled against the government of God. Before his fall he was a covering cherub, distinguished by his excellence. God made him good and beautiful, *as near as possible like Himself.*"[52] The seven churches beginning with Ephesus constituted a Roman postal route that circled within the province of Asia. Divine strategy enabled John's work to be published and made available everywhere.[53]

The Christian era spans a period of time extending from the apostolic days of the church until probation closes with the Laodicean period. God is about to define their future and reveal to them both their pitfalls and their virtues.

"Grace and peace to you from ... the *seven spirits* before his throne" (Rev. 1:4, NIV, emphasis mine).

The seven Spirits are an expression for the one Holy Spirit in whom is embodied the fullness of the *power* of salvation to the end of time.

"I saw s*even golden* lamp stands" (Rev. 1:12, NIV, emphasis mine).

Verses 12 to 17 comprise a description of the Personage speaking: (1) He was One *like* a Son of man. (2) He was dressed in a robe reaching to His feet. (3) There was a golden sash about His chest. (4) His head and hair were white *like* wool. (5) His eyes were *like* blazing fire. (6) His feet were *like* glowing bronze. (7) His voice was *like* rushing water. (8) His face was *like* the sun in its brilliance.

This passage is important to us because the Spirit of Prophecy informs us that Satan will use *this* description to personate Christ, and that will be the "almost overmastering delusion."[54]

Verse 20 explains the lamp stands, which are the seven churches, a metaphor for all the Christian churches to exist to the end of time.

---

52   Ellen G. White, *The Faith I Live By* (Washington, DC: Review and Herald, 1958), p. 66, emphasis mine.
53   "The seven churches were located on a major Roman road. A letter carrier would leave the island of Patmos [where John was exiled], arriving first at Ephesus. He would travel north to Smyrna and Pergamum, turn southeast to Thyatira, and continue on to Sardis, Philadelphia, and Laodicea—in the exact order in which the letters were dictated" (New Living Translation, Life Application Study Bible (Carol Stream, IL: Tyndale House Publishers, Inc., 2004), p. 2168 [picture caption]).
54   Ellen G. White, *The Great Controversy* (Mountain View, CA: Pacific Press, 1911), p. 624.

These golden lamp stands should not be confused with the menorah that is a seven-branched candlestick expressly crafted to accommodate the tent-like tabernacle and wilderness journeying. Solomon's Temple more nearly represented the one in heaven, and there were placed seven free-standing lamps as they are in heaven. Jesus walks *among* the seven that represent *all the churches,* present and yet future, who will testify of Him.

"In his right hand he held *seven stars*" (Rev. 1:16, NIV, emphasis mine).

Verse 20 explains the seven stars, which are seven angels of the seven churches, or all of the elders who will lead these churches down through the era. These collections of "sevens" will be instrumental in the success of God's enterprise in the earth. If any of them *fail,* God will fill their place with other more willing workers—even cause the rocks to cry out—because He holds them in His *right* hand!

"[O]ut of his mouth went a sharp twoedged sword" (Rev. 1:16).

The double-edged sword is the Old and New Testaments that would communicate God's will down through the next 2,000 years, *cutting both ways*, showing both the *justice* and *mercy* of God.

"I hold the keys of death and Hades" (Rev. 1:18, NIV).

Jesus is here declaring power over the second death, as well as the power of an eternal resurrection. It is one thing to have died; it is another thing to be resurrected from death. Here John projects a people group who will choose both eternal death and the eternal grave rather than a recognition of Jesus. Jesus now begins dictating the messages He intends for those who will contend for eternal life in the *next two millennia*. It is important for us to note that these messages are continuous and will apply to all persons and groups of worshipers claiming the name of Jesus to the end of time. Even though we parse these seven "churches" into seven periods of time within the Christian era, for us that is perhaps the least-significant aspect of the understanding. *Most important* to recognize is that the messages accumulate and are viable to every generation from John's time to the very end of time.

"The names of the seven churches are symbolic of the church in different periods of the Christian Era. *The number 7 indicates completeness,* and is symbolic of the fact that *the messages extend to the end of time*, while the symbols used reveal the *condition of the church at different periods in the history of the world.*"⁵⁵

The first message is addressed to the church in Ephesus. All the messages will follow the same format: Five parts: (1) Commendation, (2) Condemnation, (3) Counsel, (4) Challenge, and (5) Characteristic of the speaker, Jesus Christ.

I. Ephesus—Apostolic Period—AD 31 to AD 100 (Desirable)

Commendation: *"I have seen your hard work* **and your patient endurance. I know you don't tolerate evil people. You have examined the claims of those who say they are apostles but are not. You have discovered they are liars .... But this is in your favor: You hate the evil deeds of the Nicolaitans, just as I do"** (Rev. 2:1–3, 6, LASB).

This is the church of the apostles, the foundation stones of Christ's new institution for spreading the gospel. They have worked hard and persevere even unto death. They have set standards of excellence by which new members are to be guided. On the pagan side, Ephesus was the seat of Diana—the mother of the gods. At the Council of Ephesus (AD 431) the title "Mother of God" was given to Mary, the mother of Jesus.⁵⁶ The great Temple of Diana was built about 480 BC, and it was here that the apostle Paul was challenged, nearly losing his life.

The principal teaching of the Nicolaitans declares that "the gospel of Christ has made the law of God of no effect; that by "believing" we are released from the necessity of being doers of the Word."⁵⁷ Thus, *antinomianism* is the abandoning of God's law; it is said to be nailed to the cross, and is no longer binding upon Christians.

What is the legacy of the Nicolaitans that is still embraced by the world today? Many people unknowingly honor this Nicholas even in our day by observing customs associated with December 25. Christmas originally was the "Saturnalia," or birthday, of Nimrod.⁵⁸ Of course, theses customs, handed down from ancient paganism, have been renamed and made to appear innocent and good! Referring

---

55   Ellen G. White, *The Acts of the Apostles* (Mountain View, CA: Pacific Press, 1911), p. 585, emphasis mine.
56   "Council of Ephesus," Wikipedia, https://1ref.us/1jf (accessed February 8, 2021).
57   Ellen G. White, *SDA Bible Commentary*, vol. 7 (Washington, DC: Review and Herald, 1957), p. 957.
58   "Paganism," Wikipedia, https://1ref.us/1jg (accessed February 8, 2021).

to Christmas, Ellen White advises, "It is right to bestow upon one another tokens of love and remembrance if we do not in this forget God, our best friend. We should make our gifts such as will prove a real benefit to the receiver"[59]

Condemnation: "Yet I hold this against you: You have forsaken the love you had at first" (Rev. 2:4, NIV).

In their preoccupation with the second coming and the leading of the church, they had shifted away from the gospel focus, thus weakening their effort. Though their ardor was intact, their priorities had shifted! Their attention was directed away from the gospel task to one of self-dependence on leadership and concern for the second coming of Christ.

Counsel: "Remember then how far you have fallen; repent, and do the works you did at first" (Rev. 2:5, CSB).

The focus is shifting from the Person to the return of the Person. Remember how much you loved *Me* when we first covenanted? Remember the days, the loving crowds? Jesus is covetous of these things. Contrast this behavior with the concern of things now—that's the measure of the fall. Repent and refocus on the message. When repenting, one *stops* and turns around and faces a different direction. That's *repenting. Moving* in a new direction is something else. Repenting is *always* stopping the direction of error and turning the face away from it but should never be confused with *regret*. To *regret* is to wish that a thing had not happened, that something else had happened instead. But to feel deep sorrow, deep pain for what one has done (or omitted to do) is to *repent of* the cause of the sorrow and pain.

Challenge: "To the one who conquers, I will give the right to eat from the tree of life, which is in the paradise of God" (Rev. 2:7, CSB).

To those who give me *continuous permission* to recreate I will give access to the tree of life. Are we back in the Garden of Eden—the Paradise of God?

Characteristic: "[He] who holds the seven stars in his right hand and walks among the seven golden lampstands" (Rev. 2:1, NIV).

The "seven stars" are the "seven ministers," all the ministers of the church down through the ages. "He who holds," supports these

---

[59] Ellen G. White, *The Adventist Home* (Hagerstown, MD: Review and Herald, 1952), pp. 478–479.

ministers of His church down through time, and He holds them in His *right hand,* not His left. He walks among the seven golden lamp stands which are all the churches in the Christian era—from John's time until the end. When we meet together in church we are meeting with Christ, because He's there in the Person of the Holy Spirit!

II. Smyrna—Persecuted—AD 100 to AD 313 (Myrrh: Sweet-Smelling Odor of Sacrifice)

"And unto the angel of the church in Smyrna write ... *I know thy works"* **(Rev. 2:8–9, emphasis mine).**

The Smyrnan period is distinguished by persecution and death from AD 100, the reign of Diocletian, to AD 313, Constantine's time. Diocletian is considered the worst emperor in Rome's history and the greatest antagonist of the Christian faith. Under his leadership many Roman cities had public burnings of the sacred Scriptures.[60] During the second and third centuries this age saw hundreds of Christians brought into the Coliseum of Rome to be fed to lions while thousands of spectators cheered. Many were crucified; others were covered with animal skins and tortured to death by wild dogs. They were covered with tar and set on fire to serve as torches. They were boiled in oil and burned at the stake. It is estimated that during this period, 5 million Christians were martyred for the testimony of Jesus Christ. However, the church reached its greatest numbers, in proportion to world population, during this period of persecution.[61]

This church age is distinguished by its many translations and its production of hand-copied manuscripts of the Bible. Early in this period the Bible was translated into Syriac, which became the official Scriptures of the Eastern churches and from which translations were made into Arabic, Persian, and Armenian. In the second century the Bible was translated into Latin, which became the Bible of the Western churches for more than 1,000 years. Thus, Emperor Constantine established Christianity as the state church in AD 312.[62]

---

[60] "The Tenth Persecution, Under Diocletian, A.D. 303," Bible Study Tools, https://1ref.us/1jh (accessed February 8, 2021).
[61] See also John Foxe, *Foxe's Book of Martyrs* (England: John Day, 1563).
[62] "Bible translations into Armenian," Wikipedia, https://1ref.us/1ji (accessed February 8, 2021) and "Bible translations into Persian," Wikipedia, https://1ref.us/1jj (accessed February 8, 2021) and "Bible translations into Arabic," Wikipedia, https://1ref.us/1jk (accessed February 8, 2021).

Commendation: *"I know your tribulation and your poverty* (but you are rich) *and the slander of those who say that they are Jews and are not, but are a synagogue of Satan"* (Rev. 2:9, ESV, emphasis mine).

Notice the oxymoron: "You are poor, yet rich! You are afflicted, yet impervious to slander!" This same attitude characterized the life of Christ. He had put aside the divine position and prerogatives to become an innocent child of poor parents in an obscure village. Contrast this affirmation with the condemnation of the Laodicean period, who only *think* they are rich.

Condemnation: *NONE!*

There is no condemnation! Is that not a marvelous thing? But He does give some counsel.

Counsel: "Do not be afraid of what you are about to suffer …. you will suffer persecution …. *Be faithful, even to the point of death"* (Rev. 2:10, NIV, emphasis mine).

Be unafraid of affliction, of suffering, prison, and persecution. To what extent? Until death! Smyrna is the one church of the seven that is specifically indicative of martyrs. We will find that there are only two of the seven churches that receive no condemnation from God. Therefore, it appears that those in the other five must sort themselves out among these two, because in final analysis we must stand guiltless before God.

Challenge: "I will give you the crown of life …. The one who conquers will never be harmed by the second death" (Rev. 2:10–11, CSB).

Keep this concept in mind because as we unfold the rest of Revelation this will make a great deal more sense.

Characteristic: "I am the First and Last …. I was dead, but look—I am alive forever and ever" (Rev. 1:17–18, CSB).

How encouraging this is to those who will be martyred! He says, "*I* [also] was dead/martyred, and behold I am alive forever and ever!"

III. Pergamum—Indulged—AD 313 to AD 538 (Citadel/Elevation)

"And to the angel of the church in Pergamos write … *I know thy works"* (Rev. 2:12–13, emphasis mine).

Pergamum (Pergamos) was the ancient capital of the Roman province of Asia. When Medo-Persia conquered Babylon, the Babylonian priesthood escaped to Pergamum and established for themselves a temple to Zeus and to Aesclepius, the serpent god. They took with them also the Palladium stone, vestments, the title *Pontifex Maximus* (bridge between heaven and earth), keys, and the mitre (a vestment reminiscent of Dagon, the open-mouthed fish god).

Pergamum introduces the Dark Ages, which will suppress not only spiritual understanding but secular culture, as well. Literacy was limited to the very wealthy and to the leader.

In AD 313 Constantine began the absorption of paganism into Christianity. The label ascribed to this church period is "citadel," or high place, and the church at this time was riding high! They had been sorely persecuted for more than two centuries, and now suddenly they are the premier religious institution of the empire. A further subtlety in this designation connects it with the "high places" of paganism. Jesus' church will gradually adopt all the accoutrements of pagan power and influence, as well as its strategies of maintenance.

Commendation: *"I know where you live …. You are true to me and you did not abandon your faith in me"* **(Rev. 2:13, GNT, emphasis mine).**

God is still commending them! He declares to them (with the exception of Rome and Alexandria), "You've remained true, and you have not renounced your faith." The name Pergamum means "marriage" or "elevation." As the church became married to governmental authority and elevated to a place of acceptance, it declined in spiritual blessing and power.[63, 64]

---

63 See Chart 2, p. 41, "Apostasy and Reformation."
64 Francesca Romana Valente, "7 PAGAN FESTIVALS WE STILL CELEBRATE TODAY," THROUGH ETERNITY, https://1ref.us/1jl (accessed February 8, 2021).

Revelation 1–3: Introduction to Revelation and the Seven Churches

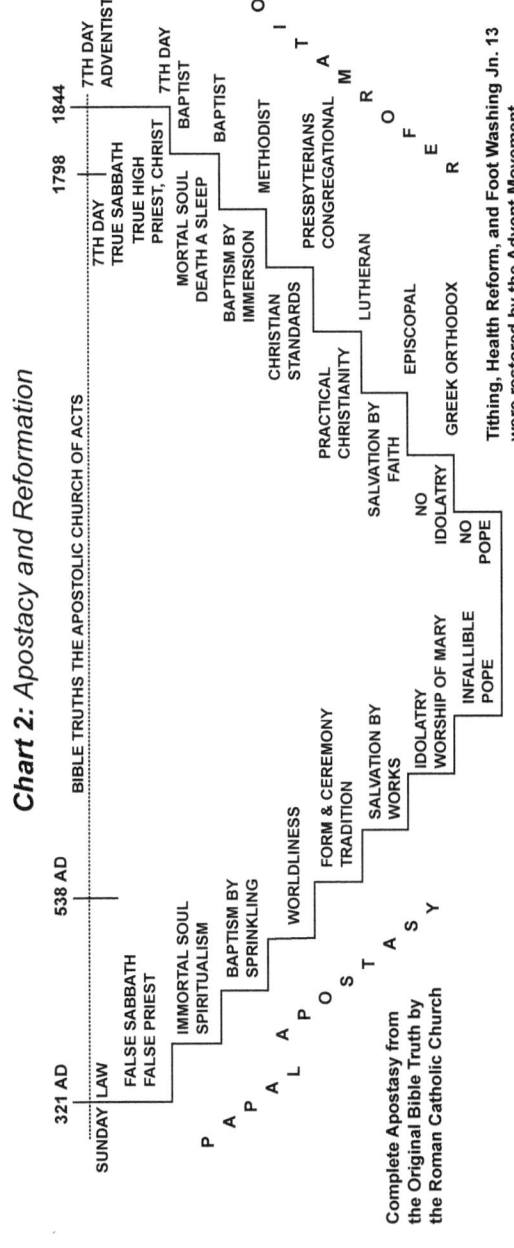

Chart 2: *Apostasy and Reformation*

As shown, the cause of so many denominations is the reformation out of the great Papal Apostasy from the original teachings of the Bible, as foretold in II Thess. 2:3-10 and Dan 7:21-25. A great reformer would protest against false teachings in the church and would originate a denomination which reformed on certain points of doctrine but then that denomination would stop and go no further with their reformation. Then another reformer would organize a church which would include all of the previous reforms, plus other important reforms. Thus many different churches were formed. Afterwards many of these original denominations divided over minor points of doctrine or organization, causing many more.

Bring God's people back from every denomination, to following the Bible and the Bible only, which includes keeping all of the commandments of God, thus fulfilling all of His requirements for His True Remnant Church. According to Rev. 12:6-17 the true church should come out of hiding and all of God's truths once again would be restored by a remnant which would keep the commandments of God and have the Testimony of Jesus which is the Spirit of Prophecy. Rev 18:4 And I heard another voice from heaven saying, Come out of her, my people, that ye be not partakers of her sins, and that ye receive not of her plagues.

Condemnation: "Some of your people follow the teaching of Balaam .... [T]hey committed sexual sins. You also have people who follow the teaching of the Nicolaitans" (Rev. 2:14–15, NIRV).

The teaching of Balaam differs from the teaching of the Nicolaitans, though they are closely related. Nicolaitanism—from *Niko* (to conquer, to overthrow) and *Laos* (the people, laity); thus, to overthrow the people—created two problems. (1) They practiced sensuality by completely separating the spiritual and physical natures, the ancient equivalent of the "holy flesh" movement, which permitted sexual ritual as part of the church worship. (2) They tried to establish an ecclesiastical order. Nicolaitanism is an effort to set up bishops, archbishops, cardinals, and popes.

The teaching of Balaam is sensual for a different reason. It seeks fellowship with unbelievers on their level of experience *in order to convert them.* It gives up standards, hoping to entice them into the fold. Christian standards were compromised during this period by the adoption of a ritualism strongly resembling Babylonian mysticism. Listed below are some of the practices inculcated into the church during this period:

> AD 300—**Prayers for the dead.**
>
> AD 300—**Making the sign of the cross.**
>
> AD 375—**Worship of saints and angels.**
>
> AD 394—**Mass first instituted.**
>
> AD 431—**Worship of Mary begun.**
>
> AD 500—**Priests began dressing differently than laypeople.**
>
> AD 526—**Extreme unction.**
>
> AD 593—**Doctrine of purgatory introduced.**
>
> AD 600—**Worship services conducted in Latin.**
>
> AD 600—**Prayers directed to Mary.** [65]

---

[65] Loraine Boettner, *Roman Catholicism* (Philadelphia, PA: Presbyterian and Reformed, 1962), pp. 7–9.

From AD 312 and forward, the church became more Roman and less Christian in its practices. The Roman Catholic Church of today cannot be traced prior to AD 312.[66] Until that time the church was a collection of independent local churches working together whenever possible but not dominated by central authority.

Counsel: "Repent" (Rev. 2:16).

One word: *repent!* How do you repent? STOP what you're doing and turn (your will) around.

Challenge: "[If you repent], I will give some of the hidden manna, and I will give him a white stone, with a new name written on the stone" (Rev. 2:17, ESV).

To receive a white stone means "to be acquitted" in a court of law.[67] But manna is a symbol of grace. Manna must be gathered early every day in a sufficient quantity for that day for each person. One cannot gather for another. It is intended to convey the notion of grace. You must rise early in the morning, individually, and go out and receive grace from God sufficient for that day, every day. Next we will look at the characteristic of the Speaker.

Characteristic: "[H]e which hath the sharp sword with two edges" (Rev. 2:12).

We have seen that Christ has selected one of the aspects of His nature as revealed to John in his vision and presented it to each individual church. To Pergamum He revealed the sharp, double-edged sword (Rev. 2:12) which, without question, refers to the Word of God. The cure for the problems of the local church at Pergamum of the Pergamum age, or indeed of any church or age, is the Word of God. Christ used that Word to sanctify His Church (John 17:17), to cleanse it (Eph. 5:25–26), and to bring it peace (John 16:33). Had the church of Pergamum heeded the Word of God, the evils of the Dark Ages could well have been avoided.

IV. Thyatira—Pagan—AD 538 to AD 1517 (Sweet Savor of Labor, Sacrifice of Contrition, Satan's Teaching)

---

66 "Roman Catholicism," EUROPEAN-AMERICAN EVANGELISTIC CRUSADES, https://1ref.us/1jm (accessed February 8, 2021).
67 *Andrews Study Bible* (Berrien Springs, MI: Andrews University Press, 2010), p. 1664.

"And unto the angel of the church in Thyatira write ... *I know thy works*" (Rev. 2:18–19, emphasis mine).

In AD 538 Justinian by decree appointed Vigilius, the Bishop of Rome, as "The Corrector of Heretics," marking the beginning of the Dark Ages—1,260 years of unprecedented persecution from AD 538 to AD 1798.

Commendation: *"I know your works,* **love, service, faith, and your patience; and as for your works, the last are more than the first"** (Rev. 2:19, NKJV, New Millennium Edition, emphasis mine).

God has yet something good to say of His church! Remember, these seven churches reflect all collective souls on earth who have entered into some formal institution or agreement proclaiming Christ—not just a denomination, or a *remnant*. Jesus is commending Thyatira for continuing to reflect love, faith, service, and perseverance *more than at first!* Spiritual corruption has been confined to Rome and Alexandria, Egypt, but the church has grown in number and influence; it has spread abroad and embraced many peoples. Storm clouds are again gathering, but from a different direction. And with His commendation, Jesus is warning them of this new danger. His words fall into three categories:

1. "I know where you live." History has revealed the evil nature of this city which Satan had made his headquarters. Through the Roman emperors during the first three centuries Satan had learned that attacking Christians would never conquer them; thus, he changed his approach to one of indulgence and elevation.

2. "Yet you remain true to my name." Criticism cannot be hurled against the doctrine of this church or age, for they were still doctrinally pure. But they sinned by taking in the ceremonies of paganism, which later were supported by artificial doctrines of an unscriptural nature that went on to pollute the true doctrines of the church, elevating traditional authority above that of scriptural. It was at this time that the Arian controversy was fought at the Council of Nicaea in AD 325. Arians insist, as do Jehovah's Witnesses, that Christ was the greatest of all *created beings,* but is not one with the Father.[68] There was no strong central body governing Christ's church at that time, nor was there intended to be. The cities of Rome and Alexandria compromised early and

---

[68] "First Council of Nicaea," Britannica, https://1ref.us/1jn (accessed February 8, 2021).

held to that stance for many years. But because the church at large held fast to Christ's name, the organized church did not teach anything but the personal deity of Jesus Christ for more than 1,000 years. Not until rationalism came in and produced nineteenth- and twentieth-century modernism could the church be found guilty of a false doctrine regarding our Lord. The devil did succeed in subverting this teaching by making it merely a dogmatic doctrine rather than a vital relationship with a Person. However, most so-called Christian churches today at least pay lip service to the deity of Christ.

3. "You did not renounce your faith in me." This characteristic has been largely covered in the discussion on doctrinal purity. However, Arianism was a distorted version of the reality of the times. The Antipas referred to in Revelation 2:13 is unknown by Bible scholars. He was probably a local Christian in the city of Pergamum who had sealed the testimony of his faith with his own blood.

Condemnation: Nevertheless, some of you tolerate Jezebel—false prophetess, sexual immorality, food sacrificed to idols (Rev. 2:20).

"You tolerate that woman Jezebel" (Rev. 2:20, NIV). Whenever a woman is used symbolically to convey a religious dogma, she always represents a religious institution. The teaching of the false prophetess, Jezebel, took two forms: (1) "By her teaching she misleads my servants into sexual immorality" (Rev. 2:20, NIV), which is a symbol of the idolatry brought in during this period and (2) "the eating of food sacrificed to idols" (Ibid.), a symbol of the mingling of the church with the world. During this time Rome sought to bring the kingdom of the world under the domination of the pope in Rome.

It was prior to this period of the Christian era that the church had embraced Sunday worship, adopted popery, and enacted holy days, similar to pagan holidays. The embracing and absorption of paganism is now in full swing. Continuing the history of the church's fall where we left off in the church of Pergamum, note the following changes and doctrines that have their source in paganism:

AD 607—Boniface III made first official pope.

AD 709—Kissing the pope's foot.

AD 786—Worshiping of images and relics.

AD 850—Use of "holy water" begun.

AD 995—Canonization of dead saints.

AD 998—Fasting on Fridays and during Lent.

AD 1079—Celibacy of the priesthood.

AD 1090—Prayer beads.

AD 1184—The Inquisition.

AD 1190—Sale of indulgences.

AD 1215—Transubstantiation.

AD 1220—Adoration of the wafer (Host).

AD 1229—Bible forbidden to laypeople.

AD 1414—Cup forbidden to people at Communion.

AD 1439—Doctrine of purgatory decreed.

AD 1439—Doctrine of seven sacraments affirmed.

AD 1508—The *Ave Maria* approved.

AD 1534—Jesuit order founded.

AD 1545—Tradition granted equal authority with Bible.

AD 1546—Apocryphal books put into Bible.

AD 1854—Immaculate conception of Mary.

AD 1854—*Syllabus of Errors* proclaimed.

AD 1870—Infallibility of the Pope declared.

AD 1930—Public schools condemned by the church.

AD 1950—Assumption of the Virgin Mary.

AD 1965—Mary proclaimed Mother of the Church.[69]

---

[69] Loraine Boettner, *Roman Catholicism* (Philadelphia, PA: Presbyterian and Reformed, 1962), p. 9.

In view of these changes and additions made, as substantiated by history, it seems ironic that "the Church of Rome today boasts that she never changes—*Semper Idem*— 'Always the Same,' a counterfeit of the divine recognition that 'Jesus Christ is the same yesterday and today and forever' (Heb. 13:8, NIV)".[70] Even more tragic is the fact that many believe this assertion.[71]

Counsel: "[H]old fast what [little] you have until I come" (Rev. 2:25, ESV).

Every period of apostasy in earth's history from Adam's fall onward has had its *remnant*, those who have discerned truth clearly and have not bent the knee. This counsel registered with those only who, during this trying period, remained steadfast despite the groundswell of popularity.

Challenge: I will give you power and authority over the nations (Rev. 2:26–27).

Power over nations is what they *most sought*. But the church declines God's offer saying, "No, I want it *my* way!" Under the popes, the church has called to her cause kings and their armies. Most of the nations of Europe have kissed her ring. And that's the fatal choice.

Characteristic: "[Son of man whose] eyes were as a flame of fire; and his feet like unto fine brass" (Rev. 1:14–15).

God sees the portending of church history and is stirred to indignation: "Eyes like unto a flame" which is divine sight of every earthly act. "Feet like unto fine brass" which is the Divine will in every earthly enterprise.

V. Sardis—Dead—AD 1520 to AD 1750

Commendation: "*I know your works*; you have the name of being alive …. Yet you have still a few names in Sardis, people who have not soiled their garments" (Rev. 3:1, 4, RSV, emphasis mine).

How is it that a person soils his clothes? He loses control, does he not?

Condemnation: "[Y]ou have a *reputation* for being alive, but you are dead …. I have not found your works complete" (Rev. 3:1–2, CSB, emphasis mine).

---

70   Ibid., p. 447.
71   See Chart 2, p. 41, "Apostasy and Reformation."

"Your deeds are incomplete." A vital element is omitted. The **Comparative Study Bible, AMP,** renders the phrase this way: "I have not found a thing that you have done—any work of yours—meeting the requirements of My God *or* perfect in His sight." This is a deplorable condition, almost as deplorable as the Laodicean Church will be. What is the difference between them? The church of Laodicea *has no works at all* that elicit from God His approval. Sardis is at least commended for her works, which must have a semblance of *rightness* about them. The problem with Sardis is that she is *dead*, going through the correct motions even though shorn of the Spirit.

Counsel: "Be alert and strengthen [*hold fast*] what remains .... Remember ... what you have received ... *and repent* **[Stop! Turn around!]" (Rev. 3:2, HCSB, emphasis mine).**

Sardis is positioned near the end of the Dark Ages and transitions into the most commendable of the seven periods: Philadelphia, the church of brotherly love. By the grace of God Sardis has preserved the essential elements of brotherly love.

Challenge: "[T]hey will walk with Me in white, because they are worthy .... I will never erase his name from the book of life but will acknowledge his name" (Rev. 3:4–5, HCSB).

How does one become dressed in white? He accepts and *lives* the character of Jesus, which is a gift. "If you will walk with Me dressed in white, I will not blot out your name from the book of life, but I will acknowledge your name before God."

> *How does one become dressed in white? He accepts and lives the character of Jesus, which is a gift. "If you will walk with Me dressed in white, I will not blot out your name from the book of life, but I will acknowledge your name before God."*

Characteristic: "[H]e that hath the seven Spirits of God, and the seven stars" (Rev. 3:1).

He who sends the Holy Spirit also directs the seven stars. The seven stars are those who have ministered, who have had oversight of the churches throughout the long history of the Christian era.

VI. Philadelphia—Loved—1750 to AD 1844 (Brotherly Love)

"And to the angel of the church in Philadelphia write ... *I know thy works*" (Rev. 3:7, emphasis mine).

The city of Philadelphia was formed in a gateway through the mountains, thus the application of an "open door." At some point in the seven-church allegory the divine view shifts from the holistic body to the particular partial view. It is obvious that Philadelphia evinces characteristics quite opposite to generally accepted Christian standards. God's comments are focused on this partial.

Commendation: *"I know thy works.* **I have set before you an open door, and no man can shut it. You have works, missions, little strength but have kept My word, have NOT denied My name"** (Rev. 3:8, Comparative Study Bible, AMP, emphasis mine).

Philadelphia has *little strength* because her numbers are so few. Nevertheless, she has been faithful in every respect.

Condemnation: *NONE!* **The fires of persecution had died down and the reformation was beginning to stir.**

Counsel: *"Hold fast what you have,* **so that no one will take your crown"** (Rev. 3:11, NASB, emphasis mine).

What does this admonition do to the doctrine of "once saved, always saved"? If after conversion one was always saved, what was the necessity to hold fast? And how is a crown of life jeopardized?

Challenge: "I will keep you from the hour of trial .... I will make [you] a pillar in the temple of my God ... I will write on [you] the name of my God ... and my own new name" (Rev. 3:12, RSV).

In the Jewish world it was customary to erect a pillar as a monument to help remember a person beyond his death, and thus immortalize the individual in the memory of the living. (Is this perhaps a precursor of tombstones today?) Here, we commemorate the dead; there, God will commemorate the living.

Characteristic: "[H]e that is holy, he that is true, he that hath the key of David, he that openeth, and no man shutteth; and shutteth, and no man openeth" (Rev. 3:7).

Why is this peculiar to the Philadelphian era? It was during this period that the fires of martyrdom and persecution were especially intense—conditions that favor purity within the church and an influx of membership. Keep the "key" and "door" in mind for future reference.

VII. Laodicea—Apostate/Judged—AD 1844 to the End

"And unto the angel of the church of the Laodiceans write … *I know thy works***" (Rev. 3:14–15, emphasis mine).**

Antiochus the Great built the city and named it after his wife, Laodicea. Independently wealthy, the city opted to rebuild itself after being destroyed in AD 60 by an earthquake, even though Rome offered to finance the job.[72]

This, the last of the seven churches, is the most disappointing. Jesus compares it with the nauseating experience of drinking a tepid substance that induces vomiting (Rev. 3:16). In the original language it would be a cause of involuntary "spewing." Today's teenager would describe it as "hurling," a violent gastrointestinal reaction to sudden sickness.

Commendation: *NONE! I know thy works! (Rev. 3:15).*

Does God have *anything* good to say to the Laodiceans? Our period is bankrupt; God can find nothing to commend us! The church of Laodicea has the distinction of being the only one of the seven churches whose conduct is so reprehensible that even the Christ of glory, who knows all about her, can find nothing for which to commend her.

Condemnation: "[Y]ou are like lukewarm water …. You say, 'I am rich …. I don't need a thing!' And you don't realize that you are wretched and miserable and poor and blind and naked" (Rev. 3:16–17, NLT).

When I toured Greece and western Turkey in May 2005, I went to Laodicea. As our tour bus approached the city from the northeast, we looked across a wide expanse of valley. Way off in the distance was a rim of white several miles long, a formidable escarpment even from that distance. The tour guide said, "That's Laodicea. Those are the springs." He took us across the valley, up the foothills, and over the top where we were able to go through the bathhouses and walk out to the springs that are still there. The lukewarm water is still flowing after many thousands of years, and hundreds of tourists are still bathing their feet in it.

---

72 "Laodicea on the Lycus," Wikipedia, https://1ref.us/1jo (accessed February 8, 2021).

Speaking of this last of the seven churches Jesus said, "You are like those springs—lukewarm. I would that you were either hot or cold."

Counsel: "[B]uy from me gold refined in the fire ... and white clothes to wear, so you can cover your shameful nakedness; and salve to put on your eyes .... be earnest and repent. Here I am!" (Rev. 3:18–20, NIV).

Another characteristic of the city of Laodicea was that it manufactured black cloth woven from the wool of black sheep. Jesus insisted that they buy of Him white raiment. Also, in Laodicea was a pharmaceutical industry manufacturing eye salve. Jesus' message to members of the Laodicean church is to buy of Him eye salve, because these articles of the city are counterfeit to the heavenly thing.

Challenge: If you will do business with me and buy these things, then I will grant you the right to sit with Me on My throne (Rev. 3:21, paraphrase).

"Buy of Me" these heavenly objects. To purchase something there must be an exchange. As a hopeless sinner, what have I to barter for eternal treasure? Jesus said, "Come as you are. Bring your own treasure and exchange it for Mine. I have righteousness for your unrighteousness, I have integrity for your dishonesty, I have generosity for your covetousness." Jesus will take away these cursed things and give us heaven's wealth.

What does it imply to sit with Christ on His throne? You will be a judge, a king; you will have responsibility for serving many.

Characteristic: "The Amen, the faithful and true Witness, the Beginning of the creation of God" (Rev. 1:5, NASB. See also Rev. 19:11; 22:6; Col. 1:15).

It could be said that of the seven churches only two will enter the kingdom of God— Smyrna and Philadelphia. Smyrna characterizes those who were martyred for Christ, and Philadelphia characterizes those faithful who lived for Christ through difficult times. Certainly, Laodicea has nothing to recommend it. Being in the most lamentable state, not only is it bereft of any saving grace, it is ignorant of the lack. And it is well said: *Indifference accompanies ignorance.* What is to be done? The door opens from the *inside!*[73]

---

73   See Appendix 5, p. 244, "From Laodicea to 144,000."

Chapter 3
Revelation 4–6: Setting Up the Judgment and the Seven Seals

The book of Revelation is unmistakably an account of John's personal experience. Forty-five times he "saw," and twenty-five times he "heard." It is thought to consist of eight separate visions or scenes, prefaced by phrases suggesting change. Chapter 4 begins with just such a phrase:

"After this I *looked*, and there before me was a door standing open in heaven. And the voice I had first *heard* speaking to me *like a trumpet* said, "Come up here, and I will show you what must take place after this" (Rev. 4:1, NIV, emphasis mine).

After what? ("After" implies that prophecy is moving forward.) *After the scene of the churches*. Whose voice had John *first* heard then? None other than Jesus Himself! Now he hears His voice once more. *"At once,"* John said, *"I was in the Spirit"* (Rev. 4:2, NIV, emphasis mine). How much of John's book describes a *reality* moment, and how much describes a *visionary* moment? Here it appears that there are two levels because John is speaking with Jesus, and Jesus says, "Come up here, and I will show you" (Rev. 4:1, NIV). Then John advances to a higher, or different, level of visionary experience.

"At once I was in the Spirit, and there before me was a *throne* in heaven with someone sitting on it" (Rev. 4:2, NIV, emphasis mine).

The significance of this arrangement didn't escape John. From his description we can be certain that he was seeing a great tribunal being set up. The One *seated* could be none other than *El Shaddai*—the mighty-breasted one.[74] No *personal feature* is described—only

---

74 The breast is one of the key symbols of sustenance and parental love passed on from God—the parent—to humanity, God's child. So instead of "God Almighty," El Shaddai should probably be translated as "God all-sufficient."

Chart 3: *The Wilderness Tabernacle*

There were three basic divisions distinguishing the tabernacle structure: 1) the court, 2) the Holy Place, and 3) the Most Holy Place; and three basic divisions distinguishing the tabernacle ritual: 1) atonement, 2) intercession, and 3) judgment. The courtyard, with its slain sacrifice on the bronze altar, signified *atonement* and pointed, in particular, to the great transaction at the cross. The Holy Place, with its incense on the golden altar, signified *intercession*, commencing at Christ's ascension and continuing to the end of human probation. The Most Holy Place, the focus of the great annual Day of Atonement (Yom Kippur), typified the antitypical day of *judgment*, commencing in 1844, and ending with the final eradication of sin and evil from the universe.

All three of these paired elements together constitute *Atonement*.

THE THREE FUNDAMENTAL DIMENSIONS OF SALVATION PORTRAYED IN THE SANCTUARY

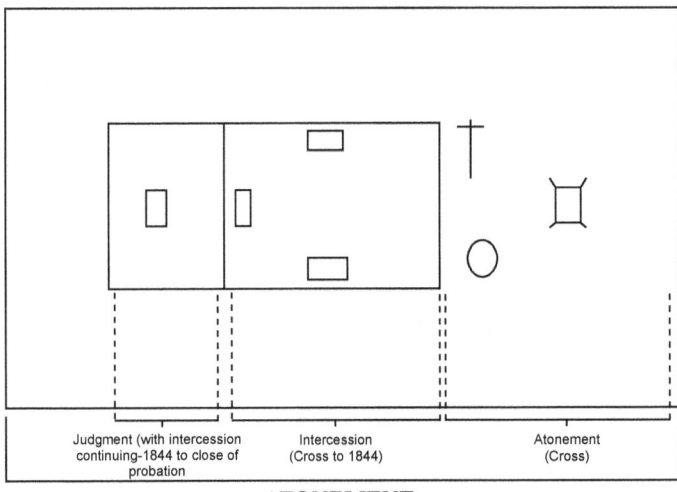

symbols of authority and presence. No one has ever seen the Father. At this point an issue much debated might be raised: where in the real estate of heaven are we—the Holy Place or the Most Holy Place? Certainly, in Revelation 4 the judgment throne room is being set up and staffed. And certainly, in Revelation chapter 6 the assemblage is in the Most Holy Place.[75] All judgment activity will take place in the Most Holy Place. The Father will enter first, followed by the entrance of Jesus a short time later. These entrances will correspond to AD 1844 earth time.[76] The question is: where in the narrative of events related in the Revelation is the passing of deity from the Holy to the Most Holy described? It is not important for us to fix the time of that passage precisely. It is enough that the passage is well-described, whether the setting up of the judgment hall took place *before* the 1844 disappointment or *after* it occurred.[77]

"And round about the throne were four and twenty seats: and upon the seats I saw four and twenty elders sitting, clothed in white raiment; and they had on their heads crowns of gold" (Rev. 4:4).

Next described are twenty-four *elders*. It is surmised that these individuals are of the human race, perhaps made up of those who are translated in Old Testament times, or perhaps of the multitude resurrected with Jesus in New Testament times—or both. They were dressed in white, had crowns of gold, and were also *seated* on thrones. These are *uniform* where each article of dress is significant of something, including the style of dress. All personages seated under similar circumstances signify judicial authority over pending issues.

Verses 5 and 6 provide visuals and sound effects: "[F]lashes of lightning, rumblings and peals of thunder" (Rev. 4:5, NIV). Two members of the Godhead are now in attendance. And there is also before the throne something that *looked like* a sea of glass, clear as crystal (reminiscent of the great iron *sea* set before Solomon's Temple,

---

75 Ellen G. White, *SDA Bible Commentary*, vol. 7 (Washington, DC: Review and Herald, 1957), pp. 766, 775.
76 Ellen G. White, *Early Writings* (Washington, DC: Review and Herald, 1882), pp. 42, 54–55, 253.
77 See Chart 3, p. 53, "The Wilderness Tabernacle."

perhaps?).[78] Remember, metaphors have specific significance; and whenever one is indicated, we must honor the structure of language and make a proper application. This is no cramped courtroom. If there is a sea of glass on which there is an innumerable multitude in attendance, then it is of stupendous dimension, capable of accommodating billions as we will see later.

"In the center, around the throne, were four living creatures" (Rev. 4:6, NIV).

Now proceeds a description that must be figurative, highly symbolic. Two of the properties ascribed to these four persons are (A) they are *living*, and (B) they are *created*. John further describes their appearance *in a particular order*:

(1) They are covered with eyes front and back (Rev. 4:6).

(2) The first of them is *like* a **lion**, the second is *like* an **ox**, the third has the face of a **man**, and the fourth is *like* a *flying* **eagle** (Rev. 4:7).

Upon the banks of the river Chebar, Ezekiel beheld a whirlwind seeming to come from the north, "a great cloud, and a fire infolding itself, and a brightness was about it, and out of the midst thereof as the color of amber." A number of wheels, intersecting one another, were moved by *four living beings*. High above all these "was the likeness of a throne, as the appearance of a sapphire stone: and upon the likeness of the throne was the likeness as the appearance of a man above upon it." *"And there appeared in the* cherubims *the form of a man's hand under their wings."* Ezekiel 1:4, 26; 10:8. The wheels were so complicated in arrangement that at first sight they appeared to be in confusion; but they moved in perfect harmony. *Heavenly beings, sustained and guided by the hand beneath the wings of the cherubim,* were impelling these wheels; above them, upon the

---

78 David Guzik, "2 CHRONICLES 4 – FURNISHINGS FOR THE TEMPLE AND ITS COURT," ENDURING WORD, https://1ref.us/1jp (accessed February 8, 2021): "The laver (basin) and its stand in the wilderness tabernacle, made of bronze, was located in the courtyard between the entrance of the tabernacle and the altar of burnt offerings. It was used by the priests to wash for cleanliness and a reminder of the need for spiritual cleansing and purification. The basin in Solomon's Temple in Jerusalem, called 'the Sea,' was made of cast bronze and replaced the bronze basin from the wilderness tabernacle—but it was MUCH grander! It was a large, completely round water container, shaped like a lily blossom, made of three-inch thick cast bronze, and measuring about fifteen feet from brim to brim. It stood more than seven feet high and was 45 feet in circumference. Filled with lots of water (enough for 3,000 baths), the basin stood on twelve cast oxen (representing the 12 tribes), in groups of three, each group facing one of the four points of the compass. The Sea was set upon the oxen, back parts pointed inward."

sapphire throne, was the Eternal One; and round about the throne a rainbow, the emblem of divine mercy.

As the wheel-like complications were under the guidance of the hand beneath the wings of the cherubim, so the complicated play of human events is under divine control. Amidst the strife and tumult of nations, He that sitteth above the cherubim still guides the affairs of the earth.[79]

To the east three tribes—Judah, Issachar, and Zebulon—belonged to the standard of the camp of Judah, the *lion* (Num. 2:3–9). The lion, nature's symbol of authority adopted by kings and monarchs, is a fitting symbol of this tribe. In Jacob's blessing and judgment on his sons, Judah received "the kingdom and the Messianic promise."[80] What is to be Judah's experience in the last days? "[T]hou art he whom thy brethren shall praise" (Gen. 49:8). Judah is the "goodly [white] horse in the battle" (Zech. 10:3).[81]

To the west three tribes—Ephraim, Manasseh, and Benjamin—belonged to the standard of the *calf* (Num. 2:18–24). Ephraim bore the standard of divine sacrifice. But why the symbol of the *calf*? The calf was a perpetual reminder of God's purpose and presence.

"They made a calf in Horeb, and worshipped the molten image. Thus they changed their glory [authority] into the similitude of an ox that eateth grass. They forgat God their saviour, which had done great things in Egypt" (Ps. 106:19–21).

"Ephraim is joined to idols: let him alone" (Hosea 4:17).

As a result, Ephraim is not represented among the 144,000 in Revelation 7 (see Hosea 12:14; 13:1–2.) There is a parallel in the red horse group who profess the name of Christ but who are left joined to their idols (Rev. 6:4).

To the south, three tribes—Reuben, Simeon, and Gad—belonged to the standard of the *man* (Num. 2:10–16). In the last days the spiritual descendants of Reuben may be described as being associated with a prostitute woman, Babylon, the mother of harlots, because Reuben lay with Bilhah, his father's concubine (Rev. 18:1–4; Gen. 35:22; Rev. 17:1–5). The face of a man also signifies trust in men rather than God.

---

[79] Ellen G. White, *Education* (Mountain View, CA: Pacific Press, 1903), pp. 177–178, emphasis mine.
[80] Ellen G. White, *Patriarchs and Prophets* (Mountain View, CA: Pacific Press, 1890), p. 235.
[81] Ibid., pp. 235–236.

Jacob predicted that in the last days the descendants of Gad, a tribe under the standard of man, would "overcome at the last" (Gen. 49:19). God's people in Babylon (black horse) come out and are the focus of the third seal, where the creature with the face of a man says, "Come and see" (Rev. 6:5). God's people in Babylon are called out at the loud cry of the three angels. Reuben and Gad are represented among the 144,000.

To the north, three tribes—Dan, Asher, and Naphtali—belonged to the standard of the *eagle* (Num. 2:25–31). In Scripture, the eagle is classed with the vulture as an unclean bird (Deut. 14:12, NIV). The name Dan means "judge." The eagle is a symbol of self-exaltation:

"Though thou exalt thyself as the eagle, and though thou set thy nest among the stars, thence will I bring thee down, saith the LORD" (Obad. 4).

The connection of the eagle, signifying those who are lost in the judgment (pale horse), is given in Luke 17:37: "Wheresoever the body is, thither will the eagles be gathered together." The eagle as a symbol of impending doom and death fits the group revealed under the fourth seal.

Each beast (authority) has six wings covered with eyes all around—fit witnesses to testify in the judgment (Rev. 4:8). In unison, by some means, they continually recognize sovereign God: glory, honor, and thanksgiving. *Their* worship inspires a response from the twenty-four elders who have their own unique expression of worship. All this is not to entertain us, but to inform us. We are to catch something of the majesty, the solemnity, the awfulness of what is about to transpire.

"Then I saw in the *right hand* of him who sat on the throne a scroll with writing *on both sides* and sealed with *seven seals*" (Rev. 5:1, NIV, emphasis mine).

Until now the scene described is thought by some to have been in the Holy Place in heaven. But notice: God the Father has possession of a document, densely inscribed and firmly secured—seven seals, no less.[82] Are the seals multiple for security sake or is there another purpose for seven of them? A mighty angel, perhaps Gabriel, introduces a dilemma. He asks the question: "Who is worthy to break the seals and open the scroll?" (Rev. 5:2, NIV).

---

82   Ancient Near East *covenant* documents were written on both sides, as evidenced by the account in Exodus 32:15, KJV: "And Moses turned, and went down from the mount, and the two tables of the testimony were in his hand: the tables were written on both their sides; on the one side and on the other were they written." Also in Zechariah 5:1, 3, ESV: "Again I lifted my eyes and saw ... a flying scroll .... For everyone who steals shall be cleaned out according to what is on one side, and everyone who swears falsely shall be cleaned out according to what is on the other side." Also see Ezekiel 2:9–10 and Revelation 5:1.

John is at a loss. Among the most notables of the *universe* at this gathering there is no one stepping forward to claim the right. Silence hangs heavy, and John is distressed to the point of tears because neither in heaven nor on earth nor *under* the earth can a search discover a worthy one. Why *under* the earth? Because that is the domain of demons, and demons have challenged God on both His mercy and His justice. One of the twenty-four elders (why them?) expresses pity for John and informs him that "[T]he *Lion* of the tribe of Judah, the Root of David, has triumphed. *He* is able to open the scroll and its seven seals" (Rev. 5:5, NIV, emphasis mine).

John is much relieved. But notice the next verse. Does it not pose *another* problem?

"Then I saw a *Lamb,* looking as if it had been slain, standing at the center of the throne, encircled by the four living creatures and the elders" (Rev. 5:6, NIV, emphasis mine).

Why a *Lamb* when it has been announced that the *Lion of the tribe of Judah* has authority only? This will be resolved in chapter 6 when the seals of the scroll are opened. The arrangement of the court has been clarified as well. The Lamb is in the center of the throne *with the Father*, encircled next by the four living creatures, and then by the twenty-four elders. Notice the rest of verse 6 that describes this Personage: "[He] had *seven horns* and *seven eyes*, which are the *seven spirits* of God sent out into all the earth. He went and took the scroll from the *right* hand of him who sat on the throne" (Rev. 5:6–7, NIV, emphasis mine).

The Lamb had *seven* horns: complete power to resolve issues until the end of time. He had *seven* eyes as well as the seven horns, *which are the seven Spirits*. The seven Spirits, we have learned, is a descriptive of the Holy Spirit, the third Member of the Trinity. Thus, all three Members of the Godhead are seen to be in attendance at this great event. The Lamb now took the mysterious scroll from the hand of Him who sat on the throne. Attention is called to a spontaneous celebration by the inner circle of court attendants. The twenty-four elders were equipped with "each one" a harp, and each a bowl full of incense, *"which are the prayers of the saints"* (Rev. 5:8, emphasis mine). This idea will become important later on. In verse 11 John's attention is called to the larger court: "Then I *looked* and *heard* the voice of many angels, *numbering thousands upon thousands, and ten thousand times ten thousand.* They encircled the throne and the living creatures and the elders" (Rev. 5:11, NIV, emphasis mine).

Revelation 4–6: Setting Up the Judgment and the Seven Seals

It appears that every intelligence in heaven is in attendance. Within the narrative of John's Revelation, how did we arrive at this point? Can we place this event in the stream of prophetic *history*? If we go back to Revelation 3:7–13 the church of Philadelphia emerges. The historical date for this church is determined to be AD 1750 to AD 1844. Notice a very significant statement made by "[H]im who is holy and true, who holds the key of David" (Rev. 3:7, NIV).

"What he opens no one can shut, and what he shuts no one can open …. See, *I have placed before you an open door* **that no one can shut" (Rev. 3:7–8, NIV, emphasis mine).**

The door to the Holy Place is now shut, and the door to the Most Holy Place is now open. Spirit of Prophecy makes plain this passage in *Early Writings*:

"Jesus has risen up and shut the door of the holy place of the heavenly sanctuary and has opened a door into the most holy place and entered in to cleanse the sanctuary …. As Jesus ended His ministration in the holy place and closed the door of that apartment, a great darkness settled upon [the rejecters of His message]."[83]

These events occurred in the year AD 1844 and bring us to chapter 6 of Revelation and John's vision of the seals. It is important for us to internalize that we have followed John's Revelation narrative from Ephesus AD 100 up through Philadelphia AD 1798 at the time mentioned, and that John has related the events in a sequential manner. *At this point* the seals are introduced. An important question to ask is should we go back and make the journey again, or is it more logical for us to assume that the narrative continues?[84] In just 12 verses, six of the seven seals are opened in cryptic language. (The seventh is not to be opened until Revelation 8:1.) Is there available to us any indication of what is contained in the densely written scroll about to be unsealed?

"The book of Daniel is unsealed in the revelation to John, *and carries us forward* to the last scenes of this earth's history."[85]

So, it appears that we are being *carried forward* by prophecy! We ask John what he *saw* and *heard* in the vision at Patmos, and he answers: [Revelation 5:1–3, quoted]. There in His open

---

[83] Ellen G. White, *Early Writings* (Washington, DC: Review and Herald, 1882), pp. 251–252.
[84] Ellen G. White, *SDA Bible Commentary*, vol. 7 (Washington, DC: Review and Herald, 1957), pp. 108–111. This reviews the metamorphosis of interpretation of the seals. The current application generally accepted by the church came originally from non-Adventist sources.
[85] Ellen G. White, *Testimonies to Ministers and Gospel Workers* (Mountain View, CA: Pacific Press, 1923), p. 115, emphasis mine.

hand [the open hand of a strong angel] lay the book, *the roll of the history of God's providences,* the prophetic history of nations and the church. Herein was contained the *divine utterances, His authority, His commandments, His laws, the whole symbolic counsel of the Eternal, and the history of all ruling powers in the nations.* In symbolic language was contained in that roll *the influence of every nation, tongue, and people from the beginning of earth's history to its close …. The destiny of every nation was contained in that book.*[86]

Here, described in language most exquisite and detailed, are the contents of the book of life.

"I watched as the Lamb opened the first of the seven seals" (Rev. 6:1, NIV).

In Revelation 5:5, the lion is authorized to open the book, but here we discover the *lamb* claiming the privilege. Of course, we understand the Lion and the Lamb to be the same Person, but why the wordplay? As the opening of the seals unfolds, it will become more evident. But a paragraph from Spirit of Prophecy will be helpful here:

"The Savior is presented before John under the symbols of "the Lion of the tribe of Judah" and of "a Lamb as it had been slain." Revelation 5:5, 6. These symbols represent the union of omnipotent power and self-sacrificing love. *The Lion of Judah, so terrible to the rejecters of His grace, will be the Lamb of God to the obedient and faithful.*"[87]

We will find that each of the seals can be none other than *topics organizing the business of the great judgment.* The first four are represented as *different-colored horses.* For an explanation of the meaning it is best that "the Bible [be] its own expositor."[88] It is not a study of the Greek language that is the expositor of Scripture (although that has its place) but a comparison among texts that gives meaning. The mysteries are "open to the study of *all,*"[89] not just to theologians or Greek scholars. Zechariah is one of the two prophets of the restoration of the temple in the Old Testament (see *Prophets and Kings,* chapters 46–48). Notice what Zechariah says:

---

[86] Ellen G. White, *Manuscript Releases,* vol. 12 (Silver Spring, MD: Ellen G. White Estate, 1990), p. 296, emphasis mine.
[87] Ellen G. White, *The Acts of the Apostles* (Mountain View, CA: Pacific Press, 1911), p. 589, emphasis mine.
[88] Ellen G. White, *Education* (Mountain View, CA: Pacific Press, 1903), p. 190.
[89] Ellen G. White, *The Acts of the Apostles* (Mountain View, CA: Pacific Press, 1911), p. 584, emphasis mine.

"The Lord of hosts hath visited his flock the house of Judah, and hath made them as his goodly *horse* in the battle" (Zech. 10:3, emphasis mine).

Support for the symbolism of horses *representing people* is found in Joel 2:1–4 in which the time frame is the "day of the LORD" (Joel 2:1) and the righteous are referred to as a "great people and a strong" (Joel 2:2) and "the appearance of them is as the appearance of *horses*" (Joel 2:4, emphasis mine).[90] The different horses could represent different classes of people in the judgment, commencing in 1844 and extending to the close of probation.

Chart 4: 7 Seals: Scenes of Judgment

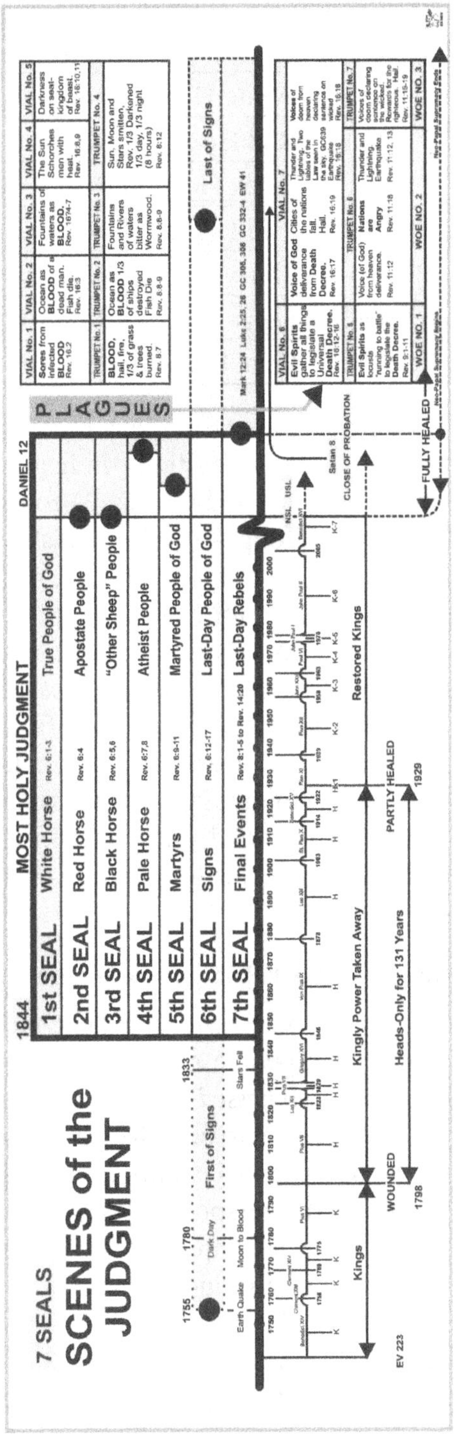

90   See Chart 4 on this page, "7 Seals: Scenes of Judgment."

1st Seal	White Horse	Rev. 6:1–3	True People of God
2nd Seal	Red Horse	Rev. 6:4	Apostate People
3rd Seal	Black Horse	Rev. 6:5–6	Other Sheep People
4th Seal	Pale Horse	Rev. 6:7–8	Atheist People
5th Seal	Martyrs	Rev. 6:9–11	Martyred People of God
6th Seal	Signs	Rev. 6:12–17	Last-day People of God
7th Seal	Final Events	Rev. 8:1–14:20	Last-day Rebels

In these representations there is much *duality* that demands our attention: (1) dual action—in heaven and in earth; (2) dual application—historical and future; (3) controlling forces—Christ and Satan; (4) people groups—loyal and disloyal; (5) consequences—good and evil.

Seals one to four can be graphically described as the "four horsemen of the Apocalypse." *For each rider in turn* (white horse, red horse, black horse, and pale horse), *apostle John is urged to "Come!"*

Each rider is *given an object* (a crown and a bow, a great sword, a pair of scales, and authority over "a fourth of the earth"); and *performs an action* (conquering and to conquer, take peace from the earth, measuring out food, and power to kill with sword, hunger, death and by beasts of the earth). [Rev. 6:1–8, ESV.] Now let's explore each seal in more detail.

SEAL NUMBER 1: The First Horse Is White—True People of God

Christ comes into judgment mounted upon a white horse. The white horse people group are all those who, since the beginning of time, have *confessed the name of Jesus.* They now come up "before judgment"—not to be judged in the sense of discovering innocence or guilt, but rather of *confirming* God's judgment of innocence. Has God not reached a personal conclusion respecting each one who has died? Has God been completely just in His verdict respecting those saved? Is it safe to reintroduce them to the community of universal harmony? In all three phases of the judgment that we will experience—and we *will all experience them*—we will not make any conclusion respecting any person in those judgments that will affect their eternal destiny. We will only endorse God's conclusion respecting each one of them. And that's the purpose of it.

"And I saw when the *Lamb* opened one [the first] of the seals, and I heard, *as it were* the noise of thunder [the first of the seven thunders to be mentioned in chapter 10], one of the four beasts [lion] saying, Come and see [Pay close attention!]" (Rev. 6:1, emphasis mine).

A subsequent chapter will discuss the subject of the seven thunders of Revelation 10. Apocalyptic *thunder* is the speaking of God, or the speaking of a nation in legislative session.

"I heard, as it were the noise of thunder, one of the four beasts [the *lion*], saying, Come and see" (Ibid.). Each of the first four seals will be introduced by one of the four beasts. "Come and see!" This invitation is addressed to the huge court where unnumbered intelligences are gathered to witness the great judgment. The sense of the invitation to "Come and see" is to bend closer, pay very careful attention to what is being done with respect to these people because universal perception of God's justice and His mercy is at stake. His mercy will repatriate sinners with whom the universe will share eternity, and His justice will damn many others to an unwaking sleep. *Pay attention*:

"For the time is come that judgment must begin at the house of God: [We understand that to be His church, don't we?] and if it first begin at us, what shall the end be of them that obey [respond] not [to] the gospel of God?" (1 Pet. 4:17).

"And I saw, and behold a white horse: and he that sat on him had a bow; and a crown was given unto him: and he went forth conquering, and to conquer" (Rev. 6:2).

Here we will see action both in heaven and on earth, the duality mentioned earlier. Jesus, the rider, is depicted with a *bow* and a *crown*. The action now shifts from the judgment hall in heaven to the battlefield of earth. The bow in His hand represents His Word according to Habakkuk 3:9. He is directing the battle for souls during the last moments of earth's history. It is also a symbol of the ongoing *judgment*.

"Thy bow was made quite naked [unsheathed], according to the oaths of the tribes, even thy *word. Selah* [*Think of it!*]. Thou didst cleave the earth with rivers [with Thy Word]" (Hab. 3:9, emphasis mine).

The *crown* in this context has a unique application. We turn to Zechariah 6 to find it:

Then take silver and gold, and make *crowns,* and set them upon the head of Joshua the son of Josedech, the high priest; and speak unto him, saying, Thus speaketh the LORD of hosts, saying, Behold the man whose name is The BRANCH; and he shall grow up out of his place, and he shall *build the temple of the LORD;* Even he shall *build the temple of the LORD*; and he shall bear the glory, and shall *sit and rule upon his throne;* and he shall *be a priest upon his throne.* (Zech. 6:11–13, emphasis mine)[91]

It's a bit redundant, isn't it? Why did John articulate the redundancy in that text? *Because it must be important.* God will be doubted whether He has the capability or the will to build a temple, to recover a kingdom, and to prepare a people. God is telling us three times in this verse, "Yes, it can be done! And yes, I will do it!" So the "crown" given to Christ in Revelation 6:2 in the first seal marks the change in His ministry as He moves to the Most Holy Place *to build the temple* and *to restore the sanctuary to its rightful state* (Dan. 8:14). Thus, these "symbols" represent authority and processes taking place in *both* heaven and earth respecting the *setting up of Christ's eternal kingdom.* In this primary action of the tribunal, only the cases of those whose names have been entered in the book of life will be considered. Names will be accepted, and names will be rejected.

SEAL NUMBER 2: The Second Horse Is Red—Apostate People

"And when he had opened the second seal, I heard the second beast [calf] say, Come and see! [*Pay close attention!*] And there *went out* another horse that was red: and power was given to him that sat thereon to take peace from the earth, and that they should kill one another: and there was given unto him a great sword" (Rev. 6:3–4, emphasis mine).

There is a reason the *four horses* are presented in the way that they are: first, the *white horse,* then the *red horse,* then the *black horse,* and finally the *pale horse.* The judgment is dealing *first* with the saints of God (those who are saved to the kingdom), *second* with those who have apostatized (abandoned purity within the church), *third* with the ignorant (those who have been uninformed or misinformed), and *fourth* with those who *deny* that Jesus Christ has the only authority to oversee

---

91 See Chart 3, p. 53, "The Wilderness Tabernacle Chart."

the affairs of salvation. "*[T]here is none other name under heaven given among men, whereby we must be saved*" (Acts 4:12, emphasis mine). And anyone who denies this Person, Jesus Christ, is an atheist.[92]

Let me share an excerpt from *Testimonies for the Church*:

> They [the *white horse* people] are powerless to stop the rushing torrent of iniquity, and hence they are filled with grief and alarm. They mourn before God to see *religion despised in the very homes of those who have had great light*. They lament and afflict their souls because pride, avarice, selfishness, and deception of almost every kind *are in the church*. The *Spirit of God*, which prompts to reproof, *is trampled underfoot*, while the servants of Satan triumph .... The class who *do not feel grieved* over their own spiritual declension [the *red horse* people], nor mourn over the sins of others, *will be left without the seal of God*. The Lord commissions His messengers, the men with the slaughtering weapons in their hands [Ezek. 9]: "Go ye after him through the city, and smite ... slay utterly old and young ... and *begin at My sanctuary* .... Here we see that the *church*—the Lord's sanctuary—was *the first to feel the stroke of the wrath of God* .... Our own course of action will determine whether we shall *receive the seal* of the living God [*white horse* people] or *be cut down* by the destroying weapons [*red horse* people].[93]

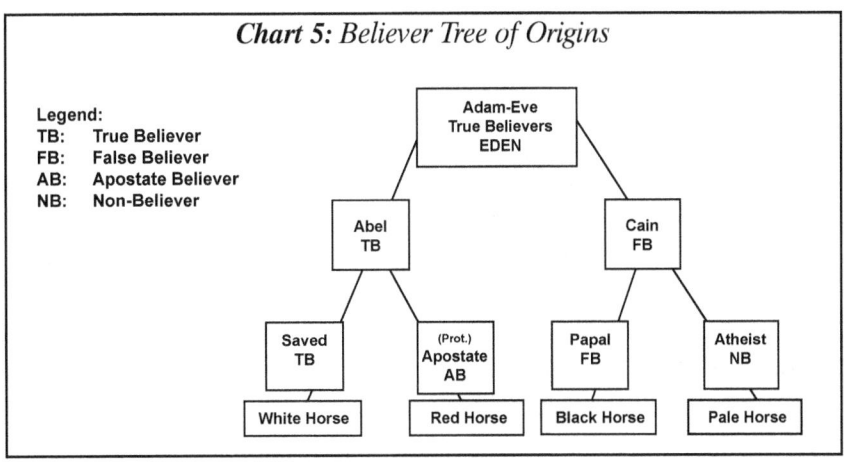

Chart 5: *Believer Tree of Origins*

We turn again to Zechariah for an interpretation of red horses:

---

92   See Chart 2, p. 41, "Apostasy and Reformation."
93   Ellen G. White, *Testimonies for the Church*, vol. 5 (Mountain View, CA: Pacific Press, 1889), pp. 210–212, emphasis mine.

> I saw by night, and behold a man riding upon a *red horse* .... Then I said, O my lord, what are these? .... And the man ... answered and said, These are they *whom the LORD hath sent to walk to and fro through the earth* [they are His chosen people] .... And they answered the angel of the LORD ... and said, We have walked to and fro through the earth, and, behold, *all the earth sitteth still, and is at rest* [Everything's fine!] (Zech. 1:8–11, emphasis mine).

This is a false report according to Ezekiel. Notice: "Thus saith the LORD GOD: Woe unto the foolish prophets, that follow their own spirit, and *have seen nothing!* ... Because, even because they have seduced *my people,* saying, Peace; and there was no peace" (Ezek. 13:3, 10, emphasis mine).

The red horse represents all those false-hearted people who have professed the name of Christ, but who misrepresent Him, giving a false message of peace to the world. They have been *surface students* and are judged in the investigative judgment as found wanting. In Ezekiel 9 this group is the first to receive God's judgment upon them when He says: "Slay utterly old and young, both maids, and little children, and women: but come not near any man upon whom is the mark; and *begin at my sanctuary*. Then they began at the ancient men which were before the house" (Ezek. 9:6, emphasis mine).[94]

It is significant that the red horse of Revelation 6 *went out* (verse 4) in contrast to the other three horses (verses 2, 5 and 8). This compares with Zechariah's statement that the members of this group are the ones whom the Lord has *sent to walk through the earth* (Zech. 1:10). This group is part of the *visible church* sent to fulfill the gospel commission but who fail to make the necessary preparation, and who do not bear the burdens of the cross (the five foolish virgins in Matthew 25). Jesus' parable of ten virgins who prepared themselves to meet and escort the Bridegroom into the wedding feast figured His church at the time of His second coming: all slept while waiting, five had brought extra oil (Holy Spirit), while five had no oil at the time of His coming.

"And there *went out* another horse that was red: and power was given to him that sat thereon to take peace from the earth, and that

---

94 Ellen G. White, *The Great Controversy* (Mountain View, CA: Pacific Press, 1911), p. 656.

they should kill one another: and there was given unto him a great sword" (Rev. 6:4, emphasis mine).

Contrary to the message of peace and safety they give by their careless and indifferent lives, *the one riding the horse* has the power to take peace from the earth. Although professing to be Christ's followers, this group is really under the control of the rider of the horse—Satan—the one that brings death and destruction.

Hebrews 2:14 speaks of "him that had the power of death, that is, the devil." In the fearful time ahead when calamities polarize humanity according to their cultivated predispositions, there will be a falling away from the body of Christ, even by the brightest among us. Consider this from the Spirit of Prophecy:

> [M]any, *even of the professed followers of Christ,* are thinking, planning, and working so eagerly for self-exaltation, that in order to gain the sympathy and support of the people, they are ready to pervert the truth, falsifying and misrepresenting the Lord's servants, and even charging them with the base and selfish motives that inspire their own hearts. By persistently reiterating falsehood, and that against all evidence, they at last come to believe it to be truth. While endeavoring to destroy the confidence of the people in the men of God's appointment, *they really believe that they are engaged in a good work, verily doing God service.*[95]

SEAL NUMBER 3: The Third Horse Is Black—Other Sheep People of God

"And when he had opened the third seal, I heard the third beast [man] say, Come and see [*Pay close attention!*]" (Rev. 6:5, emphasis mine).

These invitations by the four beasts around the throne are addressed to the great audience chamber, to those in attendance of this assize. They are the sinless worlds, the remaining angels who did not defect in Lucifer's rebellion. They are the ones to whom this judgment will make a monumental difference, because from it God proposes to introduce to the universe repatriated sinners who in intimate

---

[95] Ellen G. White, "The Rebellion of Korah," *The Review and Herald*, November 12, 1903, emphasis mine.

association will replace the lost ones of heaven. The question uppermost in the minds of all: Are they safe to save?

"And I beheld, and lo a black horse; and he that sat on him had a pair of balances in his hand" (Rev. 6:5).

Again, Zechariah gives us a clue: "The black horses which are therein go forth into the *north country*" (Zech. 6:6, emphasis mine). *North* is God's designation, and they are objects of a divine mission. Remember, the *horses* in Zechariah are *prophetic forces* preparing to act in Israel's final moment. Therefore, the black horse of Revelation is identified with the *north* whose king in Daniel 11:40–45 is the papacy during the last days. Remember also that the papacy is Christian and has been Christian since its inception in AD 321. And remember the final state of things with respect to papal power: the whole world will wonder after her. Protestantism is even now blending into the world of papal influence so that soon there will exist but one body. The black horse people are thus associated with Babylon who also professes the name of Christ but who are actually *anti*christ—in the place of Christ. The papacy has notoriously announced itself to be in the place of Christ here on earth. And all those who align themselves with the papacy buy into that philosophy. They are judged in the investigative judgment by Jesus who is represented as "[H]e that sat on him [and] had a pair of *balances* in his hand" (Rev. 6:5, emphasis mine). This is judgment language! We are weighed in the balances of the sanctuary.[96]

"And I heard a voice in the midst of the four beasts say, A measure of wheat for a penny, and three measures of barley for a penny; and see thou hurt not the oil and the wine" (Rev. 6:6).

Matthew 20:1–16 tells of the penny as the standard wage for all those laboring in the Master's vineyard. When the early workers complained of the inequity, the Master reminded them that they received just what they had agreed to. What was it that these workers did for their penny? They harvested wheat and barley until past the *eleventh hour!* And then what? The application in this parable is the end of the world where the standard reward for God's servants is *eternal life*. How many eternal lives are profitable to one person? Why would you contend with the Master for more than one eternal life?

In the parable of Matthew 13:33, emphasis mine, Jesus says, "[T]he kingdom of heaven is like unto leaven, which a woman took,

---

[96] Ellen G. White, *Testimonies to Ministers and Gospel Workers* (Mountain View, CA: Pacific Press, 1923), p. 450.

Revelation 4–6: Setting Up the Judgment and the Seven Seals

and hid in *three measures of meal,* till the whole was leavened." *Christ's Object Lessons* tells us that the leaven here "illustrates the quickening, assimilating power of the *grace* of God. *None* are so vile, *none* have fallen so low, as to be beyond the working of *this* power."[97] The *three measures of barley* tie the judgment in the third seal group to the principle enunciated in Christ's parable. It is the Holy Spirit who prepares the three measures of barley for the judgment.[98]

The voice also warns us to be careful of the *oil and the wine.* What do these symbols mean? There is a powerful statement in *Testimonies*:

> In order to secure man to Himself and ensure his eternal salvation, Christ left the royal courts of heaven and came to this earth, endured the agonies of sin and shame in man's stead, and died to make him free. In view of the infinite price paid for man's redemption, how dare any professing the name of Christ treat with indifference one of His little ones? How carefully should brethren and sisters in the church guard every word and action lest *they hurt the oil and the wine!*[99]

"Oil" is figurative of the Holy Spirit scripturally; and the warning is to not abuse—quench—the Holy Spirit. "Wine" is figurative of Christ's healing sacrifice, and the caution is to lead on gently lest the tender ones be offended.

SEAL NUMBER 4: The Fourth Horse Is Pale—Atheist People

John's introduction here is consistent with the other three: "And when he had opened the fourth seal, I heard the voice of the fourth beast [eagle] say, Come and see [Pay attention!]" (Rev. 6:7).

"And I looked, and behold a pale horse: and his name that sat on him was *Death,* and *Hell* followed with him. And power was given unto *them* over the fourth part of the earth, to kill with *sword*, and with *hunger*, and with *death*, and with the *beasts* of the earth [four things]" (Rev. 6:8, emphasis mine).

Again, Zechariah sheds light on the meaning of the symbol. Zechariah 6:6 says that the *grisled* horses (RSV: dappled grey) go toward the south country. The King of the South in Daniel 11:40 is identified

---

97   Ellen G. White, *Christ's Object Lessons* (Washington, DC: Review and Herald, 1900), p. 96, emphasis mine.
98   Ibid., p. 97.
99   Ellen G. White, *Testimonies for the Church*, vol. 5 (Mountain View, CA: Pacific Press, 1889), p. 614, emphasis mine.

as in opposition to the King of the North. In ancient times, the King of the South was Egyptian. Revelation 11:8 identifies *modern/figurative* Egypt this way:

"Their bodies will lie in the public square of the great city—which is *figuratively* called Sodom and *Egypt*—where also their Lord was crucified" (Rev. 11:8, NIV, emphasis mine).

Egypt most boldly denied the existence of the living God. No monarch ever ventured upon a more open and high-handed rebellion against the authority of heaven than did the pharaoh of Egypt. Thus, the King of the South represents *atheism,* and the fate of these anti-God forces is an *automatic exclusion from the investigative judgment.*[100]

Suppose Kellogg's Cornflakes Company featured a picture on the back of each box of cereal shipped to all the homes of America. In order to win a prize, this picture must be colored by the children and sent in by December 31. All across America children sit at their breakfast tables munching cornflakes and staring at the back of the box. Of all the children, a few cut out the picture, color it, and mail it to Kellogg's in Battle Creek, Michigan. On January 1, when the Kellogg's committee sits down to evaluate who should receive a prize, must they consider every one of the millions of children in America, or do they consider only those who have sent in a colored picture? So it is with God's kingdom. Every home has had in it a box of Kellogg's cereal. Everyone has seen and understood the issue. But only some has availed themselves of the opportunity. And of that number, many have been quite casual in their endeavor—coloring outside the lines, coloring monochrome, coloring only certain parts, scribbling over parts that initially had merit. Nevertheless, all entries will be carefully scrutinized. The pale horse people have never sent in a colored picture and will never be considered in the investigative judgment.

What is the significance of the last part of verse 8? "And power was given unto them over the *fourth part* of the earth, to kill with sword, and with hunger, and with death, and with the beasts of the earth" (Rev. 6:8, emphasis mine). The margin in the King James Version refers us to Ezekiel 14.

"For thus saith the Lord GOD: How much more when I send my *four sore judgments* upon Jerusalem, the *sword*, and the *famine*, and the *noisome beast*, and the *pestilence*, to cut off from it man and beast?" (Ezek. 14:21, emphasis mine).

---

100 Ellen G. White, *The Great Controversy* (Mountain View, CA: Pacific Press, 1911), p. 269.

The "fourth part" in Revelation 6:8 might be better interpreted in harmony with Ezekiel's statement of judgment as *"four sore judgments."* And the sense of the prophecy then would be four distinctly different instruments being used to "cut off from it man and beast."

"And power was given unto them over the ... [*four sore judgments*] ... to kill with sword, and with hunger, and with death, and with the beasts of the earth" (Rev. 6:8, emphasis mine).

The "four sore judgments"—sword, hunger, death, beasts—are self-inflicted. This quartet is applied in several scriptural contexts and is understood to be war, famine, plague/pestilence, and political persecution.

So, it is not necessary to count the population of the earth and say that X number of them will die, which is the common understanding. The first four seals encompass all of humanity. God Himself has judged every soul, and here in the investigative judgment His purpose is to satisfy the watching universe. That's why you and I aren't there. We will have our day of satisfaction in the millennium phase, but in 1844 God told the universe, "It's time for Me to bring them home. But before I bring them home, I want you to be satisfied that what I have proposed is a reasonable thing to do. I'm calling a judgment, a review of the process by which I have determined that these people are safe to save. I want you to be there, and I want you to watch, *to come and see*."

Since 1844, the entire universe who will share eternity with us are watching closely as our cases are reviewed. When this phase of the judgment is ended, they will all say, "Amen!" and they will accept the judgment of God as safe. Then He will come for us, and when we get to heaven, in looking around, we might say of certain persons, "What's *he* doing here? Where's my aunt? She was such a nice person! How can this be?" God will respond to my dilemma by saying, "I have called a judgment, and I want you to be there." We will sit down and review

> *Since 1844, the entire universe who will share eternity with us are watching closely as our cases are reviewed. When this phase of the judgment is ended, they will all say, "Amen!" and they will accept the judgment of God as safe.*

the cases of all the people missing, and when we are finished, we will understand why some are there that we didn't expect and why some are not there that we did expect.

There remains yet one other group of people who will be dissatisfied at that point: the wicked themselves, the ones who will die without salvation. At the end of the millennium God will call a third phase, and He will provide for a starkly revealing experience. From each of the lost will be stripped away all superstition and misperception. They will confront naked truth and will fall to their knees and say, "Just and true are Thy ways, Thou King of saints."[101] And then the lake of fire will be their final fate.

---

101 Ellen G. White, *The Great Controversy* (Mountain View, CA: Pacific Press, 1911), p. 671.

Chapter 4
Revelation 6 and 7: Seals Number 5, 6, and 7 and the 144,000

SEAL NUMBER 5: Martyred People of God

The judgment is set, the books are opened, the process explained. It will begin with the house of God (white horse people) and proceed to apostates within the house of God (red horse people). All God's sheep of another flock (black horse people) will have been called out, and the defiant (pale horse people) who have refused to recognize Jesus as Lord and Savior are exposed. The *four horsemen of the apocalypse* have been thus described. The opening of seal number 5 is presented in Revelation 6:9.

"And when he had opened the fifth seal, I saw under the altar the souls of them that were slain for the word of God, and for the testimony which they held" (Rev. 6:9).

Since the *book* that is held in the right hand of the Lamb contains the history of all events on both sides of the curtain since Creation, the first entry in this *martyr* chapter must be the account of Abel, Adam's second born (Gen. 4:8). Abel was certainly slain for the Word of God *and* for his testimony, which he held up before Cain. Since that time many more millions have faithfully given up their lives in testimony for God. The papacy has perversely robbed the reputation of God's heroes to garnish her own image. In every temple of Roman influence there lies beneath the altar the slain bodies of those who gave their lives for Christ at her hands. (Revelation 6:9–10 are yet future to us.)

"And they cried with a loud voice, saying, How long, O Lord, holy and true, dost thou not judge and avenge our blood on them that dwell on the earth?" (Rev. 6:10).

Why them that dwell on the earth? From the very beginning of *sin* its virulence has been inexplicably invisible to even the most perceptive of creature minds. *Sin* blatantly contradicts simple logic and holds brilliance captive. As a result, those that dwell on the earth continue to kill the messengers of God and slay His followers. In figure, God is raising an issue here for our edification. What about these people? We are astonished at their audacity and at their courage! Such are a breed apart. God, most certainly, agrees with this observation because He will honor the martyrs apart from all the other saved. Notice verse 11:

"And white robes were given unto every one of them; and it was said unto them, that they should rest yet for a little season, until their fellowservants also and their brethren, that should be killed as they were, should be fulfilled" (Rev. 6:11).

They are given *white robes* even before the judgment is concluded and before they are resurrected to life! Their reward, however, is to be delayed until *others* suffer a similar fate yet future to the context of this seal. The context must be some time since 1844, because the *first* seal was not opened until then. There have been a few martyrs since 1844, but not many. Consider this statement from the Spirit of Prophecy:

"When the fifth seal was opened, John the Revelator in vision saw beneath the altar the company that were slain for the Word of God and the testimony of Jesus Christ. *After this* came the scenes described in the eighteenth chapter of Revelation, when those who are faithful and true are called out from Babylon [black horse people group]."[102]

Implicit here is the understanding that *after the Sunday law* goes into effect and the nations of earth are troubled sufficiently by terrible calamities, *then* martyrdom will again revive and be the answer to both sides of the issue. God will permit loss of life to (a) sort out the sincere among those professing to follow Him, and (b) to impress the honest in heart among the "eleventh-hour-vineyard-people" to come out of her. The unrepentant will seek to "please God" by coercing those who refuse to fall into line. One more quote supports the context of post-Sunday legislation:

> When the defiance of God's law is *almost* universal, when His people are oppressed and afflicted by their fellow men, the Lord will interpose. Then will the voice be heard from the

---
[102] Ellen G. White, *SDA Bible Commentary*, vol. 7 (Washington, DC: Review and Herald, 1957), p. 968, emphasis mine.

graves of martyrs, represented by the souls that John saw slain for the Word of God, and for the testimony of Jesus Christ, which they held—then prayer will ascend from every true child of God: "It is time for thee, Lord, to work: for they have made void thy law."[103]

The blood of martyrs crying from the ground asks this question: "How long, O Lord, holy and true, dost thou not judge and avenge our blood on them that dwell on the earth?" (Rev. 6:10). *We can now answer that question exactly.* Since the martyr's cry was heard as the fifth seal opened, and since the fifth seal opens *after* the passing of the National Sunday Law (just before it becomes universal), then martyrdom begins at that time and ceases when probation closes. But the martyrs must wait *a little longer* until the beast is slain, which takes place during the seven *last plagues.* Revelation reveals when the beast is slain; and *that* is the avenging of the martyr's blood "at her hand" (Rev. 18:20; 19:2). It will be a poignant moment for God, for since Lucifer began his rebellion in heaven, God has yearned to abort the carnage caused by sin. The opinion of the universe stayed His hand then, but now they are crying out in agreement to purge all creation of this festering death.

"It is time for thee, LORD, to work: for they have made void thy law" (Ps. 119:126).

The martyrs are given voice from the grave wherein they ask the question that cannot be answered quite yet. The last harvest, the last suffering, and the last response are yet ahead.

These stalwarts *will not be scrutinized* in the investigative judgment! They have demonstrated with their very lives a *commitment* to God that is approved by a sinless universe. It could be said of the fifth seal group that they are "automatically" saved, while those of the fourth seal group are "automatically" lost. Spirit of Prophecy supports this position:

> When one suffers death for His sake, Christ says, "I am He that liveth, and was dead; and, behold, I am alive forevermore, ... and have the keys of hell and of death." Revelation 1:18. *The life that is sacrificed for Me is preserved unto eternal glory* .... As Christ arose, He brought from the grave a multitude

---

[103] Ellen G. White, *SDA Bible Commentary*, vol. 6 (Washington, DC: Review and Herald, 1956), p. 1081, emphasis mine.

of captives. The earthquake at His death had rent open their graves, and when He arose, they came forth with Him. They were those who had been co-laborers with God, and who *at the cost of their lives* had borne testimony to the truth. Now they were to be witnesses for Him who had raised them from the dead .... *[T]hose who came forth from the grave at Christ's resurrection were raised to everlasting life.*[104]

"[T]hen the prayer will ascend from *every true child of God*: "It is time for thee, Lord, to work: for they have made void thy law."[105]

When Lucifer defected in heaven with his mysterious philosophy later known as *sin*, the universe was in a state of fascination so that God was unable to arrest Lucifer and forestall the terrible experiment in sin. Creature intelligence would have been offended and universal rebellion would have condemned God in premature indignation. Now, after a long bath in sin we are ready for God to act in justice and expunge the universe of sin.

There is so much more that could be said about the reward of the martyrs. For example, the martyrs will wear a different robe. It will have a red border around the bottom, and there will be a temple on the new earth, which only they can enter.[106]

SEAL NUMBER 6: Signs and Wonders—Last-day People of God

The sixth seal is opened in verse 12 of chapter 6, and its contents include the remainder of the chapter and all of chapter 7. (The seventh seal is not opened until verse one of chapter 8.) *First,* certain events are outlined that must happen in the *physical world* to mark the opening and the closing of Christ's ministry in the Most Holy Place. It also tells the names of those who shall be delivered in the time of trouble. Then John asks a question that is the focal point of the sixth seal: "*[W]ho shall be able to stand?*" (Rev. 6:17, emphasis mine). He has just witnessed scenes of terrible persecution, and he is overwhelmed. The answer to that question is immediately given in chapter 7, which is a distinct reference to the same issue raised in Daniel 12:1–4, when the names of those to be delivered in the time of trouble were sealed until the time of the end.

---

104 Ellen G. White, *The Desire of Ages* (Mountain View, CA: Pacific Press, 1898), pp. 669, 786, emphasis mine.
105 Ellen G. White, *SDA Bible Commentary*, vol. 6 (Washington, DC: Review and Herald, 1956), p. 1081, emphasis mine.
106 Ellen G. White, *Early Writings* (Washington, DC: Review and Herald, 1882), pp. 18–19.

The sixth seal reads differently from the others in that the initial statement divides time into two distinct periods and infers a third: the *first of the signs* just before the investigative judgment, and the *last of the signs* just before the second coming of Christ. Between these two stupendous events are those who by surviving calamity demonstrate the virtues of God.

"And I beheld when he had opened the sixth seal, and, lo, there was a great earthquake; and the sun became black as sackcloth of hair, and the moon became as blood; and the stars of heaven fell unto the earth, even as a fig tree casteth her untimely figs, when she is shaken of a mighty wind" (Rev. 6:12–13).

The first of these events, the great Lisbon earthquake, happened in 1755.[107] The scope of this calamity boggles the mind. It was felt and recorded all around the world in a day when there were no seismic instruments to measure the movement or television cameras to broadcast the event. The second sign occurred in 1780, the day was darkened, and the moon appeared as blood.[108] The third prophetic event happened in 1833 when the stars fell.[109] *The Great Controversy* speaks to the confusion surrounding the events heralded by these phenomena and described by Daniel.[110]

"[A]nd, behold, one like the Son of man came with the clouds of heaven, and *came to the Ancient of Days,* and they brought him near before him. And there was given him dominion, and glory, and a kingdom, that all people, nations, and languages, should serve him: his dominion is an everlasting dominion, which shall not pass away" (Dan. 7:13–14).

Do you become lost in those pronouns? Can we sort them out? "And behold one like the Son of Man came with the clouds of heaven and came to the Ancient of Days." There are introduced these two—Son of Man and Ancient of Days. "And they brought Him [that would be the Son of Man] near before Him [the Ancient of Days] and there was given Him [the Son of Man] dominion." He received not only dominion but also "glory and a kingdom, that all people, nations, and languages should serve Him." Do you recall our discussion on these words? *Dominion*: Adam was given dominion of the newly created

---

[107] "1755 Lisbon earthquake," Wikipedia, https://1ref.us/1jq (accessed February 8, 2021).
[108] "New England's Dark Day," Wikipedia, https://1ref.us/163 (accessed February 8, 2021).
[109] "Leonids," Wikipedia, https://1ref.us/1jr (accessed February 8, 2021).
[110] Ellen G. White, *The Great Controversy* (Mountain View, CA: Pacific Press, 1911), pp. 299–317, 333.

earth. That is, he was inaugurated as governor, as king, over terrestrial territory. *Glory* is authority—always. A person can have the title—governor, king, queen. The Queen of England has the title, but she has no glory to rule. There are many positions that are honorary only, and in those kinds of cases there is no glory, no authority. Christ has not only the *dominion,* but He has *authority* over that dominion, and He has a *kingdom.* (Remember, a kingdom is related to people, nations.) "His dominion is an everlasting dominion, which shall not pass away."

Which shall not pass away! Why not? Because the rule is the rule of LOVE. The citizens of that kingdom give *GLORY* to God from their hearts. It comes almost as a surprise to recall a thing called moral law. It is their joy and happiness to give glory to their beloved Savior—the One who sacrificed Himself for a kingdom like this.

"The coming of Christ here described is *not* His second coming to the earth. He comes to the Ancient of Days in heaven to receive dominion and glory and a kingdom, which will be given Him at the close of His work as a mediator. *It is this coming,* and not His second advent to the earth, that was foretold in prophecy to take place at the termination of the 2300 days in 1844."[111]

There is more significance attached to 1844 than just the termination of the 2300 prophetic years. It has to do with *prophecy* and *time*—it is said that *"time shall be no more."* We've understood that in broader strokes than is warranted, and we've suffered as a consequence. We have said that *all* prophetic time was terminated in 1844. The sense of Daniel's statement is *the time of the 2300 days ended in 1844.* It's very specific, but time prophecy as a concept continues *detached from the calendar.* 1844 was the last calendar date attached to prophecy—either figurative or literal. The numbers in Daniel 12 cannot be attached to a calendar, but they can be attached to events. After 1844 *both* literal and figurative prophecies exist, attached to events. They cannot be understood any other way. By *events* we mean consequences resulting from fiat enacted by earthly governing bodies, or from pronouncements of God affecting earthly matters.

The Great Controversy makes a further clarification when commenting on these prophecies. "The revelator thus describes the **first** of the signs to precede the second advent."[112] The **last** of the signs takes place when Jesus comes to awake the sleeping saints.[113]

---

111 Ibid., p. 480, emphasis mine.
112 Ibid., p. 304, emphasis mine.
113 Ellen G. White, *Early Writings* (Washington, DC: Review and Herald, 1882), pp. 15–16.

"And the heaven departed as a scroll when it is rolled together; and every mountain and island were moved out of their places" (Rev. 6:14).

Verses 15 to 17 describe the reaction of the wicked when these signs appear and the realization of what is happening dawns. Chapter divisions in Scripture are fairly arbitrary, sometimes obscuring the author's intent. This seems to be the case with respect to the sixth seal and chapter 7. The language flows smoothly from chapter 6 to chapter 7.

After the vision of the signs and the great day of God's wrath (Rev. 6:17), John is given another scene that summarizes the judgment (the seals) quite well. Revelation 7 opens just before probation closes, near the cleansing of the church of God producing the 144,000. We must make a distinction here. The church of God is the *church militant* during this time, and the unnumbered throng has not yet been called from Babylon. Thus, there are relatively few in the church of God since the shaking and the work of Ezekiel's six angels have greatly ravished the ranks of the remnant church.

The 144,000 are a unique group, the first to fulfill a specific role in the final days of the great controversy. They will vindicate God as they live through the time of trouble without a mediator. (Christ's work as mediator is done; the 144,000 have been sealed.) And now John introduces them, tribe by tribe. There are 12 tribes, all sons of Jacob except for Dan. He is replaced by Manasseh, a son of Joseph. Just before he passed away, Jacob called his sons around him and under inspiration pronounced upon them each a blessing; but upon Joseph he pronounced a *double blessing* (Gen. 48:10–22). Jacob was not only addressing temporal issues; he was speaking in eternal terms.

The 144,000 are described as "virgins," "first fruits" (Rev. 14:4, 14–20). Virgin olive oil is that which is squeezed from the first picked fruit. Virgin wool is that which is taken at the first shearing of a lamb. These faithful are those living who first took their stand at the early morning hour. They were not called out of the harlot and her daughters during the time of trouble. They are distinguished also by a unique experience (a) they are sealed, (b) they receive the latter rain, and (c) they give the loud cry to a "remnant that were not [yet] sealed."[114]

The focus of the sixth seal is in answering the question "*[W]ho shall be able to stand?*" (Rev. 6:17, emphasis mine). Thus, there are

---
114 Ibid., p. 38.

revealed in chapter 7 two groups of those standing. The first half of Revelation 7 reveals the names of the 144,000, and then the last half of the chapter reveals a great multitude which comes out of much tribulation. *The Great Controversy* comments on these two groups.

> Servants of God, with their faces lighted up and shining with holy consecration, will hasten from place to place to proclaim the message from heaven. By thousands of voices, all over the earth, the warning will be given. Miracles will be wrought, the sick will be healed, and signs and wonders will follow the believers. Satan also works, with lying wonders, even bringing down fire from heaven in the sight of men. Revelation 13:13. *Thus the inhabitants of the earth will be brought to take their stand.*[115]

> *Thus, there are revealed in chapter 7 two groups of those standing. The first half of Revelation 7 reveals the names of the 144,000, and then the last half of the chapter reveals a great multitude which comes out of much tribulation.*

When Elijah and Ahab were on Mount Carmel and the prophets of Baal confronted Elijah, Satan was there inflaming and inspiring his 850 prophets.[116] They labored all day, even cutting themselves with knives, frantically exhibiting whatever devotion they could muster for their god, Baal. God then prevented Satan from calling down fire from heaven because that was the issue; that was the bargain. Elijah told them to make their altar, prepare their offering; and whichever one of them could call down fire from heaven, that's the god they should worship. Israel's worship was a mixture of both religions, and Elijah told them they must pick one or the other. On Mount Carmel, Satan was denied. But in the time that is yet future to us, he will not be denied. He *will* be able to call down fire from heaven (Rev. 13:13), and it will be a time of

---

115 Ellen G. White, *The Great Controversy* (Mountain View, CA: Pacific Press, 1911), p. 612, emphasis mine.
116 1 Kings 18.

terrible confusion for us to choose in that day whom we will worship *if we are not well grounded.*

The importance of revealing the sealing of these two groups as part of the sixth seal *before the close of probation* cannot be overemphasized. In Revelation 8:5, probation is closed by the angel who casts down the censer when the seventh seal opens. Let's recap the order in this unsealing/sealing work of judgment: (1) the saints of God receive first attention (the white horse group). (2) The apostates (the red horse group), those who are shaken out of their faith, become a terrible scourge to God's cause. (3) A great multitude respond to the eleventh-hour call from among the black horse group and join with the saints, while the rest join with the apostates. (4) The atheists are religionists who deny the role of Christ in the soul's intervention (the pale horse group). Atheists are very religious—they are not godless. Islam is quite ardent in its worship of Allah.

There are many Adventists among us who believe that Allah and Jehovah are the same person. They are *not* the same person. I bought a Koran at a bookstore and took the trouble to read it. Also, in my reading on the topic of Islam, I have found that Allah does not have a son, even becoming belligerent at the suggestion that he has a son. He does, however, have three goddess daughters by the sun goddess. They were called al-Lat, al-Uzza, and Manat.[117] He is the *only god*, and Mohammed is his designated prophet. Christ is recognized among followers of Islam as a prophet, but His is a very minor voice with no rank at all. So any institution that denies Christ is *a-theist.* (The prefix "a" means "not"—not Jehovah.) We are *theists*, and those who deny Christ as the only salvific agent are *atheists*.

Among the community of Christianity there are well-known institutions that deny that Christ is *deity* in the fullest sense, among them are Jehovah's Witnesses and Mormons. To Jehovah's Witnesses, Jesus had a beginning—He is a created person, a lesser God.[118] Therefore, they are atheists. The mantra of Mormons is that what God is, we shall be, and what we are, God once was. It is a perpetual evolution, and sin, the devil, will never be eradicated, being a necessary adjunct of universal life. Each of us will evolve into a god who will create a world that will be contaminated by a Satan, and we will go down and the

---

117 "The Daughters of Allah," Muslim Hope, https://1ref.us/1js (accessed February 8, 2021).
118 "The beliefs of Jehovah's Witnesses and how they differ from mainstream Christianity," BBC, https://1ref.us/1jt (accessed February 8, 2021).

savior act will go on and on, ad nauseam.[119] Anyone who denies that Christ will purge the universe of sin is atheist. By definition, atheists are defined in John 3:

"He that believeth on *him* is not condemned: *but he that believeth not is condemned already,* because he hath not believed in the name of the only begotten Son of God" (John 3:18, emphasis mine).

Remember that imagined coloring contest we talked about in chapter 3? The people described here never sent in a colored picture to Kellogg's Cornflakes, and they are condemned already. This is essentially the final position of all those lost, because they put their trust in something other than Jesus Christ.

SEAL NUMBER 7: Post-Judgment Events

"And when he had opened the seventh seal, *there was silence in heaven* about the space of half an hour .... And another angel came and stood at the altar, having a *golden censer*" (Rev. 8:1, 3, emphasis mine).

The "other Angel" should be spelled with a capital "A" because He is none other than Jesus Christ. At this time let me encourage you to read somewhat extensively from *Early Writings,* beginning on page 279 (also see Chart 4, "7 Seals: Scenes of the Judgment," p. 61). These remarks form a succinct summary of the closing up of the great judgment. The opening of the seventh seal: (1) closes the third angel's message, (2) opens the time of trouble, (3) closes the great investigative judgment, (4) is the making up of the kingdom of glory—the bride of Christ, and (5) probation for all mankind.

Revelation 8:1 announces a short period of silence *before the judgment closes*.[120] The silence consists in the cessation of harps, singing, praise, or other heavenly activity. There is *suspense!* The critical decision respecting the eternal salvation of those redeemed is coming down from the very throne of the Father. In verses 3 through 5 the golden censer is filled by the angel, its contents offered on the altar, and then filled again with holy coals to be flung to the earth

---

119 "Mormons at a glance," BBC, https://1ref.us/1ju (accessed February 8, 2021).
120 This idea of silence in heaven may be a new concept for many. Mark Finley offers this insight: "The expression 'silence in heaven' *could very well be* describing Christ, saying to the angels, 'It's time. Let's go gather My children home.'" Mark Finley, *Understanding Daniel and Revelation* (Nampa, ID: Pacific Press, 2020), pp. 244–245.
Ellen White has this to say: "Surrounded by the angelic host, He left heaven. The plagues were falling upon the inhabitants of the earth." Ellen G. White, *Early Writings* (Washington, DC: Review and Herald, 1882), p. 281.

for an eternal consequence. The judgment, however, does not close with verse 1; it closes a couple verses later. Verse 1 opens the seventh seal and ushers in *silence about the space of half an hour.* (This is prophetic time, or 15 literal days.) And then verse 2 makes an abrupt contextual turn. God's abrupt turns have occurred a number of times in Scripture. (In Genesis 2 there is one such turn at verse 18, when They decide to create Eve.)

At a recent baseball game in which there were 40,000 in attendance, the pitcher hurled a fastball across the plate. The batter responded, sending the ball directly back at the pitcher with lightning speed. The ball struck the pitcher a glancing blow on the side of his head, knocking him to the ground. The dugouts cleared, suspending the game, and the vast audience was hushed, everything was stilled—absolute silence—for 15 minutes. Do you think that the eternal fate of billions of souls is less momentous than the temporary state of one unfortunate baseball pitcher?

Verse 2 interjects:

"And I saw the seven angels which stood before God; and to them were given seven trumpets" (Rev. 8:2).

After that interjection, we commence with verse 3, which puts us back on track. Something very important and very unusual involving the censer is evidently about to take place. Continuing in verse 3 we notice the first of two distinct acts by the Angel (Christ), who came and stood at the altar, having a *golden censer.* (We know we are in the Most Holy Place when we see a golden censer because a bronze censer was used in the Holy Place.)[121]

"[A]nd there was *given* unto him *much* incense, that he should offer it with the *prayers* of *all* saints upon the golden altar which was before the throne" (Rev. 8:3, emphasis mine).

From whom did Jesus receive *much incense?* Revelation 5:8, emphasis mine, tells us that the four beasts and the 24 elders had "every one of them harps, and golden vials full of odours, *which are the prayers of the saints."* At this time which of the saints are receiving intercession? It is the *end of the great judgment* of all the confessed since Adam. The kingdom is being made up of everyone judged worthy throughout the 6,000-year rebellion. It must be *all* the saints whom Christ proposes to save. Their prayers have been logged and noted

---

[121] Heb. 9:14; Num. 16:39; Ellen G. White, *Early Writings* (Washington, DC: Review and Herald, 1882), pp. 251–252.

down through the centuries. Now they come up in remembrance and Christ puts them into the censer along with His own merit. The *Bible Commentary* offers a clarification of this event:

> He [Jesus] holds before the Father the censer of His own merits, in which there is no taint of earthly corruption. He gathers into this censer the prayers [plural], the praise, and the confessions [plural], of His people [plural], and with these He puts His own spotless righteousness. Then perfumed with the merits of Christ's propitiation, the incense comes up before God wholly and entirely acceptable.[122]

What is transpiring here? The last great office of Each of these Personages on behalf of fallen man is taking place. Jesus has had oversight of man's salvation since His creation of the earth and Adam's fall. God the Father has assumed oversight of the interests and security of the unfallen universe. It is here in Revelation 8:1–5 that they come together. On behalf of those saved, Jesus presents evidence of His effort for the Father's final consideration. Until now the focus has been on *individuals*: Adam, Eve, Cain, Abel, Noah, Job, David, etc. Now the roster for Christ's kingdom is complete and the concept of *salvation* has been tested. On behalf of the unfallen universe, the Father must consider the risks of repatriated sinners in their midst. The angels are fully aware of the issues *and are hushed to silence as they await the Father's verdict*. The consequences are many and great. Not only will former sinners be given eternal privilege, but also billions of their brethren and loved ones will be eternally snuffed out. Heaven knows God as a loving, caring, long-suffering Person; the proposed action is starkly out of character with the One known to them.

Is there a precedent for such divine action, followed by such heavenly response? Yes, there was *silence in heaven* once before. All the angelic hosts were there, as well as God the Father. Jesus' personal agony in the Garden of Gethsemane is described in graphic terms. His struggles were so great that His human nature was exhausted to the point of death. He had broken off interceding for His disciples and was now focused on the greater issue of salvation. Notice the following paragraph:

---

[122] Ellen G. White, *SDA Bible Commentary*, vol. 7A (Washington, DC: Review and Herald, 1970), pp. 485–486, emphasis mine.

But God suffered with His Son. Angels beheld the Saviour's agony. They saw their Lord enclosed by legions of satanic forces, His nature weighed down with a shuddering, mysterious dread. *There was silence in heaven. No harp was touched.* Could mortals have viewed the amazement of the angelic host as in silent grief they watched the Father *separating His beams of light, love, and glory from His beloved Son*, they would better understand how offensive in His sight is sin.[123]

Jesus died the second death of those forever lost, as well as the death of the saved. He could not see through the portals of the tomb nor grasp life again with His Father. It seemed to Him that because of His contaminating experience He was to be forever separated from the Father. Now, in Revelation 8:1 it is happening again. This time the Father is withdrawing His beams of light, love, and glory from a world hardened in rebellion, a world that has no further hope of resurrection. A world prefigured by the agony and death of Him who could have saved them, but they would not. As Jesus pours out His propitiation (the contents of the censer upon the burning altar), the silence continues, the universe holds its breath. At last the final incense offering is affirmed. Now Jesus also acts uncharacteristically. He takes the golden censer and scoops it full of coals burning with eternal fire and hurls them to the earth.

> Then I saw Jesus, who had been ministering before the ark containing the ten commandments, throw down the censer. He raised His hands, and with a loud voice said, *"It is done."* And all the angelic host laid off their crowns as Jesus made the solemn declaration, *"He that is unjust, let him be unjust still: and he which is filthy, let him be filthy still: and he that is righteous, let him be righteous still: and he that is holy, let him be holy still."*[124]

Ellen White quotes Revelation 22:11 as being the pronouncement closing out the judgment:

"Every case had been decided for life or death. While Jesus had been ministering in the sanctuary, the judgment had been going on

---

[123] Ellen G. White, *The Desire of Ages* (Mountain View, CA: Pacific Press, 1898), p. 693, emphasis mine.

[124] Ellen G. White, *Early Writings* (Washington, DC: Review and Herald, 1882), pp. 279–280, emphasis mine.

for the righteous dead, and then for the righteous living. Christ had received His kingdom, having made the atonement for His people and blotted out their sins. *The subjects of the kingdom were made up.*"[125]

Now is concluded the benign part of the judgment. We next enter into a very dark phase of the great controversy. Remember Revelation 8:2 when the seven angels were given a commission that involved seven trumpets? In verse 6 these angels take up their commission. The earth is now to be subjected to *one year* of calamity and turmoil such as has never been since there was a nation. It will take that long to work through the seven last plagues.[126] There is a divine purpose for this. You might ask What is the point of punishing a hopeless people? And it is a question that must be answered. There *is* a point in punishing a hopeless people: to demonstrate the reason of their hopelessness.

---

125 Ibid., p. 280, emphasis mine.
126 See Rev. 18:8. We will be discussing this in more detail later.

Chapter 5
Revelation 8, 9, and 16: The Trumpets and Vials, Numbers 1–4

In review, let's look at Revelation 7. Verses 1 through 8 describe the perfecting of those making up God's new kingdom. Twelve is a metaphor for *completing*—or *completed*—perfection. Twelve tribes of 12,000 each will enter the city, which has twelve foundations and twelve gates. You can see how twelve is the metaphor for a people who have survived the perfecting process. The New Jerusalem will be a city for those who have passed through just such an experience; and that's what this life on earth is for. Our entire purpose for being, from birth to death, is to pass through a perfecting process. That's why you should never be discouraged over setbacks or failures. I know it's distressing. It certainly is to me!

But look at the larger picture. Salvation is the work of an instant, an instant that must be reaffirmed every morning. Salvation isn't a difficult thing to do. It isn't necessary to save a child from a burning building, or to invent a life-saving vaccine, or to suffer privation in Africa's dark jungle. It isn't necessary to do heroic things. If you wish to do these things, God is delighted and will enter into your sanctified endeavor, but you aren't doing them for salvation. Since Jesus has already saved you, what you must do (if you are not the thief on the cross) is take up your cross (a Christlike lifestyle) and walk day by day. You must demonstrate that the power of Jesus in salvation is a viable project, because He has declared to the universe that, yes, He can recreate a sinful heart and renew a right spirit within man. Watch and see! And it does little good to present people who have deathbed conversions; He must present people who have had a lifetime conversion. That is a convincing demonstration!

The perfection presented here is not the traditional notion of perfection that is considered to be the ultimate in development, rather it is a process that *brings to* a defined state of relational maturity. Revelation 7:9–10, describe a great multitude which no man can number of all nations, kindred, tongues, and people. Verses 11 through 17 are celebratory of God's justice and His mercy in this great salvific act. Chapter 7 consists of a divine introduction of Christ's bride to the universal community. Chapter 8, verse 1, suspends that celebration for the most solemn work of officially concluding the business of ensuring that affliction will not rear its head a second time (Nahum 1:9).

> *Salvation isn't a difficult thing to do. It isn't necessary to save a child from a burning building, or to invent a life-saving vaccine, or to suffer privation in Africa's dark jungle. It isn't necessary to do heroic things. If you wish to do these things, God is delighted and will enter into your sanctified endeavor, but you aren't doing them for salvation. Since Jesus has already saved you, what you must do (if you are not the thief on the cross) is take up your cross (a Christlike lifestyle) and walk day by day.*

"And when he had opened the seventh seal, *there was silence in heaven* about the space of half an hour" (Rev. 8:1, emphasis mine).

And you remember the reason for that silence. It is said that prophecy is the luminous torch in the hands of the faithful which will lead them through earth's darkest hour.[127] It is a "light that shineth in a dark place" (2 Peter 1:19). It is the *clock* that will tell the faithful where they are in the stream of time—year by year, month by month, day by day, hour by hour.

We now enter the future, just before and after the close of probation, when calamities are mounting in disastrous proportions. We are seeing the harbingers of that already. There is much light now shining in the dark places of our understanding, but even more is to come

---

127 Leroy Edwin Froom, *The Prophetic Faith of our Fathers*, vol. 4 (Hagerstown, MD: Review and Herald, 1954), cover page.

shortly. If we have not assimilated as best we can the light available to us now, we will not understand further light when it comes.

"And I saw the seven angels which stood before God; and to them were given seven trumpets" (Rev. 8:2).

First mention of the trumpets came embedded within the discussion of the closing up of the great judgment. Verse 2 seems almost a non sequitur. Why is it *there*? The seven angels standing before God receive from Him trumpets that will signify destructive events of unprecedented proportion. The timing, duration, intensity, and the specific nature of these disasters speak of divine oversight, not of Satan's duplicity as is sometimes suggested. The trumpets are not mentioned again until verse 6, after the censer is hurled earthward.

"And the seven angels which had the seven trumpets prepared themselves to sound" (Rev. 8:6).

In between are two verses that establish the context for the sounding of the trumpets. This arrangement prevents separation of judgment activity from trumpet consequence. If God had placed verse 2 just before verse 6, intellectual expositors would have drawn a line there and separated the judgment from the consequences of the judgment. God wove these concepts together to preserve their integrity.

The question that should be asked is "Why such *punishment* after probation has closed?" The righteous are righteous still, and the wicked are wicked still. Remember, the phenomenon of angelic sympathy for Lucifer projected through the first 4,000 years of sin on earth. Only at the cross did demonic behavior sever the *last thread of sympathy* between the angelic hosts and this rebel angel. A quote from the *SDA Bible Commentary* enlarges this phenomenon:

> The holy angels were horror-stricken that one who had been of their number could fall so far as to be capable of such cruelty. [The context of this is Christ's crucifixion.] Every sentiment of sympathy or pity which they had ever felt for Satan in his exile, was quenched in their hearts. That his envy should be exercised in such revenge upon an innocent person was enough to strip him of his assumed robe of celestial light, and to reveal the hideous deformity beneath; but to manifest such malignity for the divine Son of God, who had, with unprecedented self-denial, and love for the creatures formed in His image, come from heaven and assumed their fallen nature, was such a heinous crime against Heaven that it caused the angels to

shudder with horror, and *severed forever the last tie of sympathy existing between Satan and the heavenly world.*[128]

So it is with those who are among the saved. They will have lost loved ones whom they knew as dearly beloved, and residual within each of them is a sympathy for them, even though God has judged them unfit. How will God deal with this individual phenomenon? The wicked will be dispatched forever within 1,000 years. The *punishment of the wicked* has a complex purpose. Among *this* complexity is the one complexity of our current concern. Thus, by the plagues, God is demonstrating the intractable nature of rebellion. The plagues essentially remove all earthly support of the paradigms by which men have sustained their ideas: money has failed, science has failed, politics have failed, and even religion has failed them. They have no place to turn but to God, and rather than turn to Him, they curse Him. The plagues have another application. They demonstrate to a wondering universe the faithfulness of God's reborn people, the steadfastness of their commitment to righteousness. The wicked and the righteous endure the plagues side by side. Just as the Egyptian plagues affected the Egyptians while the Israelites were spared, so God's people will be protected during this time of trouble.[129]

> And another angel came and stood at the altar, having a golden censer; and there was given unto him much incense, that he should offer it with the prayers of all saints upon the golden altar which was before the throne .... And the angel took the censer, and filled it with fire of the altar, and cast it into the earth: *and there were voices, and thunderings, and lightnings, and an earthquake.* (Rev. 8:3, 5, emphasis mine)

The Spirit of Prophecy not only places the trumpets and the vials future to Ellen White's day but also connects them in the very end time when "scenes of stupendous interest" are taking place.

Solemn events before us are yet to transpire. Trumpet after trumpet is to be sounded, vial after vial poured out one after another upon the inhabitants of the earth. *Scenes of stupendous interest are right upon us.*[130]

---
128 Ellen G. White, *SDA Bible Commentary*, vol. 5 (Washington, DC: Review and Herald, 1956), pp. 1149–1150.
129 Psalm 91:3–10; Ellen G. White, *The Great Controversy* (Mountain View, CA: Pacific Press, 1911), pp. 629, 630.
130 Ellen G. White, *SDA Bible Commentary*, vol. 7 (Washington, DC: Review and Herald, 1957), p. 982, emphasis mine.

Revelation 8, 9, and 16: The Trumpets and Vials, Numbers 1–4

Notice that the *trumpets* and the *vials* are mentioned together—trumpet after trumpet, vial after vial. *The trumpets plus the vials equal the plagues.* Spirit of Prophecy always mentions them together. Traditionally, trumpets have been instruments for calling a people to war. Jericho was warned daily by the blowing of trumpets, and on the seventh day the call was given seven times (Josh. 6:16–20).

It is important to establish boundaries with respect to future events, corollaries to the axiom, "I [God] will do nothing except I reveal it to My servants, the prophets" (Amos 3:7, paraphrase).

Corollary 1: God has ministered to previous generations through the very prophecies reserved for the last days. We are not the first ones to use these prophecies. From AD 90, when John wrote the book of Revelation, onward to AD 1798, those generations were using these prophecies to minister to their needs, and in very valid ways. Those ways are no longer valid for us, so we must now apply these prophecies consistent with our context. Which we do. As Jesus has said, everything in Scripture is there for our edification upon whom the ends of the world are come (1 Cor. 10:11). Thus, God's Word accumulates; that is, it applied then, but it applies more so now upon us who are living in the last days.

Corollary 2: God "fulfills" His Word at the *moment* of need and not a moment sooner. (Have you noticed that God practices *brinksmanship*? We could tell each other stories, could we not?)

Corollary 3: His knowledge of fulfillment exceeds our understanding of the event, and God will be sufficient for our ignorance. Therefore, in matters future, not pertaining to what is established landmark doctrine, let us not nail them too closely. We must acquaint ourselves thoroughly with everything prophetic. How else will we recognize crises events when we see them? But to dogmatically insist that a particular understanding is singular can be a reckless thing to do. Having said this, the other hand must be addressed as well. Two quotations will serve.

> *In every age* there is a new development of truth, a message of God to the people of *that generation.* The old truths are all essential; new truth is not independent of the old, but an unfolding of it. *It is only as the old truths are understood that we can comprehend the new* …. There are those who profess to believe and to teach the truths of the Old Testament, while they reject the New. But in refusing to receive the teachings

of Christ, they show that they do not believe that which patriarchs and prophets have spoken.[131]

"Now all these things happened unto them for examples: [Examples to whom?] and they are written for *our* admonition, upon whom the *ends of the world are come*" (1 Cor. 10:11, emphasis mine).

It appears reasonable that the *seven trumpets* and the *seven vials* describe the same events; they occur coincidentally. When applied *post pioneer,* they appear to be two sides of the same coin:

The *vials* explain:

> **WHAT**- - - - -happens.
>
> **WHO** - - - - -participates (and their actions).

The *trumpets* explain:

> **WHEN**- - - - -it happens (and provides the timeframe).
>
> **WHERE**- - - -the action occurs.
>
> **WHY** - - - - - - it happens (the cause and effect).
>
> **HOW**- - - - - -the action is carried on (and by what means).

The trumpets and vials together constitute the plagues. Two statements from Spirit of Prophecy are appropriate to introduce the discussion of plagues.

"[W]hen our High Priest has finished His work in the sanctuary, He will stand up, put on the garments of *vengeance, and then the seven last plagues will be poured out."[132]*

"These plagues *are not universal,* or the inhabitants of the earth would be wholly cut off."[133]

Referring to the statement in the *SDA Bible Commentary,* volume 7, that warns, "Solemn events before us *are yet* to transpire, trumpet after trumpet *is to be* sounded, vial after vial poured out one after another upon the inhabitants of the earth. Scenes of stupendous interest *are right upon us.*"[134] The trumpets and vials are not only positioned here

---

131 Ellen G. White, *Christ's Object Lessons* (Washington, DC: Review and Herald, 1900), pp. 127–128, emphasis mine.
132 Ellen G. White, *Early Writings* (Washington, DC: Review and Herald, 1882), p. 36, emphasis mine.
133 Ellen G. White, *The Great Controversy* (Mountain View, CA: Pacific Press, 1911), p. 628, emphasis mine.
134 Ellen G. White, *SDA Bible Commentary,* vol. 7 (Washington, DC: Review and Herald, 1957), p. 982, emphasis mine.

after probation closes, but are also *linked together.* The reason I am belaboring this point is because it is traditional among Adventist expositors to *recapitulate* seals and trumpets with the churches. The churches are said to be periods of time within the Christian era, and rightly so. But they say that the seals apply to periods of time within the Christian era, and that the trumpets also apply to periods of time within the Christian era. Thus, these three *sevens* are said to *recapitulate* history within the same periods of time. That approach impels the traveler into a dead end with respect to an understanding. There is nowhere to go with it. Only as the scenes of Revelation are perceived to occur *in their order* does it unfold, allowing the reader to progress.

And consistent with the strong admonition that is given by the Spirit of Prophecy, *Scripture must be understood literally unless the context indicates otherwise*, the first four plagues are literal.

TRUMPET NUMBER 1:

"The first angel sounded, and there followed *hail* and *fire* mingled with *blood*, and they [the hail, fire, and blood] *were cast upon the earth: and the third part of the trees was burnt up, and all green grass was burnt up"* (Rev. 8:7, emphasis mine).

A plague of hail and fire fell upon Egypt that affected the green herbs and trees, as well as livestock and incidental human life.

> And Moses stretched forth his rod toward heaven: and the LORD sent thunder and hail, and the fire ran along upon the ground; and the LORD rained hail upon the land of Egypt. So there was hail, and fire mingled with the hail, very grievous, such as there was none like it in all the land of Egypt since it became a nation .... And the flax and the barley was smitten: for the barley was in the ear, and the flax was bolled. (Exod. 9:23–24, 31)

The "fire ran along upon the ground .... And the hail smote throughout all the land of Egypt all that was in the field, both *man and beast*; and the hail smote every herb of the field, and brake every tree of the field .... And the flax and the barley was smitten" (Exod. 9:23, 25, 31, emphasis mine). The plagues of Egypt were literal events. There is no symbolism in them even though there are subtle applications of the objects used. (Each of first four plagues seemed to be fashioned after the gods of Egypt.)

It was not until the sixth plague that Pharaoh was compelled to say, "I will let you go, and ye shall stay no longer" (Exod. 9:28).

VIAL NUMBER 1:

"And I heard a great voice out of the temple saying to the seven angels, Go your ways, and pour out the vials of the wrath of God upon the earth .... [A]nd there fell a noisome and grievous sore upon the men *which ... worshipped his image"* (Rev. 16:1–2, emphasis mine).

> **WHAT:** Noisome and grievous sore/hail and fire mingled with blood.
>
> **WHO:** First angel.
>
> **WHEN:** The censer was hurled/trumpet sounded.
>
> **WHERE:** Upon the earth.
>
> **WHY:** Men worshiped the beast and his image.
>
> **HOW:** God's wrath poured out.

As soon as God removed the hedge from about Job, Satan destroyed his property, and attacked him physically. "So went Satan forth from the presence of the LORD, and smote Job with sore boils from the sole of his foot unto his crown" (Job 2:7). It is clear that in Job's case Satan was the agent of persecution. In the case of the Pharaoh of Egypt's first plague, Moses was the change agent. So, in the case of the last plagues of earth the *first angel "went, and poured out his vial upon the earth"* (Rev. 16:2, emphasis mine). These continue through the fifth plague. "And [they] blasphemed the God of heaven because of their pains and their **sores**" (Rev. 16:11, emphasis mine).

The first *vial* (Rev. 16:2) makes no mention of hail and fire or of blood—only sores. However, information supplied by the first *trumpet* (Rev. 8:7) completes the sense. Though Satan brought the boils on Job, affecting his body, and also brought fire from heaven, destroying his property, he did so at the permission of the God of heaven. There is a harmony in the plagues of Egypt and the seven last plagues, supporting God's directing power of earth's affairs.

TRUMPET NUMBER 2:

"And the second angel sounded ... as it were [simile—a similar effect] a great mountain burning with fire was cast [up] into the sea:

and the third part of the sea became blood; and the third part of the creatures which were in the sea, and had life, died; and the third part of the ships were destroyed" (Rev. 8:8–9).

Great mountains burning with fire have risen from the sea before—the Hawaiian Islands, for instance. But mountains rarely fall from the sky. "The third part of the sea became blood," etc.[135] Three oceans—the Atlantic, Pacific, and Indian Oceans—command the greater expanse of water on earth. If a massive volcanic eruption were to occur in *one* of these oceans, it would affect *all* of the sea creatures and ships in *one of the three oceans*.[136] Noxious fumes, gases, and burning lava could cause tremendous destruction. Remember, the plagues are not universal, else no one would survive them. This supports the notion of one-third, one-third, one-third.

VIAL NUMBER 2:

"And the *second* angel poured out his vial upon the *sea*; and it became *as* [simile] the blood of a dead man: and *every* living soul died in the sea" (Rev. 16:3, emphasis mine).

It cannot be "every living soul died in every sea in the world." Mankind could not survive. Both the second vial and the second trumpet declare that the sea became *as blood*. The second vial says, "Every soul in the sea died," but the second trumpet makes it plain that a *third part*, or *one of the three* oceans, is affected. The trumpets provide more detail. The vials are related in one chapter of 21 verses; the trumpets require two chapters of 35 verses, plus 6 verses of a third chapter because they support much more detail than the vials.

TRUMPET NUMBER 3:

"And the third angel sounded, and there fell a *great star* from heaven, burning *as it were* [simile] a lamp, and it fell upon the third part of the rivers, and upon the fountains of waters; and the name of the star is called *Wormwood*:[137] and the third part of the waters

---

135 Third Parts: A symbolic understanding of this text implies that a great mountain (religious entity) was forcefully imposed upon the sea (multitude of people). The people, consisting of three distinct groups, were affected: one of the three parts *became blood*, another third died as a consequence, and a third of the commercial activity was affected.

136 Ocean temperatures are already sufficiently high as to adversely affect much sea life.

137 *Wormwood* is sometimes translated *hemlock* and *gall*. This is what was offered to Christ on the cross and was also the substance that Socrates took as his death sentence.

became wormwood; and many men died of the waters, because they were made bitter" (Rev. 8:10–11, emphasis mine).

VIAL NUMBER 3:

"And the third angel poured out his vial upon the rivers and fountains of waters; and they *became blood* [metaphor]" (Rev. 16:4, emphasis mine).

Cause and effect: Whereas the third vial states merely that the "rivers and fountains of waters became blood," the third trumpet explains the **cause** and the **effect** in literal language: that "there fell a great star [meteor or asteroid] burning as a lamp" (Rev. 8:10, paraphrase). The technical difference between a meteor and an asteroid is one of size. This morning's newspaper posed a hypothetical situation: earth could intercept an asteroid cloud or other space debris that would cause extensive damage to its surface. Can anyone survive its disastrous consequences? For asteroids less than a mile across, only local regions will take a bad hit. For asteroids five miles across, you'd best make sure that your affairs are in order. The five-miler up to the dino-boomer (the one that supposedly destroyed the dinosaurs) releases energy billions of times more than the world's total nuclear arsenal. Rocks blown up through the atmosphere and falling back to earth would cause widespread fires, not to mention earthquakes, tsunamis, and other disastrous consequences. Such scenes are a scientific possibility, considering the language of Scripture and the imperatives of last-day calamities. Consider the apostle John's experience on the Isle of Patmos 4,000 years after the event.

> All around him the apostle beheld witnesses to the flood that had deluged the earth because the inhabitants ventured to transgress the law of God. The rocks thrown up from the great deep and from the earth, by the breaking forth of the waters, brought vividly to his mind the terrors of that awful outpouring of God's wrath. In the voice of many waters—deep calling unto deep—the prophet heard the voice of the Creator. The sea, lashed to fury by the merciless winds, represented to him the wrath of an offended God. The mighty waves, in their terrible commotion restrained within limits appointed by an invisible hand, spoke of the control of an infinite Power. And in contrast he realized the weakness and folly of mortals, who,

though but worms of the dust, glory in their supposed wisdom and strength, and set their hearts against the Ruler of the universe, as if God were altogether such a one as themselves. By the rocks he was reminded of Christ, the Rock of his strength, in whose shelter he could hide without fear. From the exiled apostle on rocky Patmos there went up the most ardent longing of soul after God, the most fervent prayers.[138]

There is no indication that a symbolic understanding is to be applied here. A consistent literal context demands that the third trumpet be recognized as simply a "great star" or burning celestial body causing many men to die. If large enough, such an impact could create noxious debris sufficient to contaminate fresh water sources.

TRUMPET NUMBER 4:

"And the fourth angel sounded, and the third part of the sun was smitten" (Rev. 8:12).

VIAL NUMBER 4:

"And the fourth angel poured out his vial upon the sun; and power was given unto him [the sun] to scorch men with fire. And men were scorched with great heat, and blasphemed the name of God, which hath power over these plagues: *and they repented not to give him glory*" (Rev. 16:8–9, emphasis mine).

"And they repented not" is a major *point* to God's post-probation punishment. He is demonstrating that stripped of all support and having God as their only recourse, they will refuse God. It's the nature of sin, and we must be impressed with that. The fourth trumpet combines elements of the fourth and fifth vials, just as the seventh vial combines elements of the sixth and seventh trumpets.[139] Vial four and the first part of trumpet four address a plague of *heat* so great that the wicked are reduced to cursing God whom they are actively appeasing on behalf of their *nation*. Does that not sound inconsistent to you? Scripture notes that *they repented not to give Him glory*—they refused to recognize His authority.

---

138 Ellen G. White, "Patmos," *The Review and Herald*, September 5, 1912.
139 See Chart 7, p. 98, "Seven Thunders: Revelation 10/Daniel 12."

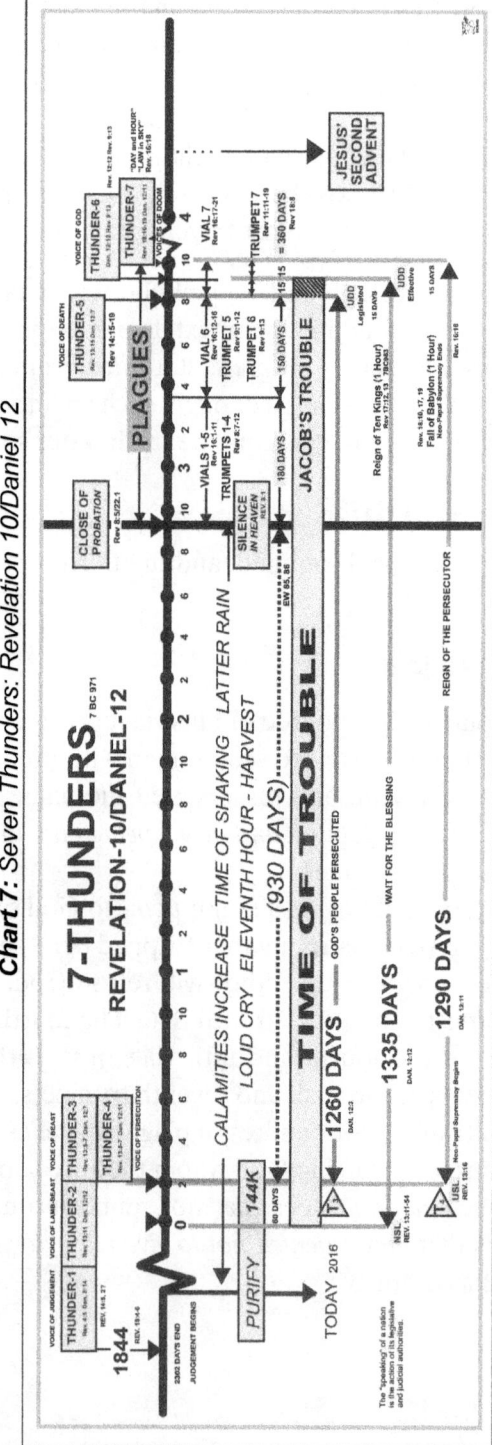

Chart 7: Seven Thunders: Revelation 10/Daniel 12

The water systems of this planet, with their cooling rains and evaporation principle, are what create the weather systems. When the oceans and rivers are affected, great drought and heat are the result. Planet earth will appear as a barren wasteland. These plagues will motivate the wicked to destroy God's people. Satan might capitalize on these disasters to accomplish his *own* goals, even enhancing their effect. But if he does, there will be tremendous collateral damage upon the wicked and upon the planet itself. Satan has no sense of loyalty or camaraderie for those held captive by him. In fact, among demons, we are told, there is only *one point of agreement:* a mutual hatred of Christ.[140] How would you like to be a demon? A demon has no friends, nor does he have pals. Each demon is isolated from all other demons respecting personal bonds of affection. Here Satan's destructive nature is demonstrated.

Cause and effect: The fourth *vial* states simply that power was given him (the sun) to scorch men with great heat. It tells *what* happens but does not tell *why* or *how*. The *trumpet* adds detail and says that these heavenly bodies were "*smitten*." The "stars" here in reference are perhaps the planets of our solar system. Satan is the "prince of the power of the air (Eph. 2:2)," bringing storms and devastation. Could he affect heavenly bodies if given the opportunity? Caution should be used respecting Satan's involvement in the plagues. Did not God select, initiate, and manage the ten plagues of Egypt? Satan attempted to duplicate the first few with dubious success. It's not necessary for us to settle these kinds of questions now. The *fifth vial* is also a consequence of that stated in the fourth *trumpet*.

"[A]nd the third part of the moon, and the third part of the stars [were smitten]; so as the third part of them was darkened, and the day shone not for a third part of it, and the night likewise" (Rev. 8:12).

"And the fifth angel poured out his vial upon the *seat of the beast;* and his kingdom was full of darkness; and they gnawed their tongues for pain" (Rev. 16:10).

The plague of darkness affects selectively *the seat of the beast—* papacy headquarters. Those most recalcitrant will be given more time to demonstrate the power of sin over man, the flower of God's earthly creation. Compare this with Exodus 10:21–23, emphasis mine:

---

140 Ellen G. White, *The Great Controversy* (Mountain View, CA: Pacific Press, 1911), p. 505.

And the LORD said unto Moses, Stretch out thine hand toward heaven, that there may be darkness over the land of Egypt, even *darkness which may be felt.* And Moses stretched forth his hand toward heaven; and there was a thick darkness in all the land of Egypt three days: they saw not one another, neither rose any from his place for three days: but all the children of Israel had light in their dwellings.

During the first four plagues the wicked will be in anguish, suffering from painful sores, parched for water, scorched with heat, and groping about in thick darkness. These calamities will bring the governments of earth to a search for the cause, and a determination to do whatever is necessary to stop them. They are unable to understand why the New World Order is not bringing peace and happiness and God's blessings on the earth. And what of the rapture? Is *everyone* to go through the seven years of tribulation? False ministers of Babylon blame the first five plagues on those who do not conform to the false Sabbath, the mark of authority of the new, one-world system. Sabbatarians are marked for extinction—the *universal death decree.*

Satan, being unable to destroy the confidence of God's people during the first five plagues, will now turn to public opinion and destroy them by legislation. The rest of the *plagues*—vials and trumpets—are for a very specific purpose. They are called "woes." Chapter 6 will cover these complex prophecies and will show how they fit the revelations given to John.

Chapter 6
Revelation 9 and 16: The Trumpets and Vials, Numbers 5–7

Passages of prophecy, being couched in symbolic terms and figures of speech, are so framed as to apply reasonably in contexts *other than apocalyptic*, and we must consider whether God has *purposely* arranged His words in such a way as to accommodate the need of *interim generations*, generations that have existed during the unfolding of the churches between Christ's day and ours. How did He minister to them? Perhaps through these very prophecies! John was given detailed information 2,000 years before the fact; and it is not as if God is limited to *John's* prophetic testimony, or that there is no one closer to the event through whom to reveal His will. We must conclude that God deliberately and purposefully did what He did for reasons that may have nothing to do with us who are the final generation.

A principle of prophetic understanding is illustrated in Jesus' own prediction of Jerusalem's destruction in AD 70 wherein He made *one* prophecy in such a way as to unmistakably apply to *two* events 2,000 years apart (Matt. 24:15–39). Why would God choose to do this? Does He not have a loving concern for *all* the faithful in *each generation* who have longed for His appearing? And those generations (at least the first few, and certainly the last few) have anticipated His coming during their lifetime. Every faithful mother for 4,000 years prior to Jesus' first appearing entertained the notion that it might be her privilege to give birth to the Messiah. That was their hope. Finally, a mother realized that dream of women, just as it has been the hope of every generation since Jesus' incarnation that He would return in their lifetime. God knew this, and I think that He established an understanding in His written Word to accommodate those interim generations as they proceeded from Christ's day to our own.

The point of all this lies in the sincere but now archaic understandings that have developed—and still persist—within the Seventh-day Adventist Church regarding the seals, trumpets, and vials. Could these *now archaic* views of prophecy have had a *divine purpose in the past?* It is not certain, but it would be unwise to quarrel with the good men of yesterday and argue with their points of view or denounce them for holding those points of view. There *is* a rather chaotic atmosphere within the current body of believers respecting many of the things being addressed here. That's exactly as it should be. Remember, Ellen White said of our spiritual intercourse, "Agitate, agitate, agitate!"[141] Understanding will not come immediately. God will unfold these things as it is necessary for us to understand them. That necessity, I believe, is sharpening daily and will continue to increase. Great men of history held apocalyptic views that occasionally jar our sensibilities. Martin Luther once claimed that the book of Revelation was "neither apostolic nor prophetic," (though he later revised his position).[142] Uriah Smith and many, if not most, of our brilliant theologians since 1844 held views of prophecy not consistent with what is unfolding before us today. The common understanding has been—and is—that the seven churches of Revelation 2 and 3, the seven seals of Revelation 6 and 7, and the seven trumpets of Revelation 8 and 9 recapitulate *time periods within the Christian era:* the seven churches is said to be a *spiritual* view; the seven seals a *judicial* view; the seven trumpets a *military* view of the same time periods within the Christian era. There may have been a time period when such a view might have been the best understanding.

The difficulty with making that position an apocalyptic view is best expressed in the words of lawmakers: "The devil is in the *detail!*" That is, as a general framework recapitulation may be recognized in history, but the prophetic details have no meaningful application *except in the future.* The details of John's prophecies wreak havoc with this approach in that *the book cannot proceed sensibly from that point.* Remember the axiom: the scenes of Revelation must be understood *in their order. ("The solemn messages that have been given in their order in the Revelation are to occupy the first place in the minds of God's peo-*

---

141 Ellen G. White, *Counsels to Writers and Editors* (Nashville, TN: Southern Publishing Association, 1946), p. 40.
142 "Book of Revelation," Wikipedia, https://1ref.us/1j7 (accessed April 7, 2021).

ple.")¹⁴³ A caveat rears its head at this point: what constitutes a *scene?* I have identified ten passages where certain phrases indicate a transition to vision.

- Rev. 1:10: "I was in the Spirit."
- Rev. 4:1–2: "After this, I looked …. I was in the spirit."
- Rev. 7:1: "[A]fter these things."
- Rev. 12:1, 3: "[T]here appeared …. there appeared."
- Rev. 13:1, 11: "I stood … I beheld."
- Rev. 15:5: "[A]fter that I looked."
- Rev. 17:1, 3: "Come hither; I will shew …. [H]e carried me away."
- Rev. 18:1: "[A]fter these things."
- Rev. 19:1: "[A]fter these things."
- Rev. 21:9: "Come hither; I will shew."

With respect to the three woes, trumpets 5, 6, and 7, the dilemma magnifies, but we are justified in making future application of these apocalyptic Scriptures by the *plainness of the Scriptures themselves*, as well as the instruction of God's prophet when she penned:

"Prophecy has been fulfilling, *line upon line* …. The more fully we accept the light presented by the Holy Spirit through the consecrated servants of God, the deeper and surer … will appear the truths of ancient prophecy …. *These messages were given, not for those that uttered the prophecies, but for us who are living amid the scenes of their fulfillment.*"¹⁴⁴

The fifth trumpet describes evil angels as they gather the kings of all nations together to legislate a universal death decree (UDD). This confrontation between the wicked and the people of God is to be known as the Battle of Armageddon.¹⁴⁵ Just as the UDD is to go into effect, the people of God are delivered by the voice of God. This voice *begins the seventh vial* and the *sixth trumpet*. When the voice of God declares, "It is done" (Rev. 16:17), the persecutions of His people are finished, and the voice pronounces the BLESSING on His people and a curse upon the wicked. The blessing is fourfold: to declare the *day*

---

143 Ellen G. White, *Testimonies for the Church*, vol. 8 (Mountain View, CA: Pacific Press, 1904), p. 302 emphasis mine.
144 Ellen G. White, *Selected Messages*, book 2 (Washington, DC: Review and Herald, 1958), p. 114, emphasis mine.
145 See Chart 7, p. 98, "Seven Thunders: Revelation 10/Daniel 12."

and hour of the coming of Jesus, to identify the people of God, to reiterate the covenant, and to glorify the righteous.[146]

The fifth trumpet is aligned with the sixth vial and is supplementary to it. Both describe the work of evil angels. John says of the sixth vial:

> I saw three unclean spirits [demons] like frogs come out of the mouth of the dragon [paganism], and out of the mouth of the beast [papacy], and out of the mouth of the false prophet [apostate Protestantism]. [Paganism, papacy, and apostate Protestantism—they are a frog each.] [T]hey are *the spirits of devils,* working miracles, *which go forth unto the kings of the earth ... to gather them to the battle* [Armageddon].[147] (Rev. 16:13–14, emphasis mine)

The sixth vial tells *what* is going on, and the fifth trumpet gives additional details describing them: *how* many, *how* they work, *who* their leader is, the *methods* they use, *how* they look and act, and the *timeframe*—how long it will take to accomplish their objective: *the universal death decree.* The dragon (paganism), the beast (papacy), and the false prophet (apostate Protestantism) comprise three divisions of Satan's synagogue.

The sixth vial introduces the main characters in the battle: "the kings of the east" (Rev. 16:12)—Jesus and His attendants. The fifth trumpet introduces the *opposing forces* in the battle—Satan (Apollyon, the destroyer) and his attendants (evil angels). This vial and this trumpet bring the two opposing forces into battle alignment—Armageddon.

TRUMPET NUMBER 5: VIAL NUMBER 6

> And the fifth angel sounded, and I saw a *star* fall from heaven unto the earth: and to him was given the key of the bottomless pit. And he opened the bottomless pit; and there arose a smoke out of the pit, *as* the smoke of a great furnace; and the sun and the air were darkened by reason of the smoke of the

---
146 Ellen G. White, *Early Writings* (Washington, DC: Review and Herald, 1882), pp. 285–286.
147 Ellen G. White, *SDA Bible Commentary*, vol. 7 (Washington, DC: Review and Herald, 1957), pp. 845, 846.
dragon = paganism (centers chiefly in worship of evil spirits)
beast = papacy (Rev. 13:1 and 17:3, 8)
false prophet = apostate Protestantism (deceives men into making an "image" to it)

pit. And there came out of the smoke locusts upon the earth: and unto them was given power, *as* the scorpions of the earth have power. And it was commanded them that they should not hurt the grass of the earth, neither any green thing, neither any tree; but *only those men* which have not the seal of God in their foreheads. And to them it was given that they should not kill them, but that they should be tormented five months: and their torment was *as* the torment of a scorpion, when he striketh a man. And in those days shall men seek death, and shall not find it; and shall desire to die, and death shall flee from them. And the shapes of the locusts were *like unto* horses prepared unto battle; and on their heads were *as it were* crowns like gold, and their faces were *as* the faces of men. And they had hair *as* the hair of women, and their teeth were *as* the teeth of lions. And they had breastplates, *as it were* breastplates of iron; and the sound of their wings was *as* the sound of chariots of many horses running to battle. And they had tails *like unto* scorpions, and there were stings in their tails: and their power was to hurt men five months. And they had a king over them, which is the angel of the bottomless pit, whose name in the Hebrew tongue is Abaddon, but in the Greek tongue hath his name Apollyon. One woe is past; and, behold, there come two woes more hereafter. (Rev. 9:1–12, emphasis mine)

That's as it is presented in John's book. Notice the many similes and metaphors. We must distinguish between *figures of speech* and *symbols*. Figures of speech are broadly understood and readily applied; symbols require interpretation and are uniquely applied.

> *Like unto:* Having a characteristic of horses in battle.
>
> *As it were:* Having a characteristic of gold crowns.
>
> *As the faces of men:* Having a characteristic seen in men's faces.
>
> *As the hair of women:* Having a characteristic ascribed to women's hair.
>
> *As the teeth of lions:* Having a characteristic of lions showing their teeth.

> *Breastplates as it were:* Having a characteristic of priestly function or of war.
>
> *Like unto scorpions:* Having a characteristic of treachery.

Let's look at Rev. 9:1. "I saw a *star* fall from heaven ... and to *him* was given the key of the bottomless pit" (emphasis mine). (A star that had *fallen* from heaven.) The "star" of the third trumpet (Rev. 8:10) is an "*it*," but the "star" of the fifth trumpet is identified by the pronoun "*him*." Let's look at a text that will identify him.

"And the great dragon was cast out, that old serpent, called the Devil, and Satan ... he was cast out into the earth, and his angels were cast out with *him* .... And *his* tail drew the third part of the *stars* of heaven" (Rev. 12:9, 4, emphasis mine).

He (Satan) opened the *bottomless pit*. The earth became the bottomless pit the instant sin was conceived in the human pair. *Sin* has rendered all victims helpless to recover their previous condition. A bottomless pit implies a hopeless state from which there is no escape, a fall from which there is no recovery. Jesus has plucked us as brands from the fire; we have escaped the pit through His intervention. Satan and his demons are incarcerated here and exist under house arrest. Also implied is a measure of control by some outside Force or Presence. In this case, the outside Presence *gave him the key*, from which can be inferred a temporary release from helplessness, a relinquishing of some measure of control. In Revelation 20 a picture is given which is just the reverse of that in the fifth trumpet.

"And I saw an angel come down from heaven, having the key of the bottomless pit and a great chain in his hand. And he laid hold on the dragon, that old serpent, which is the Devil, and Satan, and bound him a thousand years, and cast him into the bottomless pit, and shut him up" (Rev. 20:1–3).

Here the action is just the opposite of Revelation 9:1–3 where Satan is permitted to open the habitation of evil angels and release them to work without restraint for a period of *five months*. What is the effect of "work" so dire as to be labeled a *woe*?

> [A]nd there arose a smoke out of the pit, *as* the smoke of a great furnace; and the sun and the air were darkened by reason of the smoke of the pit. And there came out of the smoke locusts upon the earth: and unto them was given power, *as*

the scorpions of the earth have power. And to them it was given that they should not *kill* [those without the seal of God in their foreheads] them, but that they should be tormented *five months*. (Rev. 9:2–3, 5, emphasis mine)

In the sixth vial, out of the pit there arose *smoke*, or *communication* of some sort, that darkened the sun (Christ's presence). These "unclean spirits" are likened to frogs coming out of the mouth of the dragon (Satan), the beast (papacy), and the false prophet (apostate Protestantism) because of their voices (legal enactments and pronouncements against God's people). In the fifth trumpet they are likened to locusts and are described by the term "swarm," which represents their overmastering activity. The influence of both Jesus and the Holy Spirit is obscured by their activity. Satan is frustrated by his inability to unify his people within the first four plagues, and now he is to be further frustrated by the command to "hurt only those men who have not the seal of God in their foreheads" (Rev. 9:4, paraphrase). See how God's power is still limiting Satan's destructive efforts? It is much like He limited Satan's destructive intent to Job: "Destroy his wealth, but don't touch him." "Touch his body but spare his life." God *always* has management of things. He *always* does! God sets the timeframe of the gathering action:

> *God always has management of things. He always does!*

"And to them it was given that they should not kill them, but that they should be tormented *five months*: and their torment was *as* the torment of a scorpion, when he striketh a man .... And they had tails *like unto* scorpions, and there were stings in their tails: and their power was to hurt men *five months*" (Rev. 9:5, 10, emphasis mine).

After the first five plagues have fallen, the wicked will be desperate to discover the cause of these judgments that have fallen upon the earth. It may take several months for the first four plagues to fall; Scripture says that it will take *five months* alone for the fifth trumpet to fall. Revelation 18:8 tells us of symbolic Babylon that "her plagues [shall] come in one day," or one literal year (360 literal days).[148] The "gathering" will take five months, or 150 literal days. The "10 kings" of

---

[148] One year literal time = 365 days. One year symbolic time = 360 days.
Mark Finley, *Understanding Daniel and Revelation* (Nampa, ID: Pacific Press, 2020), pp. 243–244.

Revelation 17:12–13 (apostate Protestantism) "reign" with the beast in setting up the universal death decree for "one hour" or *fifteen literal days*. Then the fall of Babylon requires an additional "one-hour," or *fifteen literal days*. These two "hours" of fifteen days each add up to thirty more days. So, 150 plus thirty equals 180 days for just the three woes—trumpets 5, 6, and 7. This tells us that plagues 1 through 4 also take 180 days. Prophecy is intended to give God's people light so that they will recognize these events and know *exactly* where they are in the stream of time *with respect to the issues*. That's the purpose of them. It is not necessary to argue or debate the time. Keep the *issue* in mind. If any should ask you for a reason for your faith, feel free to share it with them. But we are collecting pieces of the puzzle so that as prophecy unfolds these pieces will serve as waymarks. If these prophetic pieces are missing, you *will not see the waymarks* and will be like a ship without a rudder.

> "[T]o human sight it will appear that the people of God must soon seal their testimony with their blood as did the martyrs before them. *They themselves* begin to fear that the Lord has left them to fall by the hand of their enemies. It is a time of fearful agony. Day and night they cry unto God for deliverance .... Paleness sits upon every face. Yet they cease not their earnest intercession .... The very delay, so painful to them, is the best answer to their petitions. As they endeavor to wait trustingly for the Lord to work they are led to exercise faith, hope, and patience, *which have been too little exercised during their religious experience.* Yet for the elect's sake the *time of trouble* [not the timeline][149] *will be shortened.*[150]

This test is necessary for several reasons. It reinforces in the minds of both saint and angel the absolute necessity of eternal dependence on God. It is astonishing that the elect, even *after the close of probation,* have yet a significant deficiency. Their faith, hope, and patience are in need of bolstering. Thus, they are led into an experience that will exercise them. Prophecy of future events is given to us because it is necessary that the people of God may have their bearings in times of stress when the final test is upon them. The loving Father has given

---

149 End-time events are happening rapidly—*and in their order*. However, God in mercy for His faithful ones, *shortens the length of time* the trouble lasts.
150 Ellen G. White, *The Great Controversy* (Mountain View, CA: Pacific Press, 1911), pp. 630–631, emphasis mine.

these prophecies that we may walk in the light of Scripture even in the darkest hour. The *shortening of trouble* has a precedent in the 1,260 year/day prophecy of Daniel 7:25 and Revelation 13:5. That period proved to be a time of great persecution for God's people and was prophesied to be cut short, else there would be no righteous left. The 1,260-year period was determined to end in the year AD 1798. The timeline was not shortened, but the papacy lost its power and will to persecute some sixty or seventy years earlier. Thus, the *time of persecution* was cut short, but the *prophetic time* remained consistent.

> *Prophecy of future events is given to us because it is necessary that the people of God may have their bearings in times of stress when the final test is upon them.*

RUNNING TO BATTLE: For what purpose do evil spirits torment evil men? In Rev. 9:6 evil men are not permitted relief in death, even when they so desire it. In verse 7 and onward, the answer begins to emerge.

"And the shapes of the locusts were *like unto* horses *prepared unto battle* .... [A]nd the sound of their wings was *as* the sound of chariots of many horses *running to battle*" (Rev. 9:7, 9, emphasis mine).

Like unto horses—they weren't horses; they were *like* unto horses. In some respect they had characteristics that horses have when they are prepared for battle. And the sound of their wings was *as the sound* of chariots of many horses *running to battle.* That's a key phrase. They are assuredly running to battle, "the battle of that great day of God Almighty .... into a place called ... Armageddon" (Rev. 16:14, 16, emphasis mine). The purpose of evil spirits in tormenting evil men is to force them into unity to legislate a universal death decree. That purpose is described in Revelation 19:19.

"And I saw the beast, and the kings of the earth, and their armies, gathered together to make war against him that sat on the horse, and against his army" (Rev. 19:19).

Trumpet five and vial six describe this gathering action. Notice the description of demons as they appear *in their deception* for gathering the kings of the earth and the whole world to battle against the people of God through a death decree. We must keep in mind that neither God nor Satan can accomplish their desire with the snap of a finger.

Because we have been created in the image of God, sinful or not, we are so constituted that *universal free will remains intact*, and we *will* make up our own minds respecting life and death. God's tool of persuasion is *love*. Sometimes it's tough love, but still it is *love*. And with Satan it is fear or deception or coercion. But he still must *persuade*, and these evil men that Satan desires to enlist in his effort to destroy the saints must be persuaded to gather in a place, at a certain time, to accomplish the death of these people. The period of time under our scrutiny is that period of time during which Satan is practicing his deceit to accomplish that purpose.

"[O]n their heads were *as it were* crowns *like* gold"	(Rev. 9:7, emphasis mine)
"[A]nd their faces were *as* the faces of men"	(Ibid., emphasis mine)
"And they had hair *as* the hair of women"	(Rev. 9:8, emphasis mine)
"[T]heir teeth were *as* the teeth of lions"	(Ibid., emphasis mine)
"[T]hey had breastplates ... of iron"	(Rev. 9:9)

What do these descriptions, or likenesses, tell regarding the manner in which these demons shall work?

Crowns like gold: "[T]hey are the spirits of devils ... which go forth unto the kings of the earth" (Rev. 16:14). Their mission is that which deals with *leadership* and *heads* of governments. They appear before them in the most authoritative manner to compel compliance. Why wouldn't you wear a crown of gold if your task was to persuade the kings of the earth to cooperate with you?

As the faces of men: Scripture presents these demons *in the guise of men*. Can demons assume the bodies and faces of men? "'What shall I do with Jesus, which is called Christ?' Pilate asked. Again the surging multitude roared like demons. Demons themselves, *in human form*, were in the crowd."[151]

Hair as the hair of women: A woman's hair is a symbol of her "glory," or authority, as a helpmeet (1 Cor. 11:15). The evil spirits

---
151 Ellen G. White, *The Desire of Ages* (Mountain View, CA: Pacific Press, 1898), p. 733, emphasis mine.

that appear in human form will come with beauty and charm, not with horns and pikes and intimidation. Notice the modus operandi as described in *The Great Controversy:*

> The spirits of devils will go forth to the kings of the earth and to the whole world, to *fasten them in deception*, and urge them on to unite with Satan in his last struggle against the government of heaven. By these agencies, rulers and subjects will be alike *deceived* .... As the crowning act in the great drama of *deception*, Satan himself will personate Christ .... [Remember, we are some distance past the close of probation.] In different parts of the earth, Satan will *manifest himself among men* ["manifest" means visible to the sight] *as a majestic being of dazzling brightness, resembling the description of the Son of God given by John in the Revelation* .... [Remember when I said to keep that in mind? In Revelation 1:13–16 there is a powerful description of Jesus, and Satan will imitate *that description.*] The *glory* [authority] that surrounds him is unsurpassed by anything that mortal eyes have yet beheld. The shout of triumph rings out upon the air: "Christ has come! Christ has come!" The people prostrate themselves in adoration before him, while he lifts up his hands and pronounces a blessing upon them .... His voice is soft and subdued, yet full of melody. *This is the strong, almost overmastering, delusion.*[152]

"Strong, almost overmastering delusion ...." To the righteous saints *awaiting their death by decree*, they have been praying with all their strength to be delivered, and now it appears that Christ has answered their prayers. Yet they recall the promised coming of Jesus will be in the clouds of the sky, and every eye shall see Him (Rev. 1:7).

"[A]s the teeth of lions .... as the heads of lions" (Rev. 9:18, 17, emphasis mine): Although in verse 7 "their faces were as the faces of men" and they have the beauty and charm of women, here there is also the likeness to a lion. Despite the glory and beauty, there is a cruelty which is displayed by demons, portrayed with "lion's teeth" that cannot be hidden.

"As it were breastplates of iron" (Rev. 9:9, emphasis mine): The significance of a breastplate is that it is the piece of sanctified garments

---

[152] Ellen G. White, *The Great Controversy* (Mountain View, CA: Pacific Press, 1911), p. 624, emphasis mine.

worn by high priests. It is also worn *to battle*. The reference to "iron breastplates" implies that these evil spirits might also masquerade as (papist) religious authorities, or that these evil spirits have purpose and relentless urgency to do battle.

TRUMPET NUMBER 6. VIAL NUMBER 7

And the sixth angel sounded, and I heard a voice from the four horns of the golden altar which is before God, saying to the sixth angel which had the trumpet, Loose the four angels which are bound in the great river Euphrates. And the four angels were loosed, which were prepared for an hour, and a day, and a month, and a year, for to slay the third part of men. And the number of the army of the horsemen were two hundred thousand thousand: and I heard the number of them. And thus I saw the horses in the vision, and them that sat on them, having breastplates of fire, and of jacinth, and brimstone: and the heads of the horses were *as* the heads of lions; and out of their mouths issued fire and smoke and brimstone. By these three was the third part of men killed, by the fire, and by the smoke, and by the brimstone, which issued out of their mouths. For their power is in their mouth, and in their tails: for their tails were like unto serpents, and had heads, and with them they do hurt. And the rest of the men which were not killed by these plagues yet repented not of the works of their hands, that they should not worship devils, and idols of gold, and silver, and brass, and stone, and of wood: which neither can see, nor hear, nor walk: neither repented they of their murders, nor of their sorceries, nor of their fornication, nor of their thefts. (Rev. 9:13–21)

WHEN: THE TIME FRAME— "THE VOICE OF GOD SOUNDS"

"And the sixth angel sounded, and I heard *a voice* from the four horns of the golden altar which is before God, saying to the sixth angel which had the trumpet, Loose the four angels which are bound in the great river Euphrates" (Rev. 9:13–14, emphasis mine).

Finally, we come to the place where the four angels loose whatever it is that they have been holding! *Loose:* relinquish yet another measure of divine restriction.

WHERE: THE SETTING—SPIRITUAL BABYLON

The curse is upon the wicked leadership, both harlot and daughters. The ancient city of Babylon "lived" upon the waters of the Euphrates River. Modern Babylon is portrayed as sitting upon many waters (Rev. 17:1). These are the waters of the Euphrates River, which will be "dried up"[153] to prepare the way for the kings from the east. The seventh vial words it this way:

"[T]he great city [Babylon] was *divided* into three parts ... and great Babylon came in remembrance before God, to give unto her the cup of the wine of the fierceness of His wrath" (Rev. 16:19, emphasis mine).

Just as Cyrus the Great diverted the waters of the Euphrates, allowing him access to the now vulnerable city, God will divert the multitudes that *support Babylon* in its final hour. She will come to ruin when the alliance that was formed to support her turns against her. At this point Babylon can no longer stand against God because *the unity of the city* has been broken: "The great city was divided into three parts" (Rev. 16:19). What three parts united to form an alliance against the saints? The dragon, the beast, and the false prophet. Now they are at odds again. The unity is broken up, and so the false trinity falls apart.

THE ACTION: LOOSING THE FOUR ANGELS

"[W]hen God shall bid His angels to loose the winds, *there will be such a scene of strife as no pen can picture.*[154]

"And the four angels were loosed, which were prepared for *an hour, and a day, and a month, and a year*" (Rev. 9:15, emphasis mine).

The time mentioned is not a *timeline* to be added up and fixed. *It refers to a particular point in time—a specific date.* The Greek words indicate that this is a date appointed beforehand. The idea is that God already knows this date and it is set for a certain time, so that the very hour, the very day, the very month, and the very year is an *appointed*

---

153 *Andrews Study Bible* (Berrien Springs, MI: Andrews University Press, 2010), p. 1681.
154 Ellen G. White, *Testimonies for the Church*, vol. 6 (Mountain View, CA: Pacific Press, 1901), p. 408, emphasis mine.

time. The King James Version is not as clear on this text as many others. Notice:

King James Version: "And the four angels were loosed, which were prepared for an hour, and a day, and a month, and a year, for to slay the third part of men" (Rev. 9:15).

The Living Bible: "They had been kept in readiness for that year and month and day and hour, and now they were turned loose to kill a third of all mankind" (Ibid.).

New English Bible: "So the four angels were let loose, to kill a third of mankind. They had been held ready for this moment, for this very year and month, and day and hour" (Ibid.).

Complete Jewish Bible: "And they were released. These four angels had been kept ready for this moment, for this day and month and year" (Ibid.).

WHERE: SCOPE. (The sixth vial begins the drama described by thirds, or three.)

"And I saw *three* unclean spirits like frogs come out of the mouth of the *dragon*, and out of the mouth of the *beast*, and out of the mouth of the *false prophet* .... And the great city [Babylon] was divided into *three parts*." (Rev. 16:13, 19, emphasis mine). "[T]he four angels were loosed ... for to slay the *third* part of men" (Rev. 9:15, emphasis mine). The *thirds* of the sixth trumpet are *fire, jacinth, and brimstone*; *fire, smoke, and brimstone*, (Rev. 9:17–18) the *third part* of men killed.[155]

Of what does the *third part of men* consist? *The saints!* The death decree is accomplished against God's people. They are rescued, snatched from the jaws of death. But the narrative is written as if the intent of Satan is a reality.

HOW: DETAILS OF THE BATTLE ALIGNMENT

Forces *against* God:

"And the number of the army of the horsemen were two hundred thousand thousand [200 million]: and I heard the number of them" (Rev. 9:16).

---

155 The *third part* is understood to be the saints of God targeted for the universal death decree. They seem as good as dead. The satanic intent is *to slay the third part of men*.

Revelation 9 and 16: The Trumpets and Vials, Numbers 5–7

Forces that are numbered as the people of God:

"And I heard the number of them which were sealed: and there were sealed an hundred and forty and four thousand [Plus an unnumbered throng to be called out of Babylon]" (Rev. 7:4).

When Satan sees that he cannot touch the people of God and that they have been delivered and glorified, his pent-up rage and hatred against the human race will be demonstrated in his destruction of the wicked, and he turns on those who have sided with him. The last verses of the sixth trumpet describe the destruction of the wicked and are referred to in Revelation 18 as the fall of Babylon. Remember: *sin bears within it the seeds of its own destruction.*

"I will shew unto thee the judgment of the great whore ... with whom the kings of the earth ... and the inhabitants of the earth have been made drunk .... And the ten horns [apostate Protestantism] which thou sawest upon the beast, these shall hate the whore, and shall make her desolate and naked, and shall eat her flesh, and burn her with fire" (Rev. 17:1–2, 16).

This judgment is the effect of the tripart coalition when it is broken up.

HEADS AND TAILS: CAUSE-AND-EFFECT

"For their power is in their *mouth*, and in their *tails*: for their tails were like unto serpents, and had heads, and with them they do hurt" (Rev. 9:19, emphasis mine).

This strange verse has challenged prophetic expositors for many years. The context of this verse is the *concluding* statement of the sixth trumpet, describing the battle array in which a "third part of men are killed." It is a summary. *"The third of men are killed"* is a divine view of intention, i.e., the sentence of intention is equal to the sentence of commission. At this time there are three groups left on earth: apostate Protestantism, Catholicism, and the saints of God. It is the intent of the two groups to kill the third group with a death decree, and God views the intent of the heart equal to the commission of the deed. In this case the saints of God are beleaguered by Satan's hosts and are under a death decree. A larger context, involving Satan and his evil angels, is given in Revelation 12. *HEADS:* Cause. *TAILS:* Effect.

"[B]ehold a great red dragon, having seven *heads* .... And his *tail* drew the third part of the stars of heaven, and did cast them to the earth .... [N]either was their place found any more in heaven. And the great dragon was cast out, that old serpent, called the Devil, and Satan, which deceiveth the whole world: he was cast out into the earth, and his angels were cast out with him" (Rev. 12:3–4, 8–9, emphasis mine).

Satan is here described as having "heads" and a "tail." It is the "head" which thinks up and initiates *action*. In Revelation 12 the "tail" reveals the *results* of that *action*—the evil angels were cast out of heaven. Revelation 9:19 says "their power is in their ... tails." By successfully tempting the garden pair Satan released a world of *sinful* effect. The head initiates the agitating action, and the result is the product of the tail.

"HEADS" and "TAILS" reveal CAUSE and EFFECT
TIME FRAME REITERATED

The timeframe of the trumpets is so important that it not only introduces them in Revelation 9:3–7 (after the close of probation) but reiterates them in verse 20 by the phrase, "by these plagues," after they are executed. The divine purpose of the plagues is strongly implied by verses 20 and 21:

"And the rest of the men which were not killed by these plagues yet *repented not* of the works of their hands, that they should not worship devils, and idols of gold, and silver, and brass, and stone, and of wood: which neither can see, nor hear, nor walk: *neither repented* they of their murders, nor of their sorceries, nor of their fornication, nor of their thefts" (Rev. 9:20–21, emphasis mine).

The trumpets *do not lead men to repentance. They are not warnings.* They are trumpets of war—the battle of Armageddon—happening *after* the close of probation. They reveal what evil angels will do when no longer restrained by the Spirit of God, and they reveal what evil people will do despite all that God provides for personal salvation and clear thinking. And that's their point. You and I will soon enter heaven, where our primary task will be to review the books that pertain to those whom we love dearly that are lost. Remember the thread of affection? Unless that thread is severed, the potential for resentment will always be present. God is here preparing to mercifully sever that thread of sympathy that we might still retain for those who had ample opportunity, but who spurned it. And so the plagues visited upon this body of people are for our eternal benefit. *Sin will not rear its head a second time.*

TRUMPET NUMBER 7 *(Revelation 11)*

> The second woe is past; and, behold, the third woe cometh quickly. And the seventh angel sounded; and there were great *voices* in heaven, saying, The kingdoms of this world are become the kingdoms of our Lord, and of his Christ; and he shall reign for ever and ever. And the four and twenty elders, which sat before God on their seats, fell upon their faces, and worshipped God, saying, *We give thee thanks, O LORD God Almighty, which art, and wast, and art to come; because thou hast taken to thee thy great power, and hast reigned.* [That is, You've exercised your power properly.] And the nations were angry, and thy wrath is come, and the time of the dead, that they should be judged, and that thou shouldest give reward unto thy servants the prophets, and to the saints, and them that fear thy name, small and great; *and shouldest destroy them which destroy the earth*. And the temple of God was opened in heaven, and there was seen in his temple the ark of his testament: and there were lightnings, and voices, and thunderings, and an earthquake, and great hail. (Rev. 11:14–19, emphasis mine)

TIME FRAME:

"*The second woe is past*; and, behold, the third woe cometh quickly .... [T]he seventh angel sounded" (Rev. 11:14–15, emphasis mine).

The Three Woes:

First Woe: The Fifth Trumpet: It is the work of evil angels, with stings as scorpions, gathering the kings of the earth to battle (Rev. 9:9–12).

Second Woe: The Sixth Trumpet: It is the destruction that occurs in the fall of Babylon when the cities of the nations fall after the voice of God (Rev. 11:11–14).

Third Woe: The Seventh Trumpet: It is voices in heaven that *announce heaven's legislative action* (Rev. 11:14–15).

WHAT: ACTION

"We give thee thanks, O LORD God Almighty ... because thou hast taken to thee thy great power, and hast reigned .... and shouldest destroy them which destroy the earth" (Rev. 11:17–18, emphasis mine).

Finally! The universe is prepared to accept a death sentence verdict of *conspiracy* to rebel against the Most High, to commit murder and universal insurrection. It is only until 4,000 years of wholesale ruin and destruction on earth and the shameful taunting and murder of Jesus the Christ that the angelic host divorced the vestige of sympathy for Lucifer the brilliant. It will be another 2,000 years before humanity, victim of the satanic paradigm, sin, will relent and cry out to God for divine riddance of sin.

"And the seventh angel sounded; and there were great voices in heaven, saying, The kingdoms of this world are become the kingdoms of our Lord, and of his Christ; and he shall reign for ever and ever" (Rev. 11:15).

The seventh vial (Rev. 16:18) mentions these voices but does not indicate what they say. The seventh trumpet gives added detail, telling *exactly* what they say. These voices declare in legislative action *that the time has come for Christ to reign.* They have viewed the destructive nature of Satan as he has destroyed planet earth and the wicked.

NOTE: Who was it that destroyed Jesus during His earthly ministry? *The wicked killed Jesus during His earthly ministry,* but at that time Jesus was replacing whom in His human role? Specifically, at Calvary and Gethsemane? While He died in my stead, He actually died the second death as if He were a lost sinner—the wicked. *He became sin for us*. It should have been us, but we were invited to claim His gift, while He laid down His life willingly. It is not necessary for God to personally destroy the wicked—they self-destruct. Sin bears within it the seeds of its own destruction. To declare that God exercises His whip and causes *all* end-time destruction might be inaccurate. We *do* know that God's angels are perfectly capable of destructive action when God commands, but not all destructive action is the work of God's angels. Also, of a surety, God will engineer the total destruction of earth, Satan, and all his sympathizers.

Prophetic Fulfillment:

"The kingdoms of this world are ... of our Lord ... and he shall reign for ever and ever" (Rev. 11:15).

"But the saints of the most High shall take the kingdom, and possess the kingdom for ever, even for ever and ever" (Dan. 7:18).

Amazing! God is yet prepared to reinstall the human race to self-government. How confident is He to accept the rebel co-conspirator back into His bed, to declare that *sin* shall not rear its head a second time. Lest we repatriated saints miss the point: after the completely successful demonstration of *love* as the only acceptable mode of governance, a second challenge will result in a universal outcry and the demand of immediate death.

WHO: THE VOICES THAT DECLARE THESE LEGISTLATIVE ACTIONS

"And the four and twenty elders, which sat before God on their seats, fell upon their faces, and worshipped God, saying, We give thee thanks, O LORD God Almighty, which art, and wast, and art to come; because thou hast taken to thee thy great power, and hast reigned" (Rev. 11:16–17).

The "four and twenty elders" are generally considered to be those who have been taken to heaven through translation and resurrection: Enoch (Gen. 5:24), Elijah (2 Kings 2:11), Moses (Jude 9), and "[w]hen he ascended up on high, he led captivity captive" (Eph. 4:8). These elders, now residents of heaven, are representatives of the human race. They have, themselves, known the struggle of the great controversy between good and evil. Enoch, Moses, and Elijah are now several thousand years old, thus known as "elders," or "old men."

These four and twenty elders sat before God (the Ancient of Days, Dan. 7:9–10), taking part in the investigative judgment. It is in this judgment that the legal right to the kingdom is given to Christ, and it is in this judgment that the members of the kingdom are made up.

"And there was given him *dominion*, and glory, and a kingdom, that all people, nations, and languages, should serve him: his *dominion* is an everlasting *dominion*, which shall not pass away, and his kingdom that which shall not be destroyed" (Dan. 7:14, emphasis mine).

Adam surrendered his *dominion*—his license to rule. He abdicated in favor of Satan. Jesus declares it will not happen again. "It will be Mine forever, even forever!" The four and twenty elders have witnessed the mercy of God; they have seen the destructive and deceitful way of Satan. As they view the deliverance of the people of God and see Jesus leave heaven to rescue them, they fall on their faces and exclaim:

"We give thee thanks, O LORD God Almighty, which art, and wast, and art to come; because thou hast taken to thee thy great power, and hast reigned" (Rev. 11:17).[156]

Chart 8: Prophetic Scene Sequence

SEVEN Churches
1. Ephesus
2. Smyrna
3. Pergamas
4. Thyatira
5. Sardis
6. Philadelphia
7. Laodicia

SEVEN Seals
1. White Horse
2. Red Horse
3. Black Horse
4. Pale Horse
5. Martyrs
6. Signs
7. Ceremony/Destruction

SEVEN Trumpets	**SEVEN PLAGUES**	**SEVEN Vials**
1. Fire, Hail, Blood		1. Sores
2. Sea, Blood 1/3		2. Sea as Blood
3. Water, Blood 1/3		3. Rivers as Blood
4. Sun, Moon, Stars 1/3		4. Sun as Fire
5. WOE #1		5. Total Darkness
6. WOE #2		6. Euphrates Dried Up
7. WOE #3		7. SECOND COMING

---

156 See Chart 8, this page, "Prophetic Scene Sequence."

Chapter 7

Revelation 10 and 11: The Rise of Protestantism, Communism, and Atheism: Daniel 12 and the Seven Thunders of Revelation 10

To introduce Daniel 12, let me share a part of his book that was sealed—chapter 11, verses 40 and onward to the end of the book. Significant parts of Daniel prior to this have future application, but these verses are yet future to us. Ellen White said that Daniel 11 has *almost* reached its fulfillment.[157]

> And at the time of the end shall the king of the south push at *him*: and the king of the north shall come against *him* like a whirlwind, with chariots, and with horsemen, and with many ships; and he shall enter into the countries, and shall overflow and pass over. He shall enter also into the glorious land, and many countries shall be overthrown: but these [three] shall escape out of his hand, even Edom, and Moab, and the chief of the children of Ammon. (Dan. 11:40–41, emphasis mine)[158]

Do you know what the metaphor there is? When Israel conquered Palestine, those three countries—descendants of Lot and Esau—had not yet filled up their cup of rebellion, so God carefully instructed Israel with respect to them. They were not to deal with them as harshly as with the other inhabiting nations of Canaan. There is a parallel to this event in our day.

---

157 Ellen G. White, *Last Day Events* (Boise, ID: Pacific Press, 1992), p. 12.
158 See Appendix 4, p. 238, "Daniel 11: The King of the North vs. the King of the South."

He shall stretch forth his hand also upon the[se] countries: and the land of Egypt shall not escape. But he shall have power over the treasures of gold and of silver [commerce], and over all the precious things of Egypt: and the Libyans and the Ethiopians shall be at his steps. But tidings out of the *east and out of the north* shall trouble him: therefore he shall go forth with great fury to destroy, and utterly to make away many. And he shall plant the tabernacles of his palace between the seas in the glorious holy mountain; yet he shall come to his end, and none shall help him. (Dan. 11:42–45, emphasis mine)

The positioning of this prophecy *in the end time*, and the obvious reference to Israel entering their promised land suggest strong parallelism. But to interpret prophecy according to the newspaper is a presumptuous thing to do. However, it is important for us to keep them in mind. Anything that is yet future to us should be reviewed often so that we retain a sense of the movement within it. Then when it happens, we will be able to sort it out properly.

God's business and its management are as complex as the wheels within Ezekiel's vision. In Ezekiel's first vision, recorded in chapter 1 of his book, he saw wheels within wheels on God's throne, and it overwhelmed him, registering on his mind as complete confusion. Yet the more he watched, the more he sensed complex organization. And that was exactly what God was explaining to him: the business of God may be extremely complex, but it is absolutely coordinated and organized. We accept the complexity of God's view. That complexity overwhelms us on the one hand, but on the other hand we find that were we to make some grasp of it, we are far too weak-minded to encompass God's business—even *throughout eternity*, much less here, and in twenty-five words or less. Plus, we have far too much baggage in our belief systems of which we are inordinately fond. Therefore, truth is difficult for us to accept without reducing it to our mental size. Yet when we do that, truth often becomes unrecognizable. Jesus says, "I am the ... truth" (John 14:6). Keep your mind on that!

I have found that in teaching things philosophical or spiritual, the principal difficulty doesn't lie in the abstruseness of the material as much as it lies within our belief systems. We all come to the place of learning with preconceived notions, a mindset, a paradigm, the lens through which we interpret reality. It's the mechanism by which we make sense of our environment. The atheist's paradigm accepts long eons of time, and no God. When he confronts reality, he interprets it on the basis of his belief system, and evolution is the result. The Christian's paradigm confronts the same data and interprets them in the context of a Creator God. Both of them make sense of it, and neither of them is a hypocrite. We, too, come to our issues with similar baggage, making it difficult to listen to truth. It is far more difficult to *unlearn* error than it is to *learn* truth.

I propose to illustrate the framework of end-time events by combining, superimposing, the books of Daniel and Revelation, namely, the three timelines of Daniel 12 with the *thunders* of Revelation 10.[159]

The first verse of Revelation 10 begins immediately after God's observations on the first six trumpets in Chapter 9. Remember, we left off with the sounding of the sixth trumpet. The seventh trumpet has not yet sounded. This is the passage that concludes the sixth trumpet.

"Neither repented they of their murders, nor of their sorceries, nor of their fornication, nor of their thefts" (Rev. 9:21).

God repeats this expression throughout the trumpets and the vials. He is *making a point.* When we discussed this earlier, we asked the question, "Why inflict evil men with severe punishment *after* their probation has closed?" We concluded that it is not for the benefit of evil men at all! It is for the benefit of the righteous living and for the benefit of the watching universe. It is to *set the nail*. Those of you who do carpenter work know that after a nail is cleanly driven into the board it must be struck *one more time*. That's called *setting the nail*, snugly bringing together the two pieces of material being fastened. This is what God is doing. He has exercised His judgment in a carefully documented assize, and He knows that ahead of *us* is a similar experience, and that we will entertain the same questions that are being pondered within the audience chamber of the current great judgment. We are prone to harbor certain attitudes and biases of which we know nothing. We will discover only later the nature of our thinking. And God, being aware of this, is making provision for that contingency. He exposes the wicked to a punishing process that strips them of all artificial support so that in the end they have nothing to turn to but a supreme Being. Then God says, "Watch! See what they do." They recognize that a supreme Being is behind these events, and what is their response? They curse Him!

---

159 See Chart 7, p. 98, "Seven Thunders: Revelation 10/Daniel 12."

"And I saw another mighty angel come down from heaven .... and he had in his hand a little book open .... and cried with a loud voice, as when a lion roareth: and when he had cried, *seven thunders* uttered their voices" (Rev. 10:1–3).

When I was a young fellow, my wife and I and another couple took a trip from Pendleton, Oregon, to Portland during the Rose Festival. While there, we visited the Portland Zoo. Back in those days the main zoo consisted of a huge building as large as a warehouse. All the animals were in their respective cages. They were live exhibits. As I wandered through that arena, I saw a male lion, nearly as big as a horse, in an iron-barred cage upon a concrete pedestal. He *filled the cage,* and in icy silence he observed the activity around him. After circling him a few times, I left. When I was some paces away, the lion roared. His roar filled that huge building till there was room for nothing else. Then there was utter silence. Not a bird tweeted, nor did a mouse stir. Everything stopped as if frozen in time. The voice of that lion, and the effect it had on all living creatures within earshot, made a deep impression on me. Here, in verse 3, is another example of that: "And [the mighty angel] cried with a loud voice, as when a lion roareth" (Rev. 10:3). The universe will stop and listen.

"And when the seven thunders had uttered their voices ... I heard a voice from heaven saying unto me, Seal up those things which the seven thunders uttered .... And sware ... that there should be *time no longer*" (Rev. 10:4, 6, emphasis mine).

It is peculiar that John would be presented data in an *open* book, and then be instructed to seal it. This is the only material in the book of Revelation that is sealed. Much of Daniel was sealed, but in John's book, the uttering of the seven thunders is all that is sealed. *There should be time no longer.* The deliberate phrasing here is to emphasize that the *thunders* would become significant after the 2,300-day prophecy would be fulfilled. The *time that would be no longer* is also in reference to the 2,300 year/day prophecy. This is a conclusive statement with respect to the longest prophetic time period in the history of the great controversy. It is generally accepted that the *year/day* principle is made null by this statement in Revelation. But I believe this to be in error for two reasons. (1) The ancient languages distinguish between a vision and parts of the vision. This particular reference addresses the *part of the vision* pertaining to the 2,300-day period. (2) Instead of carefully parsing the language, we tend to lurch, as did Eve

Revelation 10 and 11: The Rise of Protestantism, Communism, and Atheism 125

when speaking to the serpent. "Neither must we *touch it,* lest we die!" (Gen. 3:3, paraphrase). The principle of contextual application should always be applied. If the context of an issue is presented symbolically, then the figures within that context should be understood symbolically as well. But if the context of an issue is presented literally, then the figures within that context should be understood literally. There will be situations in this chapter where the only reasonable application of the prophecy will be literal, not symbolic, and other situations where the only reasonable application will be *year/day.*

"But in the days of the voice of the seventh angel [which is yet future to us], when he shall *begin to sound*, the mystery of God should be finished, as he hath declared to his servants the prophets" (Rev. 10:7, emphasis mine).

Remember, there are two universal *mysteries*: the mystery of iniquity and the mystery of godliness. The mystery of iniquity is mysterious because it is nonsense. It will always be mysterious. It is irrational; sense cannot be made of it. Yet, we have a tendency to respond irrationally ourselves when confronted with irrational behavior. If someone behaves contrary to rule, we might exclaim, "Why did you do that?" Early in my teaching experience I often asked, "Why did you do that?" The big-eyed response of the kids would almost always be, "I don't know!" They were telling the truth—they didn't know! It was a foolish question. There is no rational answer to an irrational question. So, the mystery of iniquity is why rationally created minds will insist on behaving contrary to their divinely created paradigms even to the point of eternal death. That will always be a mystery. If an answer could be provided to that question, sin would cease to be sin.

> *The mind of God is so limitless that we will spend eternity grappling with it. And this is God's desire. He wants us to know as much of Him as we can possibly assimilate.*

The mystery of godliness is also material that we will *never fully understand*, but not because it is contrary to logic. It will be due only to our finite minds. The mind of God is so limitless that we will spend eternity grappling with it. And this is God's desire. He wants us to know as much of Him as we can possibly assimilate. But God will *always* be a mystery to us. The mystery of godliness has to do with that which is beyond our understanding as *creatures*, as well as that which has been misrepresented to us. In this case it is in reference to the seventh angel when he shall begin to sound. So, what is happening during the days when the seventh angel sounds? Let's look again at Revelation 11:15.

"And the seventh angel sounded; and there were great voices in heaven, saying, The kingdoms of this world are become the kingdoms of our Lord, and of his Christ; and he shall reign for ever and ever" (Rev. 11:15).

At this point it is all over. The seventh angel is the last bookend on the shelf. The National Sunday Law is the first bookend. Revelation 10 returns us to earth's time when God's last people have their beginning. The action shifts from heaven to earth. In heaven the judgment has been going on and is now concluding. The revelator takes us back to earth during this time and tells us what is taking place there. The mighty angel of Revelation 10, verses 1 and 2, with the little book in his hand, refers to the time of the *disappointment event of 1844* and events beyond.

> These [thunders] relate to future events which will be disclosed *in their order* .... [The seven thunders cannot occur simultaneously, they must sound in their order, one thunder at a time.] This time, which the angel declares with a solemn oath, is not the end of this world's history, neither of probationary time ... which should precede the advent of our Lord. That is, *the people will not have another message upon definite time.*[160]

Here (1844) is where *definite* (calendar) time ran out. We will not have another message on definite (calendar) time, but we will have messages on *indefinite* (calendar) time. What is the difference? Definite time is tied to an event *on a calendar*, such as AD 538, AD 1798, etc. Indefinite time is tied to an event not yet applied to a calendar. A definite time prediction will say, for example, "The building will be finished August 7, 2021." An indefinite time prediction will say, "The building will be finished three months after the permit is signed." In this case no one knows when the permit will be signed, but when that event happens, then the clock will start.

---

160 Ellen G. White, *SDA Bible Commentary*, vol. 7 (Washington, DC: Review and Herald, 1957), p. 971.

Revelation 10 and 11: The Rise of Protestantism, Communism, and Atheism

A discussion such as this one is often branded as heretical because of "date setting." When end-time events are attached to any sort of counting or numbering, hackles are raised and cautions asserted, because it is said about the close of probation by none other than Jesus Himself that of that time knoweth no man (Matt. 24:36)! (The time is not as significant as the *event*.) Daniel 12 clocks three timelines of the final days of earth's history, and within them Michael stands up. But *where* "within them" knoweth no man. Still, it must be said, be ye also ready. Michael will stand up when certain conditions are met. It isn't cosmic hide-and-go-seek: "Here I come, ready or not!"

The mighty Angel who speaks as a roaring lion is Jesus, the Lion of the tribe of Judah. All of the seven thunders were to be mysterious until it was time for them to be understood, and that time was said to be *when the mystery of God should be finished* (Rev. 10:7). The mysteries of God are represented by the number 7—the number of the book of Revelation—the *denouement* of the Bible. For those of you who are *artists*, who read books and attend plays and are fascinated by the way a skilled writer invents her characters and spins her plots, there is tremendous mystery and tension. You may read up to page 570 and still be wondering who is who, and why is why, and there may be but few pages left in the book. Then she unravels quickly all of the mysteries that have troubled you and lays out the plot. You heave a sigh of relief and say, "What a great book!" (That part where she settles the issues is the denouement.) The entire book of Revelation is a denouement of the 6,000-year experience in sin. And every time a "7" occurs in the book of Revelation, the great Author is unraveling some mystery. That's what "7" means.

Did you ever wonder why the Sabbath is the *seventh* day? When God created Adam that Friday, and he and his lovely mate breathed life for the first time, they were equipped with a certain basic knowledge. They had a command of language, but they were only hours old and had no experience in living. Nor had they more than a cameo acquaintance with God. Thus, there was a tremendous need for education. It would take some time for them to become fully familiar with God and with the circumstances of their creation. So God said, "I want you to work six days, then on the seventh day I will come and see you. Then you will work six more days, and on the seventh day I will see you again."

What is the "work" that Adam and Eve were to attend to during the six days? They were to trim the trees and train the little vines and *cultivate* in some fashion. But in a perfect world none of that *needed* to be done. Nevertheless, they were to do it. God is very clever at left-handed directions. He *knew* that if they were out among the vines in some meaningful way, they would hear the birds sing and would see the beasties behaving as God had programmed them to behave. They had been informed that God had encoded Himself in nature, and that they could *read* it as a book of information about God. They understood that. As they spent their six days, divine characteristics registered upon their consciousness. The mother hen would nurture her chicks with ardent watchfulness, the birds would carol in joyous rapture, and the fishes would swim in aquatic coordination to boggle the mind. Then they would encounter manifestations of God that could not be decoded. They would store up these matters during the six days, and when God came, He would resolve such issues for them.

Do you see why the Sabbath is a denouement? "Six days shalt thou puzzle over My creation, and on the seventh day I will give you rest from all the issues that trouble you." God was not at all interested in how many vines could be bent to the left or to the right, or how many ticky-tackies could be put in a box. He wanted them to become preoccupied with higher things through the exercise of their marvelous faculties. All this before there was sin in the world! Now that there is sin in the world there is a double reason to study six days and anticipate a denouement on the seventh, isn't that true?

The seven thunders were to be mysterious until it was time for them to be understood, and that time was said to be when the mystery of God is finished. The mystery of God is revealed in judgment, and the judgment was set shortly after 1798—the time of the end, when Daniel's mysteries began to unfold in the early 1800s with William Miller and others.

Daniel 12

The three timelines, generated by God's answer to Daniel's question, were also sealed up until the time of the end.

"How long shall it be to the end of *these wonders*?" (Dan. 12:6, emphasis mine).

It's neither the first, nor the last, time that Daniel will ask the question. In the first timeline God is responding to how long the *persecution* will be sustained.

"[I]t shall be for a time, times, and an half [For 1,260 days God's people shall be persecuted]" (Dan. 12:7).

In the **second timeline** God is responding to how long the *persecutor* will prevail (which shall be a bit longer than his capacity to persecute); in this case, thirty days longer.

"And from the time that the daily *sacrifice* shall be taken away, and the *abomination that maketh desolate* set up, there shall be a thousand two hundred and ninety days" (Dan. 12:11, emphasis mine).

That's how long the *persecutor* will reign. The *daily* in the verse above has a much larger application than is usually given by expositors. The limited focus of this work prevents an excursion into that interesting field.

In the **third timeline** God is responding to how long *His people must wait* for the blessing promised. God promises to intervene in a special way for those who endure both the persecution and for the persecutor.

"Blessed is he that waiteth, and cometh to the thousand three hundred and five and thirty days" (Dan. 12:12).

Here is seen the coming together of all the disparate parts of prophecy into one coherent whole. Let's compare Daniel 12:7 with Revelation 13:5–7.

"And I heard the man clothed in linen, which was upon the waters of the river, when he held up his right hand and his left hand unto heaven, and sware by him that liveth for ever [Himself] that it shall be for a time, times, and an half; and when *he* shall have accomplished to scatter the power of the holy people, all these things shall be finished" (Dan. 12:7).

What will it take to scatter the power of a holy people? It will certainly take the permission of God. Thus, it will be allowed at a time of dire event and must come *when the work of God's holy people is finished*. We have just picked up a notion in the book of Daniel. Let's see if there's a similar notion in John's Revelation.

"And there was given unto him a mouth speaking great things and blasphemies; and power was given unto him to continue *forty and two months* .... And it was given unto him to make war with the saints, and to overcome them: and power was given him over all kindreds, and tongues, and nations" (Rev. 13:5, 7, emphasis mine).

Expositors will argue, of course, that it applies only in the Middle Ages. But it must be asked of them, did the blasphemers then have power over *all* kindred, tongues, and nations? They had power over many of them, even most of them, but not all of them. There will come a time, *yet future to us*, when this entity will have global power over all dwellers on the earth. Then look again at the context of Revelation 13. Chapter 13 takes its context from chapter 12. In original Scripture there were no divisions, chapter, verse, diacritical marking to interrupt the flow of thought, etc., that the author might have had in mind. The thoughts of chapter 12 should flow into the ideas of chapter 13. This brings the discussion of these two chapters into our time, and beyond. Now let's compare Daniel 12:11 with Revelation 13:12, the second timeline.

"And from the time that the daily [continuous dominion] *sacrifice* shall be taken away, and the *abomination that maketh desolate* set up, there shall be *a thousand two hundred and ninety days*" (Dan. 12:11, emphasis mine).

Remember, all of Daniel 12 is yet future, and the numbers here are *literal*. This verse is not talking about the Dark Ages.

"And he [the USA] exerciseth all the power of the first beast [the papacy] before him [the USA], and causeth the earth and them which dwell therein to worship the first beast [the papacy], whose deadly wound was healed" (Rev. 13:12).

When will the papacy be entirely healed of its deadly wound? When Napoleon unseated the power of the papacy in 1798, put the pope in prison where he died, all Europe rejoiced. But one year later the cardinals of the Catholic Church approached Napoleon for redress, allowing them to elect a pope. Napoleon acquiesced. The deadly wound was not then healed, but it was on its way. In 1929 Mussolini of Italy petitioned the pope for the votes of his church, guaranteeing his election as el Deuce, in exchange for sovereignty.[161] The pope was awarded 108 sovereign acres. The second step toward complete healing was thus accomplished. Only when the United States of America, by legal enactment, joins the papacy in a Sunday closing law will the healing be complete, and martyrdom will again flourish in the world.

And finally, let's compare Daniel 12:12 with Revelation 16:15:

---

161 "Lateran Treaty," Britannica, https://1ref.us/1jv (accessed February 8, 2021).

"Blessed is he that waiteth, and cometh to the thousand three hundred and five and thirty days" (Dan. 12:12).

"Behold, I come as a thief. Blessed is he that watcheth, and keepeth his garments, lest he walk naked, and they see his shame" (Rev. 16:15).

I would like to define the approach to these issues. We have exposed ourselves to traditional Adventist thought because we believe that there is significance and urgency to these divine statements respecting *our time*. By so doing we are thought to entertain what is considered suspicious notions.

In every age there is a new development of truth, a message of God to the people of *that generation*. The old truths are all essential; new truth is not independent of the old, but an unfolding of it. It is only as the old truths are understood that we can comprehend the new .... There are those who profess to believe and to teach the truths of the Old Testament, while they reject the New. But in refusing to receive the teachings of Christ, they show that they do not believe that which patriarchs and prophets have spoken.[162]

"Now all these things [all these things in Scripture] happened unto them for examples: and they are written for our admonition, upon whom the *ends of the world are come*" (1 Cor. 10:11, emphasis mine).

How can that be? What is the power of that statement? Things repeat, don't they? It has been said that history *doesn't* repeat, it *reapplies*. Then any prophecy pertaining to that history must reapply, as well. Our children made the same mistakes we did, and our grandchildren are making the same mistakes that their parents made. Solomon assured us that there is nothing new under the sun (Eccles. 1:9). *We can't think good thoughts ahead of God.*

The first four trumpets and the first five vials fall within 180 days following the close of probation. The fifth trumpet and the sixth vial occupy the next 150 days and describe Satan's preparation for the battle of Armageddon. They are bounded by the close of probation and the universal death decree, which concludes the 1,260 days of persecution.

Trumpets six and seven are coincident with vial seven and describe the culmination of all systems of evil, and the victory of the forces of righteousness. Here is seen the final display of seal six, as well. The

---

[162] Ellen G. White, *Christ's Object Lessons* (Washington, DC: Review and Herald, 1900), pp. 127–128, emphasis mine.

sixth seal is God's *commercials*. God is saying, "When the time comes, I will cause a great earthquake, the stars to fall, the sun to darken, and the moon turn to blood; and you will know that the judgment is imminent." That's the *first part* of the sixth seal—the *first of the signs*. The *last of the signs* are what we are discussing now. Now God produces the *law in the sky*, He announces the day and hour of His second coming, the great hail falls upon the earth, and the islands of the sea disappear.[163] Thus, the sixth seal concludes.

Revelation 10:1–4, introduces the seven thunders. Their application has been a point of puzzlement and speculation for hundreds of years. The seven thunders' *voices* are identified by voices which begin and end the timelines of Daniel 12:5–13. In Scripture, anytime there is the sounding of thunder within a context involving God, either divinity is speaking or mankind, under the influence of Satan, is defying God. Remember the description of Mount Sinai when God was organizing the camp of Israel and giving His law (Exod. 19:16)? Remember Saul of Tarsus on his way to Damascus, and his encounter with Jesus (Acts 9:3–9)? And Jesus' baptism (Matt. 3:16–17)? All of these episodes involved thunder as speech. The "speaking" of God is in His pronouncements, and the "speaking" of a nation is the action of its legislative and judicial authorities.

> *Thunder Number 1 ended the 2,300 day/year prophecy in AD 1844, but it also ushered in the beginning of the investigative judgment for the dead (Dan. 8:14).*

Thunder Number 1 ended the 2,300 day/year prophecy in AD 1844, but it also ushered in the *beginning* of the investigative judgment *for the dead* (Dan. 8:14).

Thunder Number 2 is identified in Revelation 13:11 when the Lamb-like beast "spake as a dragon" and enacts the National Sunday Law. This thunder marks the *beginning* of the 1,335-day timeline with its instruction to wait for the blessing (Dan. 12:12).

Thunder Number 3 is the voice of the beast *enacting* the National Sunday Law. Sixty days after thunder number 2 it marks the *beginning* of 1,260 days of persecution for God's people.

---

163 Ellen G. White, *Early Writings* (Washington, DC: Review and Herald, 1882), pp. 285–286.

Thunder Number 4 is the voice of the beast opening "his mouth in blasphemy against God" and exercising power to make war with the saints to overcome them (Rev. 13:5–7). This *begins* the 1,290 days of the reign of the *persecutor.*

Thunder Number 5 is the voice of the *image of the beast* "that as many as would not worship the image of the beast should be killed" (Rev. 13:15). This *ends* the 1,260 days of persecution and sets up the *universal death decree. The effect will be to "scatter the … holy people"* (Dan. 12:7, emphasis mine).

Thunder Number 6 is the voice of God out of the temple of heaven saying, *"It is done!"* (Rev. 16:17, emphasis mine). It *ends* the 1,335 days and ushers in the long-awaited blessing. The "kings" (apostate Protestantism) have reigned with the beast for one hour in expectation of victory and are about to experience a great disappointment.

Thunder Number 7 is the chorus of the "voices of doom," accompanied by thunders and lightnings and a great earthquake "such as was not since men were upon the earth" (Rev. 16:18). It *ends* the 1,290-day reign of the *persecutor*, and all that remains is for the small, black cloud to appear, which is the hope of all who read and understand the prophecies written in this book.

"And after these things I heard a great voice of much people in heaven, saying, Alleluia; Salvation, and glory, and honour, and power, unto the Lord our God" (Rev. 19:1).

Let's go back and flesh out these understandings with the texts of Revelation 10 and 11.

"And the voice which I heard … said, Go and take the little book [that had the thunders in it] …. and eat it up; and it shall make thy belly bitter, but it shall be in thy mouth sweet as honey. And I took the little book out of the angel's hand, and ate it up … and as soon as I had eaten it, my belly was bitter" (Rev. 10:8–10).

The context of this event was the great disappointment of 1844—the *first thunder.*

"And he said unto me, Thou must *prophesy again before many peoples, and nations, and tongues, and kings"* (Rev. 10:11, emphasis mine).

The *larger* context here is the *second Protestant Reformation* that began in the late 1700s. These Protestant institutions will fall, twice, and become *apostate Protestantism.* Verse 11 includes the great movement that is yet future. Revelation 11:1–13, describes the birth of modern *atheism (Communism)* in the French Revolution—January

21, 1793.[164] That nation, in a reaction to papal supremacy and dominance, purged itself of all things Christian. For a period of three and a half years it worshiped "reason" alone. The experiment was both a colossal effort and a dismal failure. But the seeds sown there yielded a harvest that is flourishing even to this day. For years, Communism dominated more than half the world.

"And the holy city shall *they* [those that worship therein/the temple] tread under foot *forty and two months*. And I will give power unto my two witnesses, and they shall prophesy a *thousand two hundred and threescore days*, clothed in sackcloth" (Rev. 11:2–3, emphasis mine).

The French Revolution raged for nearly ten years before Napoleon brought stability to the government. However, within that span, *three-and-a-half years* of particular lawlessness stand out. The *two witnesses* here identified are the Old and New Testaments. Engel, Marx, and eventually Lenin formulated their theory of Communist governance out of the ashes of the French Revolution.[165] Look at verses 8, 9, and 11:

"And their dead bodies shall lie in the street of the *great city*, which spiritually is called *Sodom and Egypt,* where also our Lord was crucified. And they ... shall see their dead bodies *three days and an half* .... And after *three days and an half* the spirit of life from God entered into them, and they stood upon their feet" (Rev. 11: 8–9, 11, emphasis mine).

These verses are an example of prophecy that ministers to *interim generations. The Great Controversy* applies them to the long years between 538 and 1798 but does so within the context of the French Revolution.[166] Certainly, the context of chapter 11 addresses that event. Uriah Smith explains verse 13 as referring to France: "And the *tenth part of the city* fell." The "city" is the 10 nations of Europe, of which France is *a tenth part.*[167] This is how the early pioneers understood chapter 11. Verse 14 introduces the *third woe*, which we have discussed in chapter 5.

In review: Revelation 10 presents the rise of Protestantism and the beginning of its demise. Chapter 11 presents the roots of modern

---

[164] Ellen G. White, "The Bible and the French Revolution," in *The Great Controversy* (Mountain View, CA: Pacific Press, 1911), p. 265.
[165] "The Communist Manifesto," Wikipedia, https://1ref.us/1jw (accessed February 8, 2021).
[166] Ellen G. White, *The Great Controversy* (Mountain View, CA: Pacific Press, 1911), pp. 278, 282, 287.
[167] Uriah Smith, *The Prophecies of Daniel and the Revelation* (Mountain View, CA: Pacific Press, 1944), p. 542.

atheism.[168] These three represent the *tabernacle of Satan*, as well as the three *unclean spirits*, like frogs, that come out the mouth of the *dragon* (Rev. 16:13). The sounding of the seventh angel in Rev. 11:15 covers the rest of Revelation to the second coming of Jesus—all the events that transpire beyond the close of probation. Verses 16 through 18 are devoted to praise and benediction for the certain outcome of God's great acts during this time. Verse 19 announces the closing of Daniel's 1290-day prophecy.

Explaining THE SEVEN THUNDERS CHART[169]

How is it possible to defend these numbers on the chart? The timeline is in terms of years and months: one year after the National Sunday Law, two years after the National Sunday Law, three years after the National Sunday Law, and four years. Notice the months—two, four, six, eight, ten months. That's the way it's laid out. Prophecy may play out this way; it may play out *close* to this way. We must not cast any of this in concrete but entertain the notion that we have interpreted to the best of our ability. We have prayed before, we have prayed after, and we have confidence that the Holy Spirit has led us as far as we need to see. We are preparing ourselves for entering into this time, the time when the dominos fall. And they are beginning to fall as we speak.

The next prophetic event that we expect will be the *sanctification of the saints*. God's Sabbath-keeping people will be subjected to the most fearful inspection since Adam's rebellion. It is here that I refer the reader to Appendix 3, page 222, "Ezekiel 9: Countdown to Harvest--The Sealing of the 144,000. The experience recorded there describes the formation of the 144,000. The second domino to fall is the National Sunday Law. Mounting calamities leading up to those events will throw the nations of the earth into a tremendous crisis. These will be of such a nature that the world's resources will be insufficient to manage them, compelling leaders to turn to spiritual remedies to accommodate the issues that are devolving upon them. Their finances will fold, military efforts will be fruitless, and science will fail them. So, turning to the Jerry Falwells, Pat Robertsons, and the other spiritual leaders of the world, they will be advised that the only solution is to honor God's Sunday sabbath. We can now see that coming

---

168 See Appendix 1, p. 190, "Daniel 1-12, The Book of Daniel."
169 See Chart 7, p. 98, "Seven Thunders: Revelation 10/Daniel 12."

rapidly. The elements are already in place. We're waiting for the winds of strife to be loosed.

How can it be said that the final movements will be *rapid ones* if this chart is approximate? Wouldn't you say that three and a half years out of 6,000 is fairly rapid? Sometimes a point must be driven carefully and certainly. And what will you do with the prophetic numbers? They say what they say, and we cannot shorten them. Shortness of time depends on the activity involved—60 seconds kissing your amour versus 60 seconds sitting on a hot stove.

How long will Satan be *personating* Christ? It will be a short time. We are not told the time frame for that event. There is a margin of time, 150 days, where Satan must muster unanimity among the nations of the earth with the intent to annihilate the saints—the universal death decree. If you are watching the news, how could anyone establish working harmony among the Shiites, the Sunnis, and the Kurds? Among the Israelis and the Palestinians? Among the British Protestants and the Irish Catholics? Among the United States' democrat blue and the republican red? Something dire must happen to make *strange bedfellows* of us all. *There will be unanimity!* And Satan will have to use *persuasion* to do it. It will happen during the fifth plague. He will then bring everything together. For a short time.

Chapter 8
Revelation 12 and 13: Three Allegories—The "7/10s" of Prophecy

Between the *seventh trumpet* (Rev. 11:15–18) and the *seven vials of God's wrath* (Rev. 16:1–21) is recorded *justification* for such divine action. The sense of Revelation 11:19 belongs to chapter 12. Between the two records of punishment are chapters 12, 13, 14, and 15. Commencing where the prophet Daniel left off in his chapter 11, John begins in Revelation 12. There he presents the figure of an *enormous red dragon* with seven heads, ten horns, and seven crowns on the *heads* (verse 3). In Revelation 13 he presents a *leopard-like* beast coming out of the sea, having seven heads, ten horns, and ten crowns on his *horns* (verse 1). The presentation of these two visions prepares the way for a third manifestation of the dragon beast. In chapter 17 John is taken to a wilderness to view a woman sitting on a *scarlet beast* that has *seven heads and ten horns* (verse 3). The ten horns are explained to be ten kings who have not yet received a kingdom (verse 12)*;* therefore, no mention is made here of crowns.

What are we to make of this discussion? Beasts in prophecy prefigure political powers, but then so do horns. Perhaps there is a connection between the beasts of Daniel and these beasts of Revelation. Certainly, the fourth beast of Daniel and the first beast of Revelation are said to be the same—pagan Rome. But the subsequent viewing of John's beasts appears to be simply *other* manifestations of the same beast. First, the beast appears as a *red dragon* (Rev. 12:3)*;* next, the beast appears as a *leopard-like beast* (Rev. 13:2); and lastly, he appears as *scarlet-colored beast* (Rev. 17:3)*.* What of the ten horns? The dragon of chapter 12 is clearly identified in verse 9 as the devil, or Satan. The horns, or political powers, are nations under his control. In our discussion of Revelation 17 we will have more to say on this notion.

In Revelation, chapters 12, 13, and 17, the seven-headed beast in all three manifestations traces the history of God's people and their nemesis (Satan) from the Babylonian captivity to the Battle of Armageddon. It is here in this interval that Satan's cunning strategies to confuse are revealed—the great red dragon, the leopard-like beast, and the scarlet-colored beast. The diadem of God's anointing conferred at Mount Sinai passed from Israel to Babylon, from Babylon to Medo-Persia, from Medo-Persia to Greece, and from Greece to pagan Rome. The diadem was won back by the death of Christ, to be held in trust until Adam is reinstated in the new earth. The newly-founded church of Jesus met the same fate as the newly-founded race in Eden, as the newly-purged earth in Noah's time, and as the newly-formed nation in Moses' time. Each quickly apostatized. The church of Christ became a nest of satanic activity: intrigue, deceit, ambition, war, and cruelty when Constantine, by decree, brought paganism and Christianity together. Intending to weld a kingdom of peace, he little knew what a future of misery he was creating. The remnant that refused to accommodate the new system of compromise were ostracized and persecuted terribly. They scattered into the mountains and holes in the rocks and for years were hunted down like wild animals. Their brethren, now known as Catholics, unable to exterminate them or even to diminish their numbers, chose instead to distract attention from this fairly large contingent of dissenters by identifying small fragments of them, the Albigenses, Huguenots, Waldenses, and Vaudois. Another group of separationists later became known as Protestants. The history of their painful attempt to recover is another story. But how does the Bible predict this chapter in the great controversy?

John uses a "7/10" allegory to outline three major phases within the rebellion era. We are familiar with "lucky 7" and with "unlucky 13." In John's day a family of highly developed "completion" metaphors helped illustrate the future:

1——Complete unity.

2——Complete choice: yes/no, right/wrong, obey/disobey.

3——Complete understanding: repetition, reinforcement, emphasis, realization, the Trinity.

4——Complete geographic inclusion: as in compass directions (NEWS).

7——Complete solution: mysteries revealed, issues resolved, burdens relieved, disclosures made plain; denouement; the most amount necessary; the defining moment, the rest/completion of the story.

10——Complete necessity: the least amounts necessary, as in the Decalogue; as in the number of souls sufficient to spare Sodom.

12——Completing perfection: brought to perfection, maturity, finished, prepared; a process.

24—— (See 2 and 12.) Through a process of complete choice: a product of completed perfection being realized.

144K——Special, unique preparation or experience as in 12^2, (12 x 12) or 144; "K" or "thousand"—a metaphor for "host" or "many."

The third woe is not announced until Revelation 11, verses 14 and 15. Just as the symbolism under the first two woes identifies who were to be punished, so it is with the symbolism under the third woe. The third woe symbols begin with Revelation 12 and continue through chapter 17. This review of the turbulent past reveals more than only the identity of those institutions comprising Satan's tabernacle; it serves also to justify God in withdrawing His light, love, and glory from the wicked of the earth. That action was first described in Revelation 8:1–5, as God's strange act, so uncharacteristic of divine behavior, in contradiction to the paradigm of LOVE.

Three things are necessary in understanding prophecy: time—place—event.

"And there appeared a great wonder in heaven; *a woman* clothed with the sun, and the moon under her feet, and upon her head a *crown of twelve stars:* and she *being with child* cried, travailing in birth, and pained to be delivered" (Rev. 12:1–2, emphasis mine).

Three things are necessary in understanding prophecy: *time— place—event.* What is the time represented here in this text? AD 1. What is the place? Judea. And what event is here illustrated? The first coming of Jesus. Having answered these three questions, we are now prepared to make an application of the symbols being used.

Great Wonder: The Bible commentary tells us that the Greek derivative of the word is a sign, a mark, a token, to signify, to indicate.[170]

Heaven: (In the heaven.) The sky that is visible to John. Heaven is a general term for space. There is a space between earth and where the atmosphere ends—the first *heaven*. Then between where the atmosphere ends and God's abode begins—the locus of the stars is the second *heaven*. The space where divinity is present is the third *heaven*. Thus, there is said to be three spaces, or three heavens. The one that John sees is the one that we breathe, and there he saw a woman.

A Woman: The church, in one of its various states—good, bad, or indifferent.

Sun: Representing the glory (authority) of God.

Moon: Representing the system of types and shadows. Remember, Satan perverts everything divine. God invented the moon and the sun for *signs and seasons*. Satan has taken the sun and the moon and the stars and generated a whole false system called astrology. In the case of the vision, it was the *divine* system in reference.

Crown: *Stephanos* (a victor's crown) NOT *diadema* (a kingly crown). When we get to heaven, we will not wear *diademas*; we will wear *stephanos*.

Twelve Stars: The *Bible Commentary* speculates on whether apostles or patriarchs are inferred here. It is more likely that the completion metaphor is intended. Thus, the new church in the offing will be *brought to perfection* by the experiences she will have during this time.[171]

With Child: The promised Messiah, born to earth through much travail and pain in heavenly places. It was with great difficulty that God gave Him up. This reflects the divine pathos, the tremendous sacrifice that took place within the Godhead. We don't often dwell on that, but we ought to do so. The struggle that the Father, the Son, and the Holy Spirit had in breaking up Their unity in order to accomplish our salvation was terribly painful for Them.

---

170 Ellen G. White, *SDA Bible Commentary*, vol. 7 (Washington, DC: Review and Herald, 1957), p. 807.
171 Ibid.

"And there appeared another wonder in heaven; and behold a *great red dragon*, having *seven heads* and *ten horns*, and *seven crowns* upon his heads" (Rev. 12:3, emphasis mine).

Another Wonder in Heaven: Another *mark*, or *sign*, portending forthcoming events.

Red Dragon: As we will find in the next verse, the red dragon is identified as "that old serpent, called the Devil, and Satan." He is here represented as *working through pagan Rome*, the power ruling the world when Jesus was born. His *redness* connects him with his role as a persecutor and a destroyer. (This is reminiscent of the *red horse* of Revelation 6.)

The *seven heads* and *ten horns* require more discussion because of the myth and the speculation surrounding them. Here the crowns are upon the *seven heads*, not upon the ten horns. This fact helps us separate metaphor from symbol. A metaphor is not to be confused with a symbol. Metaphors can be present in either literal or symbolic contexts. A symbol is *never* literal. It must be interpreted, translated. In reality, heads that wear crowns are political rulers. So, we should look for a literal understanding of the seven heads. Notice the comment in *The Great Controversy*:

> The line of prophecy in which these symbols are found begins with Revelation 12, with the dragon that sought to destroy Christ at His birth. The dragon is said to be Satan (Revelation 12:9); he it was that *moved upon Herod* to put the Saviour to death. But the *chief agent of Satan* in making war upon Christ and His people during the first centuries of the Christian Era was *the Roman Empire*, in which paganism was the prevailing religion. Thus while the dragon, primarily, represents Satan, it is, in a secondary sense, *a symbol of pagan Rome.*[172]

Verses 4 and 5 are cryptic descriptions of the life and ministry of Jesus. "His tail" refers to *consequences* of behavior. *Heads* are cause—*tails* are consequence. In this case Satan, through Rome, denied Israel *one-third* of its ruling body, its kingship, leaving two-thirds: priests and the Sanhedrin. "Her *child was caught up* unto God, and to his throne" (Rev. 12:5, emphasis mine) refers to the ascension of Jesus Christ.

---

[172] Ellen G. White, *The Great Controversy* (Mountain View, CA: Pacific Press, 1911), p. 438, emphasis mine.

Verse 6 describes the persecution of the remnant through 1,260 years. Verses 7 to 9: *"And there was war* [literally] *in heaven"* (Rev. 12:7, emphasis mine) is a review of the event that sets the stage for the terrible struggle during those years and identifies the origin of it. In verses 10 to 12 is the assurance that God has firm management of this darkness. Verses 13 to 16 tell of the divine protection given through the mountain fastness of Europe and the isolation of the North American continent until the remnant church became strong enough for the final battle in the history of sin. Verse 17 brings us down to *today* and *tomorrow.*

Red Dragon Beast Let's go back to verse 3 and the seven heads with seven crowns upon them. There were seven kings called Herod ruling during the life and ministry of Jesus. Satan used (1) *Herod the Great* to make a decree to kill all the children in Bethlehem who were 2 years old and under (Matt. 2:16). He ruled *all of Palestine* at the time of Jesus' birth. His son, (2) *Herod Archelaus,* ruled Judea and Samaria during Jesus' childhood. (3) *Herod Antipas* ruled Galilee and Perea during Jesus' ministry. (4) *Herod Philip* was tetrarch of the territories northeast of the Sea of Galilee from 4 BC to AD 33. (5) *Herod Philip, brother of Antipas and first husband of Herodias*, held minor office. (6) *Herod Agrippa I* was king of Judea and all of Palestine; he persecuted the apostles, executed James, and imprisoned Peter. (7) *Herod Agrippa II ruled the northeast and was son of Agrippa I.*[173] He is the one who heard Paul.[174]

---

[173] See Chart 6, p. 143, "The Seven Heads/10 Horns of Revelation 12."
[174] Ellen G. White, *SDA Bible Commentary*, vol. 5 (Washington, DC: Review and Herald, 1956), index.

> ***Chart 6:*** *The Seven Heads/10 Horns of Revelation 12*[175]
>
> 1. **Herod the Great** (40 BC – 1 BC) (Jesus' birth)
>   Salome I (Sister)
>
>   Sons:
>   2. **Herod Archelaus** (Jesus' childhood)
>   3. **Herod Antipas** (Jesus' ministry)   Herodias (wife)
>   Aristobulous
>   Alexander
>   4. **Herod Philip Tetrarch** (4 BC—34 AD)   Salome II (wife)
>   5. **Herod Philip**   Herodias (wife)
>   6. **Herod Agrippa I** (Son of Aristobulos, Persecuted the Apostles)
>
>   Children:
>   Bernice
>   Mariamne
>   Drusilla
>   7. **Agrippa II** (Son of Agrippa I, Heard Paul)
>
> Herod the Great was brother of Salome I.
> Herod Agrippa I imprisoned Peter, slew James, died of worms.
> Herodias (wife of her two uncles, Herod Philip and Herod Antipas).
> Salame II, was the daughter of Herodias.
> Herod Antipas, "the fox" (slayer of John the Baptist, presided at Jesus' trial).
>
> In the *10 Horns* of **Revelation 12** is represented the *power of the Roman Empire* exercised against the Messiah and His *Church*. It is the minimum player necessary in the equation to exploit the vulnerability of God while in human form.

---

[175] *The SDA Bible Commentary*, vol. 8, (Washington, DC: Review and Herald 1957), pp. 479-483.

Certainly, the incarnation of God would be the most opportune time for Satan to gain his coveted victory since, in the garb of fallen humanity, divinity was incredibly vulnerable.[176] Can you imagine God taking on human flesh after 4,000 years of sin and linking Himself to the limits of human flesh? When Jesus was here, He had no memory of His life in heaven. He had to accept by faith who He was. Of course, His mother recited to Him the peculiar circumstances of His birth, and He was told who He was by His mother. When He went to the temple at the age of twelve, He had sufficient background to recognize that what was taking place there pertained to Him. And when His parents chided Him, He said, "Know ye not that I must be about My *Father's* business?" (Luke 2:49, paraphrase). Since He was not referring to Joseph, it can be inferred that He had an intellectual grasp of His divine mission at the age of twelve, but He had to struggle the same as do you and me. He had to exercise a monumental faith to accept that He was the Messiah and had the Messiah's mission.

The ten horns of Revelation 12 are symbolic of pagan Rome. Remember, "ten" is a metaphor for "the least amount necessary" and must be understood here symbolically. It was at least necessary for Rome to exist to enable Satan to carry out his plan at that time. The primary evil power in this scene is, of course, Satan, but he was working through the *secondary* power of Rome, which in the affairs of men was necessary. God works out His will through the agency of man; Satan achieves his goals through the cooperation of evil men, even the seven crowned heads of the Herod dynasty.

Leopard-like Beast The same symbolism is used 500 years later to identify another beast. This beast has the characteristics of a leopard, a bear, and a lion (the reverse order of their historic appearance in Daniel's book—looking backward), and receives his power, seat, and great authority *from the dragon.*

"And I stood upon the sand of the sea, and saw a beast rise up out of the sea, having *seven heads* and *ten horns,* and upon his horns *ten crowns,* and upon his heads the name of blasphemy" (Rev. 13:1, emphasis mine).

"And the beast which I saw was *like unto* a leopard, and his feet *were as* the feet of a bear, and his mouth *as* the mouth of a lion: and

---

[176] Ellen G. White, *The Desire of Ages* (Mountain View, CA: Pacific Press, 1898), chapter 74, "Gethsemane."

the dragon gave him his power, and his seat, and great authority" (Rev. 13:2, emphasis mine).

A prophetic *beast* is understood to be a political entity; and one rising up out of a sea is one emerging from among existing nations. This second beast also had seven heads and ten horns, but this time the crowns were upon the *horns*. And each of the heads was guilty of blasphemy. The fit of beast number two in history is *after* the apostolic church was established (see Rev. 12:17), but *before* the United States emerged (see Rev. 13:11). The *remnant* of chapter 12, verse 17, are those who resist the great merging of Christianity and paganism begun in AD 321 by Constantine the Great. Two hundred years later (AD 538), the Germanic hordes have overrun the Italian peninsula, the governing body of the Roman Empire has relocated on the Dardanelles at the new capital, Constantinople, and the bishop of the Roman Church is left to defend the city. Through collusion with Emperor Ferdinand, the crisis is met, and the church is established as a formidable power. The year is about AD 538.[177]

Notice in verse 2 that the characteristics of the beast are identical to those of previous beasts we have studied: a lion, a bear, and a leopard (Dan. 7). These were *pagan* powers—powers derived from the *dragon*. The beast in question received from the dragon not only *power* but also his *seat* (territory) and *great authority*. From this description we note the transfer of *civil power* to an *ecclesiastical institution*.

What do the symbols (seven heads/ten horns) here represent? The ten horns wear the ten crowns, so it is apparent that we should look for something literal. The ten Germanic tribes that overran Rome have been understood to apply here, especially since *three were uprooted* and in their place another fearsome power emerged. The seven heads are explained in *The Acts of the Apostles*, where the number is applied to the seven churches:

"The number 7 indicates *completeness,* and is symbolic of the fact that the messages extend to the end of time, while the symbols used reveal the condition of the church at different periods in the history of the world."[178]

Here, the number 7 indicates *completeness* and is symbolic of the *heads of the church* and extends to the end of time, beginning with

---

[177] "THE ROMAN EMPIRE FROM 313–538 AD," Lineage Journey, https://1ref.us/1jx (accessed February 8, 2021).

[178] Ellen G. White, *The Acts of the Apostles* (Mountain View, CA: Pacific Press, 1911), p. 585.

Vigilius in AD 538 and running to Francis I. Daniel was given a view of the *little horn* on at least two occasions, once in chapter 7.

"I considered the horns, and behold, there came up among them another *little horn*, before whom there were three of the first horns plucked up by the roots: and, behold, in this horn were *eyes* [paradigm] like the *eyes* of man, and a *mouth* [government] speaking great things" (Dan. 7:8, emphasis mine).[179][180]

"And I saw one of his heads *as it were* wounded to death; and his deadly wound was healed: and *all the world* wondered after the beast" (Rev. 13:3, emphasis mine).

History will repeat! And the reason it will do so is because of the nature of things earthly. Sin expresses itself in basic ways, and the consequences follow predictably. Listen to Daniel again in verse 11.

"*I beheld* then because of the voice [edict] of the great words which the horn spake: *I beheld even till the beast was slain*, and his body ... given to the burning flame" (Dan. 7:11, emphasis mine).

Daniel saw in his verse 11 what John saw in his verse 3: one of his heads, as it were, wounded; and his deadly wound was healed. This wound is understood to have taken place in 1798 when Berthier, the French general, took Pope Pius VI captive, ending his capacity as a sovereign ruler. He was left with mere ecclesiastical powers, a condition that would persist until 1929, when Benito Mussolini would cut a deal with Pope Pius XI, granting him 108 acres of sovereign territory and national independence in exchange for the Catholic vote. Thus, the deadly wound was healed a second time. There is a final healing yet future, as well as a marvelous *wondering after the beast*. Verses 3 to 8 are examples of history repeating.

---

179 Why the Ostrogoths, Vandals, and Heruli were the chosen three horns to be uprooted is a fascinating story (not necessarily consistent with popular history). The little horn of Daniel 7 corresponds with the apostle John's leopard-like beast.

180 Elias Brasil de Souza, Adult Sabbath School Bible Study Guide, 1st Quarter 2020, p. 66. "After the collapse of the Roman Empire (which came about by attacks from barbarians from the north), the bishop of Rome took advantage of the overthrow of three barbarian tribes and established himself as the sole power in Rome as of A.D. 538. In this process he adopted several institutional and political functions of the Roman emperor. From this emerged the papacy, invested with temporal and religious power until it was deposed by Napoleon in 1798. This did not bring an end to Rome, but only to that specified phase of persecution. The pope not only claimed to be the vicar of Christ but also introduced several doctrines and practices contrary to the Bible. Purgatory, penance, auricular confession, and the change of the Sabbath commandment to Sunday are among many other changes of the 'times and law' introduced by the papacy."

And I saw one of his heads as it were wounded to death; and his deadly wound was healed: and all the world wondered after the beast. And they worshipped the dragon which gave power unto the beast: and they worshipped the beast, saying, Who is like unto the beast? who is able to make war with him? And there was given unto him a mouth speaking great things and blasphemies: and power was given unto him to continue forty and two months. And he opened his mouth in blasphemy against God, to blaspheme his name, and his tabernacle, and them that dwell in heaven. And it was given unto him to make war with the saints, and to overcome them: and power was given him over all kindreds, and tongues, and nations. And all that dwell upon the earth shall worship him, whose names are not written in the book of life of the Lamb slain from the foundation of the world. (Rev. 13:3–8)

So it would happen in an earlier time, and would happen again in the ending of time with almost the same numbers—1,260 figurative days in history, and 1,260 literal days yet future (Dan. 12:7). These were wonderfully fulfilled between AD 538 and AD 1798, but will be fulfilled again in a more complete and dramatic way. Hence the warning: "*If any man have an ear, let him hear!*" (Rev. 13:9, emphasis mine).

"And I beheld *another* beast coming up *out of the earth*; and he had two horns like a lamb, and he spake as a dragon. And he exerciseth all the power of the first beast before him, and causeth the earth and them which dwell therein to worship the first beast, whose deadly wound was healed" (Rev. 13:11–12, emphasis mine).

Another beast is coming on the scene as the first beast is receiving a deadly wound in 1798. What nation emerged during that time and was separate from civilizations of the world? The United States is prophesied to speak as a dragon, to exercise *all* the power of the first beast, and to cause them which dwell on the earth to *worship* the first beast. Verse 13 adds to this unbelievable drama by declaring that the United States will do great wonders, even to bringing fire down from heaven on the earth in the sight of men. It will deceive them that dwell on the earth by means of miracles favorable to the first beast and will force an *image to this beast.* The United States will breathe life into the image such that all should worship the image or be killed (verses 14 and 15). How can that happen?

What is the image to the beast? What is the beast? The beast is an ecclesiastical body exercising political power. When the beast was formed, it was an ecclesiastical power, Pope Vigilius, that received secular power from Ferdinand. In this latter case, a secular power, the United States, will exercise ecclesiastical power. When looking into a mirror, the image is reversed—your right is its left. Your image is the reverse of you. The image here, the United States, has its origin in the reverse of the first one. The first one was an ecclesiastical body expressing secular power; the second one is a secular body expressing ecclesiastical power. *This will happen when the United States in legislative session will pass laws enforcing religious tenets.* Two statements from the Spirit of Prophecy will bring clarity here:

"What is it that gives its kingdom to this power? *Protestantism,* a power which, while professing to have the temper and spirit of a lamb and to be allied to Heaven, speaks with the voice of a dragon. It is moved by a power from beneath.[181]

"[W]hen the state shall use its power to enforce the decrees and sustain the institutions of the church—then will *Protestant America* have formed an *image to the papacy,* and there will be a national apostasy which will end only in national ruin."[182]

The United States of America was formed as a Protestant sanctuary for those who protested the persecution and crimes committed by the Catholic Church and enforced by the powers of Europe and England. Reading the literature of that early day up through the Civil War years leaves one with the impression of the fear the United States had regarding Catholicism and the pope. USA Protestantism is prophesized not only to embrace the Catholic institution but to lend her power to carry out her ancient practice of martyrdom.

Verses 16, 17, and 18 have been inspiration to the most sensational movies, books, and sermons—the mark of the beast and the number of his name. In our fervor to translate God's ideas, we stray often into gross error. In these two cases the jumping off place is a phenomenon called *anthropomorphization*: attributing human shape or human characteristics to gods, objects, or animals, i.e., the trees waved their hands, the sun smiled on the earth, etc. The mark of the beast under discussion is not tangible in a sensory way; it's not a tattoo or a microchip. Let's look at the texts and then at some clarifying references.

---

181 Ellen G. White, *SDA Bible Commentary*, vol. 7 (Washington, DC: Review and Herald, 1957), p. 983, emphasis mine.
182 Ibid., p. 976, emphasis mine.

"And he causeth all, both small and great, rich and poor, free and bond, to receive a mark in their right hand, or in their foreheads" (Rev. 13:16).

"Or" means one or the other, but not necessarily both. "And" is both of them. In order for "and" to apply, both components must be active. In order for "or" to apply, either one may be active. In this case it is "or."

"And that no man might buy or sell, save he that had the mark, *or* the name of the beast, *or* the number of his name" (Rev. 13:17, emphasis mine).

In verse 16 it is noted that no one is exempt from the marking. All will be marked in some way. Later, we will discover that there are two marking processes, both a matter of personal choice. And that is the intent of the last phrase in verse 16, "in their right hand, or in their foreheads." The forehead is the place of belief or conviction. Some will respond out of sincere belief. The hand is the place of doing. Many will respond out of cowardice or inertia. Either one will do.

The coercive element in this action is *commerce*. Life cannot proceed without commerce, buying and selling. Verse 17 expands the description of this marking phenomenon: the mark contains the name, or authority, of the beast, which is signified by a number designation, or a counting.

"Here is wisdom. Let him that hath understanding *count* [compute] the number of the beast: for it is the number of a man; and his number is *Six hundred threescore and six*" (Rev. 13:18, emphasis mine).

The number of completion and clarity is "7," and applied personally to God it would be "777," would it not? Throughout Scripture, the number of man has always been "6." (On what day was man created? Gen. 1:26, 31). Scripture recognizes this fact, so the metaphor of man is "6." The number of the evil beast that controls man would be a number designating incompletion, confusion on a colossal level. Whether or not it can be calculated from a name or title may be disputable. But when the conditions for this crisis are met, there will be no question regarding its application. So even though we may not settle certain prophetic issues here, if we are in possession of them, they will be clarified to us in a timely fashion.

"When the test comes, it will be *clearly shown* what the mark of the beast is. *It is the keeping of Sunday*."[183]

---

183 Ibid., p. 980, emphasis mine.

"Sundaykeeping is *not yet* the mark of the beast, and *will not be* until the decree goes forth *causing men* to worship this idol Sabbath. The time will come when this day *will be the test,* but that time has not come yet."[184]

The Revelation has much more to say respecting this subject. In future chapters the mark, or seal, of God will be revealed. In the next chapter we will be looking at the third 7/10 metaphor found in Revelation 17. It is germane to us because it is yet future, or it is even now presently emerging. We must decide upon examination. There are many variant understandings of Revelation 17. I have entertained several of them myself. The next chapter will consider the most recent understanding, based on a fuller grasp of inspired fact. It doesn't necessarily contradict all previously held views, and the reason is because the larger view has been mostly ignored. God is so dimensional that we cannot readily grasp His notions. Thus, we tend to pare them down to fit our size, and whenever we do that, *truth is diminished.* Recently, I have made my focus the more global view of whatever is under discussion, rather than the narrow one, but that doesn't exclude the narrow one. It keeps God in better focus.

---

[184] Ibid., p. 977, emphasis mine.

Chapter 9
Revelation 17: The Third "7/10" of Revelation 17

The three 7/10s of Revelation are allegories. An *allegory* is a multiple metaphor, or a description of an event under the image of another event. A *metaphor* is a figure of speech that makes *one point*. An allegory is a figure of speech that makes many points. It is a mistake to allegorize a metaphor, but it is often done—pushed to make more points than it was designed to do. An allegory is a linguistic device that can be applied to several ideas that are not necessarily related.

The last chapter presented two beasts, each with seven heads and ten horns—the first two allegories. The seven heads in the first allegory (Revelation 12) were the seven Herods of Palestine during the apostolic period, beginning with the life and ministry of Jesus and reaching to the death of John. The ten horns were a figurative symbol of pagan Rome, the power behind the Herods. In the second *7/10s* allegory (Revelation 13), the ten horns were literal, and were the ten Germanic tribes that overran the Roman Empire. The seven heads figuratively describe the emergence of the papacy and represent all the heads of that church until the end of time. This allegory takes us from the beginning of the papal power down through time to when one of the heads was wounded. The context of chapter 13 is shown to be the emergence of papal power within the Christian church. The wounding of one of its heads introduces an era of "is, is not, and not yet come" (Papal Wilderness, Rev. 17:8)[185] before the emergence of the third and terrible beast.

Verse 19 of chapter 16 prepares for chapter 17, and the remembering of God. When God *remembers*, there is a fullness of time, in

---
185 Ibid., p. 853.

this case with respect to institutions or individuals and the consequences, or the *tails* of their doings. Chapter 17 prepares for chapter 18, and chapter 18 is where the great apostate church of God, having become the synagogue of Satan, is destroyed. God will be victorious! He purged heaven of its defilement when he cast out the "great red dragon" and the stars that were with him. The newly created earth then fell to Satan's sophistries, God's chosen nation became like other nations, and His carefully nurtured church soon became corrupted. It appears that every enterprise that God launches falls into the corruption of the great red dragon. But through it all there were always remnant people refusing to bend the knee. The question arises: are God and His nemeses so nearly equal in power that history is an accurate measure of divine strength? The flaw lies in fallen man's shallow examination of revealed truth. The world through Adam chose sin as its default paradigm, which requires an excess of exposure to sin to awaken in man an abhorrence to it. Now God recaps that history in chapter 17, before the great whore comes to her calamitous destruction in chapter 18.

"And there came one of the seven angels which had the seven vials, and talked with me, saying unto me, Come hither; I will shew unto thee the judgment of the great whore that sitteth upon many waters" (Rev. 17:1).

A significant connection is made in this verse between the judgment of the papal institution and the seven last plagues. The judgment here referred to is not that which began in 1844, the review that selects candidates for God's kingdom. When the plagues fall, the papal institution is the last man standing. All other human institutions have ceased to exist, absorbed into Babylon. The angel offered to show John the judgment of the whore that sits upon many waters. This is a punitive judgment, not an evaluative one. The kings of the earth have shared illicit pleasures with her, and "the inhabitants of the earth have been made drunk with the wine of her fornication" (Rev. 17:2).

The angel with whom John spoke who had the vial carried him away in the Spirit into the wilderness. We saw another woman of quite a different character in chapter 12 who had fled into a wilderness. Do you remember the figure of a prophetic wilderness? A place isolated by circumstance from the commerce of civilization and power. At what time was Roman Catholicism unable to exercise fully her powers of control and persecution? Her *wilderness* is defined between the loss of *persecuting power* in 1798 and the restoring of *persecuting power* by the enactment of a Sunday law. Almost immediately she began to recover, but it wasn't until 1929 that a significant advance was made when she regained sovereign power, but her universal persecuting powers are yet future. In the wilderness, what sight caught John's visionary eye?

"[A]nd I saw a woman sit upon a scarlet coloured beast, full of names of blasphemy, having seven heads and ten horns" (Rev. 17:3).

The woman, a church, is seated upon a scarlet colored beast, a civil power by which she is upheld and which she controls and guides to her own ends. Scarlet is the color of royalty. The beast is further distinguished by names of blasphemy. The beast-horn of Daniel 7:8, 20 astonished Daniel by speaking great things. The beast of Revelation 13:5–6 also speaks blasphemies against God. These entities are identical. Also identical are the metaphors presented in verses 9 and 10 of Revelation 17. Heads, mountains, and kings are identical in the sense that they are inclusive.

Biblical perspective fixes the beast of Revelation 17 at the end-time judgment. Indeed, the angel tells John that five of the beast's heads/mountains/kings are fallen. In Daniel 2, Babylon is followed by Medo-Persia, followed by Greece, followed by pagan Rome, followed by the feet and toes, followed by the stone cut out without hands that smashes the image and grows into a great mountain. Daniel 7 recapitulates this notion with the figures of lion, bear, leopard, a dreadful beast, and a little horn. Daniel 8 recapitulates the same notion with the figures of a ram, goat, and a little horn. Here the little horn embraces both manifestations of Rome: pagan and papal. The little horn of Daniel 8 makes no distinction between these two—it's all one piece with them. Why do you think that might be? When the church absorbed paganism, the only changes made were the names of pagan icons to names of Christian icons. When Catholic missionaries went into a new civilization to proselytize them, their strategy would be to study carefully the religious structure of the pagan system, and then to superimpose a Christianized layer over the existing system.

John produces his own array of beast powers: (1) the red dragon of Revelation 12, (2) the sea beast of Revelation 13, (3) the land beast of Revelation 13, (4) the image of the beast of Revelation 13, (5) the scarlet beast of Revelation 17, and (6) the ten horns of Revelation 17. The angel speaking to John will now reveal the mystery of the woman and the beast that carries her.

"And the angel said unto me, Wherefore didst thou marvel? I will tell thee the mystery of the woman, and of the beast that carrieth her, which hath the seven heads and ten horns" (Rev. 17:7).

The angel gives the formula in a sequence of three cycles with four phases each: verses 8, 10, and 11 recapitulate. We will examine the *parts of each verse.*

(Rev. 17:8)

A. 1. The beast that thou sawest was,

2. And is not,

3. And shall ascend out of the bottomless pit,

4. And go into perdition.

(Rev. 17:10)

B. 1. Five are fallen,

2. One is,

3. The other is not yet come,

4. And when he cometh, he must continue a short space.

(Rev. 17:11)

C. 1. And the beast that was,

2. And is not,

3. He is the eighth, and is of the seven,

4. And goes into destruction.

The three cycles, while recapitulating, do not duplicate but expand on the beast under discussion. Before continuing we must take note of verses 9 and 10:

"And here is the mind which hath wisdom. The seven heads *are* seven mountains, on which the woman sitteth. And there [they] *are* seven kings" (Rev. 17:9–10, emphasis mine).

This is the second time John calls us to wisdom. The first was in Revelation 13:18. (Let him that hath wisdom count/calculate the number of the beast.) A mountain in the Bible symbolizes religious power. The seven heads *are* seven mountains of power, where the woman sits upon them, and they *are* seven kings. Thus: Heads = Mountains = Kings. (In the ancient context, pagan religion was indistinguishable from secular life.)[186]

The first cycle covers the five historical periods of Babylon, Medo-Persia, Greece, Rome, and the little horn (papal Rome) up to 1798:

The beast, which thou sawest, *was*—prior to 1798.

That was the beast of Revelation 13, the sea beast. It had the characteristics of kingdoms prophesied by Daniel in his chapter 7: leopard, bear, lion, and a dreadful beast. (The seven heads are obvious when you count as follows: lion—1 head; bear—1 head; leopard—4 heads; dreadful beast—1 head = 7 heads.)

The second cycle covers the *"is not, yet is"* (Papal Wilderness) period and is marked by the absence of church-state union.

Five are fallen, one is, and the other is not yet come.

This period corresponds to the deadly wounding of the head (1798) in Revelation 13:3 and following, when in 1929 a partial recovery was realized. The time of the deadly wound was imposed by Napoleon through his General Berthier, who took the pope captive in 1798. This cycle is the time of the sixth king/mountain/head! It will continue until the Sunday closing enactment restoring the powers of persecution taken away in 1798.

The third cycle announces that the wound has been healed and the beast is coming up out of the bottomless pit. This language is dealing with the beast that the woman rides. The woman, the Roman Catholic Church, the great whore, rides and controls the beast once again, but it has a new element: it is the eighth, the sum, substance, the total of all that have gone before, all the combined evil and persecuting power of the seven taken together. The third cycle covers the short time noted in verse 10: "[A]nd when he cometh, he must continue a short space."

"And the beast that was, and is not, even he is the eighth, and is of the seven" (Rev. 17:11).

The seven powers, also the one that is, is also the eighth! How can that be? Let's read the whole passage in one piece:

---

[186] "Heads" (religious power) = "Mountains" (where woman sits) = "kings" (political power). "The fact that Satan, the apostate church, and this scarlet beast all share similar characteristics suggests that this is a composite symbol of the forces arrayed against God at the end of time …. [The] combined aspects of the religious and political components of that power, all intertwined with Satan himself." Mark Finley, *Understanding Daniel and Revelation* (Nampa, ID: Pacific Press, 2020), p. 349.

"The seven heads are seven mountains, on which the woman sitteth. And there are seven kings: five are fallen, and one is, and the other is not yet come; and when he cometh, he must continue a short space. And the beast that was, and is not, even he is the eighth, and is of the seven" (Rev. 17:9–11).

Mervyn Maxwell explains this very well:

"Let's not make the problem too hard. The beast isn't an eighth head! It's a beast, and the seven heads all belong to it!"[187]

Do you see the difference between them? There are seven heads upon one beast. And aren't the seven heads parts of the one beast? And isn't the beast part of the seven heads? "And the beast that was, and is not, even he is the eighth [power]" (Rev. 17:11), and the seven all belong to it. These entities are all *powers*. And when Satan emerges during the fifth plague in his attempt to muster unanimity among the wicked nations of the earth for his great assault on the remnant people of God, his point is *genocide*, to exterminate the faithful of God. That's the whole purpose of this effort. He will take his place at the head of the sole remaining institution on earth—the papacy. All of the heads (seven) of other powers belong to it/come under it. When we add up seven numbers, we get an eighth number—the sum of the seven. So it is with the powers of Revelation 17: the sum of the seven powers is the eighth power. But what of the ten horns?

"And the ten horns which thou sawest are ten kings, which have *received no kingdom as yet*; but *receive power as kings* one hour with the beast" (Rev. 17:12, emphasis mine).

There is much erroneous discussion with respect to these ten kings. However, anything that has had a *crowned king* in it must be excluded. They cannot be considered here because these ten horns *have had no kingdom as yet*. So an entity must be found that will *act as king* during this short period of time, but has not been a king prior to that time. Let's see if we can do that. "[T]he ten horns which thou sawest are ten kings, which have received no kingdom as yet; but receive power *as kings* one hour with the beast" (Rev. 17:12). How long is one prophetic hour? Fifteen days. There are two end-time fifteen-day periods, and this is in reference to the first of the fifteen-day periods. What kind of powers could be represented by horns that are not civil (crowned) powers? Religious power acting as civil authority is

---

[187] C. Mervyn Maxwell, *God Cares*, vol. 2 (Boise, ID: Pacific Press, 1985), p. 475.

not yet the vogue, but it is prophesied that it will gain the ascendancy soon. Spirit of Prophecy clearly gives the answer:

"What is it that gives its kingdom to this power? *Protestantism*, a power which, while professing to have the temper and spirit of a lamb and to be allied to Heaven, speaks with the voice of a dragon. It is moved by a power from beneath."[188]

"[W]hen the state shall use its power to enforce the decrees and sustain the institutions of the church—then will *Protestant America* have formed an image to the papacy, and there will be a national apostasy which will end only in national ruin."[189]

In another chapter we will define the precise time when the ten horn power will reign as kings one hour with the beast. There is a reason that there are ten horns and not seven, or other. Remember "10" is the numeric metaphor for the least amount *necessary* for completion. What is being completed in this metaphor? *Satan's power to enact a universal death decree*! And he must persuade a following in order to accomplish this. But to what does he appeal? He is appealing to the protestant churches of the United States to make an image, that is, to exercise the same religious power here that has been exercised in Europe by the papacy for 1,200 or 1,300 years. Allan Fine, a retired Seventh-day Adventist minister and a high-ranking member of the *Christian Coalition*, was in conversation with Ralph Reed, then top officer in the organization. Reed proposed an action in close cooperation with the papacy that elicited some consternation from Allen. Allen asked him then, "How could you do that? Aren't you a Protestant?" To which Reed replied, "What do I have to protest!" Allen's conclusion is that the Protestants have now taken possession of the Republican Party, and the Catholics have taken possession of the Protestants.[190] So who controls the Republican Party? Thus, we are two-thirds on the way. To close the circle, the Christian Coalition

---

188 Ellen G. White, *SDA Bible Commentary*, vol. 7 (Washington, DC: Review and Herald, 1957), p. 983, emphasis mine.
189 Ibid., p. 976, emphasis mine.
190 "[J]ust about every Republican hoping for a shot at the GOP nomination for president will metaphorically kiss the ring of Ralph Reed and schmooze his conference crowd .... Reed is known as an evangelical whisperer .... 'Ralph invented the game and how to play the game. He's got a PhD in political science,' said Dr. Richard Land, the head of the public policy arm of the Southern Baptist Church, the nation's largest Protestant denomination with 16 million members. 'He's one of them. He's an evangelical. He understands the evangelical and the conservative Catholic positions. He understands what rings their chimes and what doesn't.'" Eric Marrapodi, "Why Ralph Reed matters," CNN Belief Blog, https://1ref.us/1jy (accessed February 8, 2021).

is a metaphoric "10"—the least amount necessary for completion of a process. In this case, the beast is the primary power, operating to achieve his own ends. Being bound to solicit help where it is available, he finds a ready ally in Apostate Protestantism. *A view of the "beast" should not be limited to the papacy.* A beast is always the power behind visible institutions, good or evil. Thus, the eighth beast is the full combined power of all the agencies of evil in the history of the world, which shall make war with the Lamb in the person of His saints.

"[A]nd the Lamb shall overcome them [The Lamb is overcoming whom? All of these combined beasts]: for he is Lord of lords, and King of kings: and they that are with him are called, and chosen, and faithful" (Rev. 17:14).

Let us recap the main points so far: there is a terrible judgment in the offing for the institution identified as the great whore—terrible judgment, an executive judgment. Cohorts and allies who delight to share in her plunder and power surround her. But John's manifestation is only an end-time revelation of the mystery of iniquity ever since Nimrod founded ancient Babylon.[191] Chapter 17 uses three symbols that are equivalent players in the drama: 7 heads, 7 mountains, and 7 kings. Here is the list:

1.	Babylon	67 years
2.	Medo-Persia	208 years
3.	Greece	163 years
4.	Pagan Rome	706 years
5.	Papal Rome	1260 years
6.	Is not-Yet is	c. 207 years
7.	Neo-Papacy	1290 days
8.	THE BEAST	Goeth into perdition

---

[191] "'Cush begot Nimrod; he began to be a mighty one on the earth. He was a mighty hunter before the Lord .... And the beginning of his kingdom was Babel.' Nimrod, the son of Cush, is linked to Mesopotamia .... The founder of the city of Babylon and several other prominent cities in Mesopotamia." *Andrews Study Bible* (Berrien Springs, MI: Andrews University Press, 2010), pp. 18, 500.

It might be profitable to interject something here respecting prophetic beasts. John's second beast, the beast of Revelation 13, is descriptive of previous beasts we have met in the book of Daniel. Looking at Daniel 7:3-8 will be a helpful review:

> And four great beasts came up from the sea, diverse one from another. The first was like a lion, and had eagle's wings: I beheld till the wings thereof were plucked, and it was lifted up from the earth, and made [to] stand upon the feet as a man, and a man's heart was given to it. And behold another beast, a second, like to a bear, and it raised up itself on one side, and it had three ribs in the mouth of it between the teeth of it: and they said thus unto it, Arise, devour much flesh. After this I beheld, and lo another, like a leopard, which had upon the back of it four wings of a fowl; the beast had also four heads; and dominion was given to it. After this I saw in the night visions, and behold a fourth beast, dreadful and terrible, and strong exceedingly; and it had great iron teeth: it devoured and brake in pieces, and stamped the residue with the feet of it: and it was diverse from all the beasts that were before it; and it had ten horns. I considered the horns, and, behold, there came up among them another little horn, before whom there were three of the first horns plucked up by the roots: and, behold, in this horn were eyes like the eyes of man, and a mouth speaking great things. (Dan. 7:3–8)

Now let's look at John's second beast in Revelation 13:2:

"And the beast which I saw was *like unto* a leopard, and his feet were *as* the feet of a bear, and his mouth *as* the mouth of a lion: and the dragon gave him his power, and his seat, and great authority" (Rev. 13:2, emphasis mine).

We find that the beast of Revelation 17 is a consequence of the previous two beasts (Rev. 12 and 13). The first one opposed Christ during His ministry on earth; the second one opposed His church until it received a deadly wound; and the third is a resurrected manifestation of the other two. Let's see if there are any other consistencies from the past. In Daniel, where have we encountered a leopard, a bear, a lion, and a dragon? In the vision of Daniel chapter 7, we see the lion of Babylon, the bear of Medo-Persia, the leopard of Greece, and the dragon of Rome. Let's now look at verse three in Revelation 17.

"So he carried me away in the spirit into the wilderness: and I saw a woman sit upon a scarlet coloured beast, full of names of blasphemy, *having seven heads and ten horns*" (Rev. 17:3, emphasis mine).

> *A wilderness in prophecy is a place, or circumstance, that is beyond commerce. There is no potential for trade, barter, or the free exercise of political power.*

In the context of the scenes shown here to John, the beast and the woman are found in the wilderness. A wilderness in prophecy is a place, or circumstance, that is beyond commerce. There is no potential for trade, barter, or the free exercise of political power. The woman, or the church, is being carried by the beast, a satanic icon, with the potential of political expression, scarlet in color. Scarlet typifies royalty, the power to rule. That the beast assumes powers akin to God is reflected in the names "full of blasphemy." The seven heads have been a point of much discussion and controversy for many years. One Protestant understanding considers the seven heads to be seven popes reigning since the healing of the deadly wound in 1929. (Even Catholic scholars subscribe to this notion. However, the Catholic version culminates with [false] Christ himself upon Peter's throne rather than a personating of Christ there.)[192]

According to this understanding, the next scene must be a national Sunday closing law. In traditional SDA understanding the seven heads are seven political powers that have been closely connected with the people of God since the diadem passed from Judah at the Babylonian captivity. There are variations in understanding this interpretation, but several aspects favor this view over the other one. Among them is its universal scope harmonizing with the grand scenes of Revelation. God is summarizing all the way through the apocalypse, and this is no exception; it is consistent with the summary notion. The beast of Revelation 13 is summarized as follows: it bears characteristics of all the beasts of prophecy previous to it. But it carries two additional distinctions. The first distinction is that God selected each of those four beasts to serve His purpose. Didn't God select Babylon and Medo-Persia and Greece and Rome? He did! And the second distinction is that

---

[192] Ranko Stefanovic, "The Seven Heads of the Beast in Revelation 17," *Ministry Magazine*, https://1ref.us/1jz (accessed February 8, 2021).

Satan perverted each one of them to serve *his* purpose. Let's review what has been learned so far.

God selected Babylon to preserve the line of David and the sanctuary system. But Satan gave it the mouth of a lion, which is the doctrine of astrology.[193] God selected Medo-Persia to liberate His chosen people and to restore the sanctuary system, which He did under Cyrus. But Satan gave it the feet of a bear, the doctrine of Mithraism, and the universal death decree which emerged in the time of Esther, Haman, and Mordecai. God selected Greece to provide a culture in which both Scripture and the Messiah could flourish. But Satan made it like unto a leopard where spots provide camouflage for sinister doctrines (Mithraism). Out of Greece came the doctrines of eternally burning hell, an immortal soul, and the spirits of the dead.[194] All three of those are integral to the Christian churches of today, and they came straight from pagan Greece. God selected Rome to provide open borders, highways of travel, and the Pax Romana, the fabled Roman peace. All these to incubate the new church and to help it to flourish. But Satan gave it teeth of iron to persecute and destroy.

Do you see all these characteristics coming together here at the end? Is it possible that the *seven kings* could be Babylon, Medo-Persia, Greece, pagan Rome, papal Rome, the wilderness Rome—an interval identified as "was, is not, yet is"—and Neo-Babylon, the restored power of persecution, then the emergence of Satan in his grand deception?

All four of the beasts presented here practiced emperor worship—all four of them—which translated into papal supremacy. Isn't papal eminence essentially papal worship? That is the fifth head of the beast. The papal head ruled and persecuted for 1,260 years, just as prophesied. At the end of that period, in 1798, the world entered an era free from overt persecution and religious domination. The dark powers are still there, but they are muted. And thus, it is as if the beast that was, is NOT—yet is. What better way to describe that period between 1798 and the Sunday closing? The beast appears *not to be,* yet it is. That's the sixth head. The dormant beast has not changed, but is, as it were, in a wilderness. Isn't that where John saw this entity? He saw her during this period between 1798 and the Sunday closing,

---

193 Gavin White, "Babylonian Star-lore," Sky Script, https://1ref.us/1k0 (accessed February 8, 2021).
194 Loraine Boettner, *Roman Catholicism* (Philadelphia, PA: Presbyterian and Reformed, 1962), pp. 228–234.

where we are today. The whore is still in the wilderness, and we don't feel the full effect of her influence yet. The power that is not will be restored when apostate Protestantism supports her in a Sunday closing law, and that's when the seventh head emerges.

A succinct recap might look as follows:

> **Rev. 12:** 7 Herods (literal)
> 10 Pagan Rome (figurative)[195]
>
> **Rev. 13:** 7 Popes (figurative) (1929–2013)
> 10 Tribes (literal)
>
> **Rev. 17:** 7 Power bases: mountains, heads, kings (literal)
> 10 Apostate Protestantism (figurative)

Verses 16 and 17 are a fitting, even a macabre, climax for the whore's successes.

"And the ten horns [apostate Protestantism] which thou sawest upon the beast, these shall hate the whore, and shall make her desolate and naked, and shall eat her flesh, and burn her with fire. For God hath put in their hearts to fulfil his will, and to agree, and give their kingdom unto the beast, until the words of God shall be fulfilled" (Rev. 17:16–17).

There is a parallel passage in the Spirit of Prophecy in which all these political entities are under the influence of a divine appeal during the three angels' messages, which they reject. They reject truth, insisting on believing something other than truth. Now probation closes, and God essentially says, "You wish to believe something other? OK!" "God hath put in their hearts to agree with each other" (Rev. 17:17, paraphrase), thus bringing them together into a final coalition where

---

[195] **Rev. 17:3:** "So he carried me away in the Spirit into the wilderness. And I saw a woman sitting on a scarlet beast *which was* full of names of blasphemy, having seven heads and ten horns."
Scarlet Beast = worldwide political power in support of end-time Babylon.
Rev. 12:3: "[A] great, fiery red dragon having seven heads and ten horns, and seven diadems on his heads."
Fiery dragon = Satan (v. 9; Gen. 3:15). Also represents the civil power of Rome (v. 5).
Diadems = crowns.
Rev. 13:1: "I saw a beast rising up out of the sea, having seven heads and ten horns, and on his horns ten crowns, and on his heads a blasphemous name."
Blasphemous name = a religious power in opposition to God and His people. The crowns have *shifted* from the *heads* to the *horns*.
Mark Finley, *Understanding Daniel and Revelation* (Nampa, ID: Pacific Press, 2020), p. 350.

they will give their kingdom unto the beast for fifteen days until the words of God shall be fulfilled. The great battle of Armageddon stops the coalition in their tracks—that's the second *hour*, or second fifteen days—and Satan is there unmasked. At this time the merchants of the earth and the falsely spiritual people become furious at the duplicity of the papal institution. Here God is seen to have so managed the affairs of end-time earth as to bring these rebellious minds to (1) fulfill His will, (2) agree, or unite, and (3) give their kingdom power to the beast. In Revelation 18 through 20 will be shown in detail the fate of both these final people groups—the saved and the lost. In verse 18, the final verse in chapter 17, is given this affirmation:

"And the woman which thou sawest is that great city, which reigneth over the kings of the earth" (Rev. 17:18).

Chapter 10

Revelation 14 and 15: The Three Angels' Messages and Two Consequences

Chapter 14 of Revelation emerges from the dark side of chapter 13. Chapter 13 describes several beasts that are to be major players in the end-time drama. Here, in chapter 14, God presents *His* people, *His* influence in the affairs of men at this critical time. John's attention is called to these people by a scene of Mount Sion. There he sees the Lamb and a group of 144,000 favored ones, each having his Father's name in their foreheads. The first five verses of Revelation 14 describe a group with special characteristics to be used for a unique mission at a critical time in earth's history. John sees them *as if in God's presence* receiving their commission. Let's take a look:

"And I looked, and, lo, a Lamb stood on the mount Sion, and with him an hundred forty and four thousand, having *his Father's name written in their foreheads*" (Rev. 14:1, emphasis mine).

Verse 2 describes the voice of God announcing something, accompanied by the voice of harpers. They are singing, *as it were*, a new song, and it is taking place in the throne room of God before the great judgment audience that is described in Revelation, chapters 1 and 2. The song is unique because its theme is of their peculiar salvation experience. They are the only ones that can sing that song.

"These are they which were *not defiled with women;* for they *are virgins.* These are they which follow the Lamb whithersoever he goeth. These were redeemed from among men, being the firstfruits unto God and to the Lamb" (Rev. 14:4, emphasis mine).

There are several descriptors that set them uniquely apart from all the rest of the redeemed: (1) they were not defiled with women, (2) they are virgins, (3) they follow the Lamb wherever He goes,

(4) they are first fruits unto God and unto the Lamb, (5) in their mouth was found no guile, and (6) they are considered by God Himself to be without fault. Let's consider them, one at a time, to get the sense of John's meaning.

They were not defiled with women. (That's the masculine view. Women in this context are apostate churches.) They are found free from defiling doctrine.

They are virgins. (That's the feminine perspective.) They have entered into this crisis time fully informed, fully committed to Christ, and are purified [not having come out of another religious body].

They follow the Lamb withersoever He goeth. They have not been remiss in anything required of them. They have been faithful to the Lamb in every respect, and they will continue to follow the Lamb in every respect.

They are first fruits unto God and the Lamb. They are first harvested; they are the earnest fruit of those yet to be called out.

In their mouth was found no guile. These are people not taken in by deceit or subterfuge. They have rightly divided the Word of truth, perceiving the way in which to walk. Remember, of Jesus it was said that He was without guile.[196] And Jesus testified of Nathaniel, a man without guile (John 1:47). Guile was an ancient word for fish bait. If a fish has taken bait in his mouth, he has accepted something that he shouldn't have and was caught thereby. During the times under discussion there will be tremendous incentives to be deceived. All manner of false Christs and false prophets will abound. And those of us who survive this era must be very careful not to take bait into our mouth; we must be able to rightly divide the Word of truth. Of these people it will be said that there was no guile in their mouths. They were not fooled—taken in by false doctrine.

> *Guile was an ancient word for fish bait. If a fish has taken bait in his mouth, he has accepted something that he shouldn't have and was caught thereby.*

They are considered by God Himself to be without fault. They have been sealed and marked for eternity at this point.

---

196 Ellen G. White, *The Desire of Ages* (Mountain View, CA: Pacific Press, 1898), p. 69.

Whenever the *Lamb* appears, Christ is representing the *redeemed;* when the *Lion* appears, Christ is addressing the *condemned.* Here is a small group distinguished by having God's name written in their foreheads. From a previous discussion we understand a writing in the forehead to be a firmly held belief, one from which a person will not be moved, a manifestation of character.

We must keep in mind that the discussion in Revelation is of *end-time events, culminating actions.* There are two (maybe three) important defaults in the study of prophecy: (1) we must always make a literal application as opposed to a symbolic application, unless the context indicates otherwise. (2) Prophecy always addresses current or future events as opposed to past events unless the context indicates otherwise.[197] (3) *Prophecy always moves forward.* That's an axiom, a rule.

The context of verse 4 is looking back on those traumatic days concluding earth's history in sin. This group had an important part to play and were made up of those *not defiled with women.* A pure woman is a church organization adhering to *truth* about God. An impure woman is a church organization corrupted with *untruths* about God. The crisis here is a Sunday closing law. There will be at that time those who are already positioned and committed to God's finishing truth; they are virgins. Yet there are *many* sincere ones among the daughters of Babylon who will commit to God's finishing truth. They have affiliation with institutions that misrepresent God in specific ways. Therefore, they are said to be *defiled with women.* These people await an invitation and an experience to commit to God.

First fruits are still often described as *virgin:* the first-picked olives produce the sweetest oil, the first-sheared wool the most beautiful fiber, and the first-committed to God in this great final time of crisis the most durable service. They are further described in verse 5:

"They were purchased [redeemed] from among mankind and offered as *firstfruits* to God and the Lamb. No lie was found in their mouths; they are blameless" (Rev. 14:4–5, NIV, emphasis mine).

Was a lie found in Eve's mouth on that day in her conversation with the serpent? The serpent, being very crafty, asked Eve, "Is it true that you cannot eat of *any of the trees* in the Garden?" And Eve replied, "Oh, no! We can eat of *all of them* except the one, and of that

---

197 Even when regressing (historical view), the point of prophecy is being served. "The solemn messages that *have been given in their order* in the Revelation are to occupy the first place in the minds of God's people." Ellen G. White, *Testimonies for the Church,* vol. 8 (Mountain View, CA: Pacific Press, 1904), p. 302, emphasis mine.

we should not eat it, *neither should we touch it*, lest we die." That was not true (Gen. 2:17; 3:3). Eve, in adding to God's command, gave the serpent an advantage, thus contributing to her own destruction. Revelation 22:18–19 contains an admonition for those of us who are living in earth's final days: we must not add to, or take away from, the words of this book, lest our part be taken out of the book of life.

The SDA Bible Commentary suggests two commonly held views of the virgins who were selected from among men and presented to God: (1) being the first installment, or pledge, of a great harvest; or (2) as simply being an offering to God.[198] Verse 5 introduces the next 8 verses: these (the 144,000) are the ones who will proclaim the last three warning messages to a doomed world. They are the three angels of Revelation 14.

"And I saw [yet] another angel fly in the midst of heaven, having the *everlasting* gospel to preach unto them that dwell on the earth, and to every nation, and kindred, and tongue, and people, saying with a *loud* voice, Fear God, and give glory to him; for the hour of his judgment is come: and *worship* him that made heaven, and earth, and the sea, and the fountains of waters" (Rev. 14:6–7, emphasis mine).

It is necessary to state what to us appears obvious, because there are very few on earth who worship in that way or who fear God. We give assent to and recognition of what ought to be, and we will even declare that *we do*. But, in fact, we have close to our hearts something else that is dearer to us than the One who created the heavens, the earth, the sea, and the fountains of waters. It is this latter-day experience that will open our eyes and force from us a very frank decision with respect to our soul.

Both the "mighty angel" of Revelation 18:1 and the first angel of Revelation 14:6 respond to the divine mandate and mission proclaiming the last warning of prophecy to every nation, and kindred, and tongue, and people. The first angel's message, with its announcement of the heavenly judgment hour, found its most direct fulfillment in the messages of William Miller and his associates.

This warning message began to sound shortly after 1798, the official starting point for the time of the end. Like the messages to the seven churches, the messages of the three angels are to sound until the close of probation. Notice that God disabled His opposition at a very

---

198 *The Seventh-day Adventist Bible Commentary*, vol. 8 (Washington, DC: Review and Herald Publishing Association, 1960), p. 826.

crucial time—the awakening of the neo-Protestant movement. There was then a tremendous fervor of missionary activity. During this time Stanley went to Africa in search of Dr. Livingston and became himself a power for God, Finney began preaching, and Whitehead and the great preachers of the past that did such marvelous things. That peaceful era was needed to root the remnant church deeply in gospel soil so it could withstand the fires of Satan's final deceptions. God is in control of *all.*

> *Since Adam, God has been unfolding His character through patriarchs, prophets, and saints down through the generations. Now in our time the data are complete, the verdict is in, God is innocent, and we are commissioned to publish that truth. All that God has claimed to be respecting Himself from time immemorial has always been true and will be everlastingly true! That's the everlasting gospel.*

What is it that distinguishes the *everlasting gospel* message from other gospel messages? Lest we be taken to task for suggesting that there are multiple gospel messages, consider the good news to the shepherds on the hills of Judea that Christ was born. Haven't there been messages of other good news respecting Christ's work that have applied specifically to times past? And why is John the Revelator instructed to use the adjective *everlasting* gospel if there was only one gospel message? From the inception of iniquity in the heart of Lucifer to the lake of fire, post millennium, God will be misrepresented and accused before the universe, and yet He claims to be unchanging, the same yesterday, today, and forever (Heb. 13:8). Since Adam, God has been unfolding His character through patriarchs, prophets, and saints down through the generations. Now in our time the data are complete, the verdict is in, *God is innocent*, and we are commissioned to publish that truth. All that God has claimed to be respecting Himself from time immemorial has *always been true* and *will be everlastingly true!* That's the everlasting gospel. The lies of Satan are annulled. Whatever he has lodged against God since before the world was created has been shown false. It has been delivered to us, and it is our responsibility to proclaim this. It will be proclaimed to those on earth, but those throughout the universe will hear it as well. They are interested in what is happening here.

The world will be called to consider its own disrespect of God. What is the disrespect of the world? (1) We have no fear of God who has said, *fear God*—the first angel's message. And it is the first message because there is no possible transaction until we can fear God. (2) We do not recognize His glory (His authority in our lives). To *fear God* is to shed the mantle of a fool. Fools rush in where angels fear to tread. The awesome presence of divinity inspires overwhelming respect, sanctified uncertainty. Recall Manoah and his wife when they were told to expect Samson (Judges 13). Their experience was very unsettling because of the divine manifestation that brought the message. Other encounters with God or His messengers were similarly frightening—Isaiah, Daniel, Ezekiel, John, and Paul, all encountered the divine. No matter how impeccable their lives, there was always the fearful response. The reason that is so is because of the vast distance between the Creator and the creature. There is no way to bridge that gap; it will always exist. When we as creatures encounter the presence of God, we will have a fearful reaction, and God will always say to us, *fear not*. His love for us is perfect, and perfect love casts out all fear (1 John 4:18). And the closer we come to Him, the less power fear has over us because we feel God's continual presence, His strength, His comfort, and His guidance. "There will be no more curse," He promises. "You will see My face—My name will be written on your forehead" (Rev. 22:3-4, paraphrase).

It is an *everlasting* feature of creature life. There's nothing that God or creature need do about it. The fear that dominates *our* lives now is of the perverted kind: dread, trepidation, alarm. But that is not to be part of our relationship with God. We, however, do have a nonchalant, casual view of deity that we must address. We are comfortable slouching into His presence chewing our gum, snapping our fingers, and laughing loudly in His sanctuary. Have I overstated that? Remember, we are addressing more than Seventh-day Adventism when talking about God's church. Included in our discussion are all the various institutions that claim the name Christian, and necessarily so, because the over-bounding number of the righteous living in the last days are yet among them, and it will be our responsibility to lead them out. We are even now being prepared for that.

Since the context of this message is literal, the time figures should be understood literally. The metaphoric hour, the time, of His judgment has arrived, and the world is being called back to *worship* of the Creator. We will discover that this is the crux of all three messages. The *worship* in question is the antithesis of selfishness that is at the core of our sinful being. We are called to shift our values from self to God. Why? Because we are in a dire strait, and our attention should be on the One who saves. The One who saves presents His credentials here: He that made heaven, and earth, and the sea, and the fountains of waters.

If you are in a crevasse or in a swelling tide and are helpless to help yourself, completely dependent on someone above to throw you a rope or other rescue device, wouldn't you be well advised to keep your eye upon him? But if you are examining your fingernails or the set of your hair you might miss the rope. And we are in a worse state than someone in that circumstance. We must keep our eyes on Christ.

"And there followed another angel, saying, Babylon is fallen, *is fallen*, that great city, because she made all nations drink of the wine of the wrath of her fornication" (Rev. 14:8, emphasis mine).

> *Why is God repeating here? Every word scriptural has its place. Ancient language was bereft of periods and accent marks, so for emphasis it relied on repetition.*

Why is God repeating here? Every word scriptural has its place. Ancient language was bereft of periods and accent marks, so for emphasis it relied on repetition.

Babylon, that institution fully defined and revealed, God's *church* in the earth, is declared to be *fallen*. Fallen from a state of grace. That's what makes her Babylon. The pioneers identified that fall to have taken place in 1844 when the leading churches of the day turned their backs on the *second angel's message*. There is to be yet *another fall*—the reason for the repetition. Remember the prophecy, "*I will overturn, overturn, overturn*" (Ezek. 21:27, emphasis mine)? There were then three entities to which God's diadem would yet pass. God said, "I will pass the diadem to them, to them, and to them." And now in Revelation

Revelation 14 and 15: The Three Angels' Messages and Two Consequences

14:8 the church will fall once, have a second chance, and then it will fall again. There will be no more chance after that. When the leading churches of our day clasp hands with Catholicism and, in union with federal power, make a law enforcing false worship, then the fall will be complete.

> The Bible declares ... they that "received not the love of the truth, that they might be saved," will be left to receive "strong delusion, that they should believe a lie." 2 Thessalonians 2:9–11. *Not until this condition shall be reached, and the union of the church with the world shall be fully accomplished throughout Christendom, will the fall of Babylon be complete.* The change is a progressive one, and the perfect fulfillment of Revelation 14:8 is yet future.[199]

What constitutes Babylon's fall is *drinking the wine of wrath that comes from fornication* and causing others to do likewise. The focus here is the part of Babylon that is Protestant but does not exclude the part that is of the papal institution. "Wrath" is separation from God, distance from God's presence and providence. When Christ was on the cross, God separated His beams of light, love, and mercy from Him, and it so devastated Christ that He cried out, "Why have you done this?" He was dying the death of the wicked. He was separated from God. He felt a distance that broke His heart. Thus, the wrath of God is not to be considered after the manner of man's wrath. When a man becomes wrathful, everyone in the house knows it. When God becomes wrathful, there is a ringing in the ears because of the profound silence. We might clarify here who has moved by a parable.

An old married couple was driving in a car with the wife positioned tightly against the right-hand door, the husband firmly behind the steering wheel. After traveling in silence for some time the wife looked at her husband and said, "Horace, what has happened to us? When we were young, we sat so close together." Horace was silent for a moment and then replied, "I ain't moved!"

When we consider the distance between us and God, the question should be, which of us has moved? What is said to cause this devastating distance between God and us? *Wine* that is connected to *fornication*. Wine is doctrine, false doctrine that alienates from God. *Rain* is

---

[199] Ellen G. White, *The Faith I Live By* (Washington, DC: Review and Herald, 1958), p. 285, emphasis mine.

true doctrine (Deut. 32:2). *Fornication* is profiting from false doctrine, becoming rich at God's expense.

"And the third angel followed them saying with a loud voice, If any man *worship* the beast and his image, and receive his mark in his forehead, or in his hand, the same shall drink of the *wine of the wrath of God* [there will be *two* servings],[200] which is poured out without mixture into the cup of his indignation" (Rev. 14:9–10, emphasis mine).

I went out to the garage one morning and mixed up some chemicals to put on weeds that plague my yard. I read the label that instructed me to use three-quarters of an ounce in two-and-a-half gallons of water. So my concoction is *mixed,* isn't it? It's that little bit of poison mixed with quite a bit of fairly healthy water. For 6,000 years we have experienced that kind of wrath from God. God has very carefully measured His wrath to us, the distance between us, calculated to make us lonely enough to cry out to Him. But here is a time described where there is no mixture. It is total, utter, eternal distance from God for which there is no amelioration. The rejecters of God's mercy are left fully exposed to Satan's malignant wrath.

First came the proclamation of the *everlasting gospel* (verse 6), followed by a universal summons to *fear God* and glorify Him as Creator and Judge. The final verdict on Babylon is announced in the third angel's message. It contains the most dreadful warning ever sent from heaven to mortal beings, the warning concerning the wrath of God in the seven last plagues.

Babylon's apostasy has gone beyond remedy—she is condemned to drink the wine of God's wrath. This warning message specifically alerts all true believers to the inexorable consequences of drinking the wine of Babylon. Doesn't that behoove us to re-examine our doctrine? Spirit of Prophecy tells us that truth can bear close scrutiny, and it does no harm for us to re-examine the truths that we hold. "No line of truth that has made the Seventh-day Adventist people what they are is to be weakened. We have the old landmarks of truth, experience, and duty, and we are to stand firmly in defense of our principles, in full view of the world."[201] Why are we admonished to examine often the *landmark* truths? Let me illustrate the point.

---

[200] The wine of God's wrath is manifest when He abandons a sinner to his own false beliefs as He did with Israel: "Ephraim is joined to his idols; let him alone" (Hosea 4:17).

[201] Ellen G. White, *Testimonies for the Church*, vol. 6 (Mountain View, CA: Pacific Press, 1901), p. 17.

When I was seven or eight years of age my parents converted to Seventh-day Adventism. I went to Sabbath school and learned the memory verses. I could recite them for the entire year. As a child I did this more than once. I attended the fifth and sixth grades in church schools, and then attended academy for two years. After that time, I went another way and left the company of church for fifteen years. At the age of thirty I had a confrontation with God of a thoroughly fearful nature. Being not completely stupid, I returned to my father's God. I was enthusiastic in my new church experience and would sit among the good people of the Central Acres Church and enter into the discussions with them. I remembered the doctrine learned as a child at my mother's knee. In expressing my recollection of that far-off learning, the church people were very gentle with me. They would say to me, "No, brother, that's not the way it is. It's like this." In those fifteen years that I had been gone, much of my doctrine had turned 180 degrees. And to this day I have no idea how it happened. But it did! We must re-examine our doctrine, especially in these times, because we might be in difficulty—and completely unaware of the fact.

Whoever drinks of the wine of Babylon *will drink of the wine of God's fury*, which has been poured full strength into the cup of His wrath. The *wine of God's fury* is the doctrine of justice: "[T]he soul that sinneth, *it shall die* (Ezek. 18:4, emphasis mine). What is the other side of justice? It is mercy, is it not? We have been drinking of God's mercy all these years. Mercy has run out, and now it's time for justice to reveal itself. The *cup of His wrath* is eternal separation from God, without hope of resurrection. It symbolizes the way God has acted, and will act, against sin and impenitent sinners. Wrath, *unmixed with mercy*, expresses God's *total absence*. The saint's confession that they have been making all this time is also mixed with the incense of Christ's propitiation before the mercy seat of God's throne.

Have you ever wondered why the word "propitiation" is used in Scripture? It is borrowed from paganism. God does this. He delights in the unexpected, and it's a jarring thing for Him to use this word because to *propitiate* is to bring an *appeasing* sacrifice to an angry god, most likely your firstborn son. When you approach an angry god with a sacrifice intended to make him tractable to you, that is a *propitiation*. God said, *I* will provide a propitiation for this situation. *And the propitiation was Himself to Himself.* He brought Himself to Himself a living sacrifice, and *He* died. Now, isn't that ironic!

There is no mercy for unrepentant sinners. What doctrines obviate the message of the third angel? (1) Once saved, always saved. (2) Rapture, and its second chance. (3) God's unmitigated mercy—everyone will be saved. (4) Purgatory—works intervention.

> [A]nd he [those who hold erroneous notions respecting God] shall be tormented with fire and brimstone in the presence of the holy angels, and in the presence of the Lamb: and the smoke of their torment ascendeth up for ever and ever [is that as long as they are burning, or is it literally forever?]: and they have no *rest* day nor night, who *worship* the beast and his image, and whosoever receiveth the mark of his name. (Rev. 14:10–11, emphasis mine)

To digress a moment, the word "rest" in this context has nothing to do with fatigue and repose. It is the same rest that is bound up in the Sabbath rest. As we saw in earlier chapters, it has to do with the tension of perplexity when discovery escapes you, when the resolution of a dilemma persistently evades, especially respecting God. That's what the Sabbath is about—*understanding the nature of God*. He gave us the Sabbath, of which He said, "I will come on the seventh day and resolve all of the issues you might have respecting Me. I want you to labor six days on this topic. And if you labor six days, struggling to understand Me, you will arrive at the seventh day with a number of questions. Those are the questions that I will address, and *I will give you rest*. I will relieve your tension."

The individuals in Revelation 14:11 will have no rest from their tension. Remember, it is said that they will go from coast to coast, seeking some word of mercy, and they will not find it. Throughout eternity that question will for them remain unresolved. Their eternal sleep will have no end.

This passage moves past the millennium to the *lake of fire*, the time when *every* knee shall bow and *every* tongue confess, *"Just and mighty are Thy ways, O God"* (Rev. 15:3, paraphrase). This they will do in the presence of holy angels and the Lamb. How, though, does the *smoke of their torment ascend up forever and ever*? Smoke is symbolism for *communication*—it always is in Scripture. When the priest took the censer and swung it before the veil, the smoke of incense would rise up and go over the top into the Most Holy Place, symbolizing the prayers of mercy on behalf of the penitent. There were billows of smoke surrounding Mount Sinai, and there will be smoke at the second coming of Christ.

What is the torment of the wicked? Separation! Eternal separation. *Loss of life!* No hope of resurrection! The message here is inherent in the telling and retelling of the salvation story throughout eternity. When our loved ones die today, we are not terribly distressed because we know that the separation is temporary. I attended a funeral one time where the pastor opened his remarks by leaning over the podium and, pointing to the casket, said, *"This body shall rise again!"* He made no judgmental remarks, good or ill. He simply assured us that this body would rise again. Was he right? Absolutely! There was a sort of comfort in the notion that the one celebrated that day was but temporarily asleep. But when the wicked die in the lake of fire, can the preacher say that? Those dead *will not rise again!* What will be the theme of the saved throughout eternity? What will be their testimony? The story of divine rescue! God's unutterable intervention! Alive forevermore! For how long will the saved bear this testimony? Forever and ever! Testimony is symbolized by smoke, isn't it? Is not this the smoke that will ascend forever and ever? The testimony of the salvation of God, and how death is forever cast into the lake of fire.

> *What will be the theme of the saved throughout eternity? What will be their testimony? The story of divine rescue! God's unutterable intervention! Alive forevermore! For how long will the saved bear this testimony? Forever and ever!*

"Here is the patience of the saints: here are they that keep the commandments of God, and the faith of Jesus" (Rev. 14:12).

This is a prescription for patient endurance, steadfast loyalty, unshaken love, a description of those who so aligned themselves with God as to achieve full compliance with His holy life—and this by *promise!* Just as a doctor prescribes a specific medicine for a specific condition, this is God's prescription for achieving full compliance with His holy life. These twelve verses conclude a discussion of a special people and their mission. The next eight verses describe the fate of those who defy the last message of mercy to this sinful world. Revelation 15 is a summary of these two groups. Verse 1 introduces the seven angels and the seven vials, and chapter 16 presents them in their order. We have moved to the space between two accounts of divine retribution—Revelation 8 and 9, the trumpets, and Revelation 16, the vials. Two sides of the same coin.

These chapters relate the same events. They describe God's culminating effort in fairness to the last generation, and its response to His final appeal. God must not only act in fairness, He must also be *perceived* as One acting in fairness. My mother advised me often: it is not enough to be right—you must also *appear* to be right.

Leviticus 16 presents a prototype of these judgments. There, the Lord warned Israel of the consequences of idolatry, which she was yet to commit, and of willful rejection of His law, notwithstanding repeated calls for repentance. The King James Version refers to a *sevenfold punishment* and a virtual declaration of divine war against the covenant people. The Septuagint version of the Old Testament translates Leviticus 26:21 like this:

"And if after this you should walk perversely, and not be willing to obey me, I will further bring upon you *seven plagues* according to your sins" (Lev. 26:21).[202]

The understanding of this thematic unfolding in Revelation 14 through 16 caused the founding fathers of Adventism to include the seven last plagues as *an integral part of the third angel's message.* And the angel's reference to *restless torment* with *burning sulfur in the presence of the holy angels and of the Lamb* (Rev. 14:10) led James White to the conclusion that *more than death* is involved here. A remarkable truth! There *is* more than death involved here. He saw in this judgment the *terrors* of the second death at the end of the 1,000 years of Revelation 20. Only at the end of the millennium, when the hosts of Gog and Magog (the *root* and *branch* of evil) gather around the camp of God's people, will fire come down from heaven to devour the wicked (Rev. 20:9).

"And I heard a voice from heaven saying unto me, Write, Blessed are the dead which die *in the Lord* from henceforth: Yea, saith the Spirit, that they may rest from their labours; *and their works do follow them"* (Rev. 14:13, emphasis mine).

---

202 Albert Pietersma and Benjamin G. Wright, III, *A New English Translation of the Septuagint* (New York, NY: Oxford University Press, 2007).

Revelation 14 and 15: The Three Angels' Messages and Two Consequences 177

The scene changes. John is back on the Isle of Patmos but still oriented within the context of the judgment. He is told to preserve a beatitude for those who will die during the judgment. The judgment may be longer than an age. It has been longer than 175 years. There may also be those who will yet forfeit their lives. He assures them that *their* works, their good deeds, will bear fruit.

Verses 14 to 20 turn to the fate of the wicked. Here is the *second* harvest, the harvest of the tares, of the grapes. Harvest *one* is of wheat. Harvest *two* is of grapes. Wheat is righteous. Grapes are wicked. The language in these verses is very graphic, painting a horrifying picture of loss and despair. This is the first consequence.

The second consequence is found in chapter 15. While seven angels prepare for the first consequence, John is shown, as it were, a sea of glass mingled with fire.

"[A]nd them that had gotten the victory over the beast, and over his image, and over his mark, and over the number of his name, stand on the sea of glass, having the harps of God" (Rev. 15:2).

They sing the same song that Moses and the Lamb were able to sing. Then they ask a rhetorical question: "Who shall not *fear* thee, O Lord" (Rev. 15:4)? There are no more fools. All creation gladly *glorifies* His name, recognizes God's authority. God alone is holy, and all nations now *worship* before Him because "[T]hy judgments are made *manifest*" (Rev. 15:4, emphasis mine). The righteous say, "We're so glad, God! Your judgments are made manifest!" That is, we *saw* them! Remember how the wicked appear before God and have a confession experience? It's a terrible thing, but the righteous *see* within it God's justice. To be manifest is to be visible, plain, revealed, obvious (verse 4). Now the scene changes again: the seven angels emerge from the temple. They are dressed and equipped for their grisly task. What task is that? The seven last plagues. The temple is filled with smoke (divine statements are being made), and is placed *off limits* to man until the seven plagues are fulfilled. What does that mean? The saints are not yet glorified, the sea of glass is still future. Probation has closed. Christ has put off His priestly robes and donned garments of victory. His temple work is done. He has left the sanctuary (temple). There is now no intercessor; man will not have access to the temple until the plagues are finished.

"While Jesus had been standing between God and guilty man, a restraint was upon the people; but when He stepped out from between man and the Father, the restraint was removed and Satan had entire control of the finally impenitent."[203]

"And the temple was filled with smoke [communication] from the glory [authority] of God, and from his power; and no man was able to enter into the temple, till the seven plagues of the seven angels were fulfilled" (Rev. 15:8).

All eyes in the universe are now focused earthward. There is no more heavenly business to do until the saints are brought home.

---

203 Ellen G. White, *Early Writings* (Washington, DC: Review and Herald, 1882), p. 280.

Chapter 11

Revelation 18 and 19: The End—Last Call, Last Reward, Last Battle

Chapter 18 of Revelation is yet *future*. Beginning with verse 1, John introduces a new scene or vision.

"And after these things [that's our cue to John's new scene] I saw another angel [the fourth angel] come down from heaven, having great power; and the earth was lightened with his *glory* [authority]" (Rev. 18:1, emphasis mine).

The first three verses of Revelation 18 give the last *end-of-time* message, just before probation closes. The rest of the chapter explains the state of the earth that has prompted God's destroying wrath, because Revelation 19 is the battle of Armageddon, which is the expression of God's destroying wrath.

"And he *cried mightily* with a *strong voice*, saying, Babylon the great *is fallen, is fallen,* and is become the habitation of devils, and the hold of every foul spirit, and a cage of every unclean and hateful bird" (Rev. 18:2, emphasis mine).

The second angel's message is here repeated. The first "is fallen" applies to 1844, when the Protestant churches disfellowshipped the Millerites and refused the three angels' messages. The second "is fallen" now occurs and is the final one. Babylon is fallen and:

    1. Has become the habitation of:

        —Devils.

        —Foul spirits.

        —Unclean and hateful birds.

2. Has caused all nations to:

    —Drink of her wine.

    —Commit fornication with her.

    —Wax rich at God's expense.

"For all nations have drunk of the wine of the wrath of her fornication, and the kings of the earth have committed fornication with her, and the merchants of the earth are waxed rich through the abundance of her delicacies" (Rev. 18:3).

Wrath in this sense is a distancing, a separation from things spiritual, brought about by false teaching (fornication). The institution of the papacy is one of the most powerful on earth with a broad base of influence—political, financial, and commercial, as well as social. A visit to the Vatican, especially to St. Peter's Basilica, boggles the imagination by its opulent wealth and size. Gold, art, artifact, stone, space, antiquities are unparalleled. The papacy is engaged in the business of the world. When President Reagan engineered the collapse of the Russian Empire, he worked through the papacy. Of the two involved in that particular enterprise, the primary player was undoubtedly Pope John Paul II. Influence peddling is the widest gate for wealth, and no one is better positioned than the pope for such activity. The one who can pull strings controls finance, and this is the business of the Vatican.

Yet within Babylon are many of God's people (verse 4). God calls for their *immediate* separation, just as Lot's family was called from Sodom. Remember how urgent the angels were with respect to Lot and his family. Lot pleaded, "I must go warn my children!" The angels were reluctant to allow him that. They knew something he didn't know, and they told him, "The breaking of the day is coming on, so you'd better hurry!" Lot went out, but his sons-in-law and his daughters ridiculed him. Coming back empty-handed, such was the urgency that it was necessary for the angels to physically take Lot, his wife, and his two unmarried daughters by their arms, ushering them out of the doomed city. In earth's final harvest there will be the same urgency. God has remembered her iniquities (verse 5). That is, the time has come for divine action. How is this to be done? By what instrumentality will God bring about the final separation of wheat and tares?

Earth's last harvest takes place *during* the time of the loud cry (Rev. 18:1–4). Indeed, it is the loud cry that effects earth's last harvest.

Revelation 18 and 19: The End—Last Call, Last Reward, Last Battle

Recall the vision shown to John wherein the 144,000 are sealed *before the four winds are released* (Rev. 7:1–4), before the time of trouble such as never was since there was a nation.

"Just *before* we entered it [the time of trouble] we *all* received the seal of the living God. Then I saw the four angels cease to hold the four winds."[204]

The loosening of the four winds declares the introduction of the seven last plagues. Ever since AD 1905 the four winds have been held in abeyance. Now they are loosed, bringing on catastrophe, plague, disruption, and confusion.

The 144,000 are sealed *before* the time of trouble, but as we continue our study, we will find *another group of saints* who are sealed *during* the time of trouble! However, let's find out what happens to the 144,000 after they are sealed, at the *commencement* of the time of trouble.[205]

"The commencement of *that* time of trouble, here mentioned, *does not refer to the time* when the plagues shall begin to be poured out, but to a *short period just before they are poured out,* while Christ is in the sanctuary …. At that time, the *'latter rain,'* or refreshing from the presence of the Lord, will come, to give *power* to the loud voice of the third angel."[206]

"And I heard another voice from heaven, saying, Come out of her, *my people,* that ye be not partakers of her sins, and that ye receive not of her plagues" (Rev. 18:4, emphasis mine).

Who are *my* people in reference here? Are they Seventh-day Adventists? No, they are not. They are faithful Sunday keepers, or Friday keepers, or Wednesday keepers. They are other persons of other persuasions who are very precious to God. He calls them *My people* because they are honest in heart. His invitation is for them to come out before the sulfur falls on Sodom and Gomorrah. Verse 4 is likened to the 1844 movement, and to the Day of Pentecost: "[The] message will close with power and strength *far exceeding* the midnight cry."[207] The book, **Last Day Events,** speaks to this future time:

---

[204] Ellen G. White, *SDA Bible Commentary*, vol. 7 (Washington, DC: Review and Herald, 1957), p. 968, emphasis mine.
[205] See Appendix 3, p. 222, "Ezekiel 9: Countdown to Harvest—The Sealing of the 144,000," for an in-depth discussion of the topic.
[206] Ellen G. White, *Early Writings* (Washington, DC: Review and Herald, 1882), pp. 85, 86, emphasis mine.
[207] Ibid., p. 278, emphasis mine.

The sick were healed, [speaking of this time] and other miracles were wrought .... Servants of God [you and I], with their faces lighted up and shining with holy consecration, will hasten from place to place .... The Lord will work ... in a manner very much out of the common order of things .... The Comforter is to reveal Himself, not in any specified, precise way ... but in the order of God .... In the last solemn work *few* great men will be engaged .... The laborers will be qualified rather by the unction of His Spirit than by the training of literary institutions .... Children are impelled by the Spirit to go forth and declare the message from heaven .... [A]ngels of heaven are moving upon human minds to arouse investigation in the themes of the Bible .... Angels will do a work which men might have had the blessing of accomplishing had they not neglected to answer the claims of God.[208]

These statements validate our current attention to these things.

Many [of us] will have to stand in the legislative courts; some [of us] will have to stand before kings and before the learned of the earth, to answer for their faith. Those who have only *a superficial understanding of truth* will not be able clearly to expound the Scriptures, and give definite reasons for their faith .... Let no one imagine that he has no need to study, because he is not to preach in the sacred desk. You know not what God may require of you.[209]

When we are admonished to take no thought of what we shall say (Matt. 10:19). It is not an admonition excusing us from study because when we stand in a circumstance where it is necessary for us to say something, the Holy Spirit will bring to mind that which is already there, and present it in a timely fashion. But if there is nothing there, the Holy Spirit will allow us to be embarrassed. We must inculcate truth in all its various facets. It isn't necessary for us to *organize* it. That's what the Holy Spirit is saying here.

---

208 Ellen G. White, *Last Day Events* (Boise, ID: Pacific Press, 1992), pp. 202–207.
209 Ellen G. White, *Fundamentals of Christian Education* (Nashville, TN: Southern Publishing Association, 1923), p. 217, emphasis mine.

Revelation 18 and 19: The End—Last Call, Last Reward, Last Battle

"When the storm of persecution really breaks upon us, ... then will the message of the third angel swell to a loud cry, and the whole earth will be lightened with the glory of the Lord."[210]

The message of the *third angel* is to be compared to a cry when fire is engulfing a house, or a tidal wave is crashing upon a beach. Those endangered must be warned of the impending disaster in no uncertain terms. "The crisis is right upon us!" Verses 5 and 6 of Revelation 18 proclaim the *reason* to vacate Babylon:

"For her sins have reached unto heaven, and God hath remembered her iniquities. Reward her even as she rewarded you, and double unto her double according to her works: in the cup which she hath filled fill to her double" (Rev. 18:5–6).

When God "remembers" something, it is an indication that He will take imminent action. When will God take the action threatened in this passage?

Another interesting question: at what time will her *sins have reached unto heaven?* Answer: "When the law of God is *finally* made void by legislation."[211]

A third interesting question: and when is the law of God *finally* made void? The answer:

"When our nation, in its legislative councils, shall enact laws to bind the consciences of men in regard to their religious privileges, enforcing Sunday observance, and bringing oppressive power to bear against those who keep the seventh-day Sabbath, *the law of God will, to all intents and purposes, be made void in our land,* and national apostasy will be followed by national ruin."[212]

Of further interest is a series of verses that appear in this chapter of Revelation respecting God's action against the self-styled "Queen" (verses 8, 10, 17, and 19). Let's take them one at a time for the sense of each:

"Therefore shall *her plagues come in one day,* death, and mourning, and famine; and she shall be *utterly burned* with fire" (Rev. 18:8, emphasis mine).

A literal understanding of the thought here expressed implies that the seven last plagues will do their destructive work in one *prophetic* day's time—one year.

---

210 Ellen G. White, *Last Day Events* (Boise, ID: Pacific Press, 1992), p. 208.
211 Ibid., p. 198, emphasis mine.
212 Ibid., p. 134, emphasis mine.

"[The kings of the earth] [s]tanding afar off for the fear of her torment, saying, Alas, alas that great city Babylon, that mighty city! *for in one hour is thy judgment come*" (Rev. 18:10, emphasis mine).

"*For in one hour* so great riches is come to nought. And every shipmaster, and all the company in ships, and sailors, and as many as trade by sea, stood afar off ... when they saw the smoke of her burning" (Rev. 18:17–18).

"And they ... cried, weeping and wailing, saying, Alas, alas that great city, wherein were made rich all that had ships in the sea by reason of her costliness! *for in one hour is she made desolate*" (Rev. 18:19, emphasis mine).

Verse 8 states that *in one day* shall her plagues come. The other three texts state that *in one hour* the following shall take place:

1. Thy judgment is come [reached].
2. So great riches are come to naught.
3. She is made desolate.

Throughout the first six plagues she has apparently prospered as never before in her history, insofar as international support is concerned. This is the time when Satan is building his unanimity, and he prospers those who are the objects of his attention.

Verse 7 expresses her perception this way:

"How much she hath glorified herself, and lived deliciously, so much torment and sorrow give her: for she saith in her heart, *I sit a queen, and am no widow, and shall see no sorrow*" (Rev. 18:7, emphasis mine).

She has been so adored and glorified that arrogant self-confidence has made her certain of success in obliterating God's remnant people and to reign supreme over the earth.[213] She is saying in her heart, "I sit a queen," at the time the angel of verse 4 delivers his message of warning, *as well as* later during the sixth plague. As a widow she would have no legal status or claim upon the allegiance of the people of earth (Isa. 47:8, 10).

We turn now to chapter 19, where heaven anticipates something with great joy: the game is essentially over, the numbers on the scoreboard are so advanced that there is no possibility of loss.[214] All that

---

213 Ellen G. White, *SDA Bible Commentary*, vol. 7 (Washington, DC: Review and Herald, 1957), p. 862.
214 See Appendix 2, p. 212, "Daniel 2: The Mystery Stone of Daniel 2."

Revelation 18 and 19: The End—Last Call, Last Reward, Last Battle

is left is to run out the clock. In verse 9 John is commanded to write another beatitude—his sixth:

"Blessed are they which are called unto the marriage supper of the Lamb .... These are the true sayings of God" (Rev. 19:9).

In verse 11 John is presented another scene: "[H]eaven [is] *opened,* and behold a white horse; and he that sat upon him was called *Faithful and True,* and in righteousness he doth *judge and make war*" (Rev. 19:11, emphasis mine). Verse 12 gives a description of His majesty and His crown: it was a crown of many crowns. The last time we saw this Person mounted on a white horse He wore one crown (Rev. 6:2)—the beginning of the judgment, the opening of the first seal. Now judgment is over, and it's time to bring the redeemed ones home. We are through the first of two fifteen-day periods. The battle of Armageddon is about to be joined, the over-confident queen and her beast on the one hand, and the King of kings and His army on the other:

"And I saw the beast, and the kings of the earth, and their armies, gathered together to make war against him that sat on the horse, and against his army" (Rev. 19:19).

Do you want to know the outcome of this epic battle? Read Revelation 19:20–21:

> And the beast was taken, and with him the false prophet that wrought miracles before him, with which he deceived them that had received the mark of the beast, and them that worshipped his image. These both were cast alive into a lake of fire burning with brimstone. And the remnant were slain with the sword of him that sat upon the horse, which sword proceeded out of his mouth: and all the fowls were filled with their flesh. (Rev. 19:20–21)

The beast is the papacy, now become itself a remnant; and the false prophet is apostate Protestantism. The miracles performed by the false prophet and done before the beast are yet to be discovered. However, the *mark* is well defined. Let me share a paragraph or two from the book, *Last Day Events,* that graphically illustrate the moment of divine intervention:

> Satan's host and wicked men will surround them and exult over them because there will seem to be no way of escape for them [reminiscent of Israel at the Red Sea]. But in the midst

of their revelry and triumph there is heard *peal upon peal of the loudest thunder.* The heavens have gathered blackness, and are only illuminated by the blazing light and terrible glory from heaven, as God *utters His voice* from His holy habitation.[215]

Let me quote further from the same book. We recognize the time as being the last fifteen-day period of earth's history, the seventh plague that brings total destruction to the earth, the special resurrection promised to those who gave special service, and final liberation to the saints of God. Now is come a "great earthquake, such as was not since men were upon the earth, so mighty an earthquake, and so great" (Rev. 16:18).

> When the protection of human laws shall be withdrawn from those who honor the law of God, there will be, in different lands, a simultaneous movement for their destruction. As the time appointed in the decree [universal death decree] draws near, the people will conspire to root out the hated sect. It will be determined to strike in one night a decisive blow, which shall utterly silence the voice of dissent and reproof [reminiscent of Mordecai and Hamen]. The people of God—some in prison cells, some hidden in solitary retreats in the forests and the mountains—still plead for divine protection, while in every quarter companies of armed men, urged on by hosts of evil angels, are preparing for the work of death .... [Satan's goal is to exterminate every righteous soul on earth. And if he can do that, then God has no reason to return. That's his insane thought process.] With shouts of triumph, jeering, and imprecation, throngs of evil men are about to rush upon their prey when, lo, a dense blackness, deeper than the darkness of the night, falls upon the earth.[216]

Is that a plague? Of course, it is! We are deep into the seven last plagues, and this is the plague of darkness.

"It is at midnight that God manifests His power for the deliverance of His people .... In the midst of the angry heavens is one clear space of indescribable glory, whence comes the voice of God like the

---

[215] Ellen G. White, *Last Day Events* (Boise, ID: Pacific Press, 1992), p. 269.
[216] Ibid., pp. 269–270.

Revelation 18 and 19: The End—Last Call, Last Reward, Last Battle

sound of many waters, saying, "It is done" (Revelation 16:17). That voice shakes the heavens and the earth."[217]

The seventh plague and the special resurrection are introduced here. Have you ever wondered when the special resurrection would occur?

> The firmament appears to open and shut. The glory from the throne of God seems flashing through. The mountains shake like a reed in the wind, and ragged rocks are scattered on every side .... The whole earth heaves and swells like the waves of the sea. Its surface is breaking up. Its very foundations seem to be giving way. Mountain chains are sinking. Inhabited islands disappear. The seaports that have become like Sodom for wickedness are swallowed up by the angry waters .... Great hailstones, every one "about the weight of a talent," are doing their work of destruction [Rev. 16:17–19]. [At that time] [g]raves are opened, and "many of them that sleep in the dust of the earth ... awake, some to everlasting life, and some to shame and everlasting contempt" (Daniel 12:2). All who have died in the faith of the third angel's message come forth from the tomb *glorified* [marked with divine authority] to hear God's covenant of peace with those who have kept His law. "They also which pierced Him" (Revelation 1:7), those that mocked and derided Christ's dying agonies, and the most violent opposers of His truth and His people, are raised to behold Him in His glory, and to see the honor placed upon the loyal and obedient.[218]

These are the final scenes in rapid succession:

1. Dark heavy clouds come up.
2. The atmosphere is parted and rolled back.
3. We look up through the open space in Orion, whence came the voice of God.
4. We hear the voice of God give us the day and hour of Jesus' coming.

---

217 Ibid., p. 270.
218 Ibid., pp. 271–272, emphasis mine.

5. The living saints understand the voice, but the wicked think it is thunder and an earthquake. "He [God] spoke one sentence, and then paused, while the words were rolling through the earth .... At the end of every sentence the saints shouted, 'Glory! Hallelujah!'"
6. "The wicked are filled with regret ... because God has conquered. They lament that the result is what it is, but they do not repent of their wickedness."
7. "There appears in the east a small black cloud, about half the size of a man's hand."
8. "Jesus rides forth as a mighty conqueror .... [H]oly angels ... attend Him on His way."
9. "The King of kings descends upon the cloud, wrapped in flaming fire."
10. "The sound of music is heard ... [and] the graves are opened and the dead are raised."
11. "The child of God will be terror-stricken at the first sight of the majesty of Jesus Christ .... But the word comes ... 'Fear not!'"
12. The saints are changed in a moment, in the twinkling of an eye.
13. "[T]he wicked are blotted from the face of the whole earth—consumed with the spirit of His mouth and destroyed by the brightness of His glory."[219] (They are *not* changed in a moment, in the twinkling of an eye, therefore they are consumed.)[220]

Just as darkness cannot exist in the presence of light, sin cannot exist in the presence of God (see 1 John 1:5–9).

[It is an act of mercy.] [T]hey have never learned the language of heaven .... [P]urity, holiness, and peace would be torture to them; the glory of God would be a consuming fire. They would long to flee from that holy place .... The living righteous are .... made immortal, and with the risen saints are caught up to meet their Lord in the air. Angels "gather together His elect

---
219 Ibid., pp. 272, 274, 276–278.
220 See Chart 8, p. 120, "Prophetic Scene Sequence."

from the four winds, from one end of heaven to the other." Little children are borne by holy angels to their mothers' arms. Friends long separated by death are united, nevermore to part, and with songs of gladness ascend together to the city of God.[221]

The great controversy is ended. Sin and sinners are no more. The entire universe is clean. One pulse of harmony and gladness beats through the vast creation. From Him who created all, flow life and light and gladness, throughout the realms of illimitable space. From the minutest atom to the greatest world, all things, animate and inanimate, in their unshadowed beauty and perfect joy, declare that God is love.[222]

With arms spread wide in love, Jesus welcomes His children home, and in a voice that reverberates throughout the universe He declares:

"These are they which came out of great tribulation, and have washed their robes, and made them white in the blood of the Lamb. Therefore are they before the throne of God, and serve him day and night in his temple…

They shall hunger no more, nor thirst anymore;

   the sun shall not strike them, nor any heat;

      For the Lamb who is in the midst of the throne will shepherd them

      And lead them to living fountains of waters.

   And God will wipe away every tear from their eyes"….

"They shall see His face, and His name shall be on their foreheads.…

   "And they shall reign forever and ever.…

      Even so, come, Lord Jesus! Amen!"

         —Rev. 7:14-17; 22:4-5, 20, NKJV

---

[221] Ibid., pp. 279–280.
[222] Ellen G. White, *The Great Controversy* (Mountain View, CA: Pacific Press, 1911), p. 678.

Appendix 1
Daniel 1–12: The Book of Daniel

Introduction

The probable date for the completion of Daniel's book is circa 530 BC, shortly after the capture of Babylon by Cyrus in 539. (Daniel chapter 10 records a vision received in 536 BC.)[223] Although higher critics debate its validity, the text of Daniel mentions him as the author several times. Jesus Himself affirmed Daniel's writings in Matthew 24:15.

Nabopolassar, the father of Nebuchadnezzar, was a trusted general in the service of the Assyrian king in 625 BC when he was called upon to suppress a revolt against Assyria, coordinated by the vassal states of Media, Babylon, and Egypt. His performance was so exceptional that he was rewarded with the title, "King of Babylon." Not long afterward, Nabopolassar himself orchestrated a successful revolt against Assyria, leading to the ruin of Nineveh and the separation of the Assyrian Empire into three great divisions.[224]

Daniel 1

In 607 BC, Nabopolassar associated Nebuchadnezzar, his eldest son, as co-regent with himself, and in 605 BC dispatched him to engage the army of Pharaoh-Necho at Carchemish on the banks of the Euphrates River. The sovereignty of Egypt extended north from the Nile River to include all of Palestine, up to the Great River Euphrates. Nebuchadnezzar scoured the land of Israel in the third year of the reign of Jehoiakim. Being ill at the time of the dispatch, Nabopolassar

---

223 Ellen G. White, *SDA Bible Commentary*, vol. 4 (Washington, DC: Review and Herald, 1955), p. 743 and *Andrews Study Bible* (Berrien Springs, MI: Andrews University Press, 2010), p. 1106.
224 N.S. Gill, "Nabopolassar," ThoughtCo, https://1ref.us/1k1 (accessed February 9, 2021).

died while Nebuchadnezzar was on the march, necessitating his son's immediate return to Babylon to secure the throne. Passing through Jerusalem on his northward trek, Nebuchadnezzar collected a bounty for the kingdom, and Daniel begins his narrative at this point (chapter 1, verse 1).[225] Verses 3 to 5 reveal the superb qualifications of those taken captive, of whom Daniel and his three companions were part. The remainder of the chapter defines the moral character of these four servants of the most high God.

Daniel 2

Chapter 2 describes the metal man of Nebuchadnezzar's dream. Why did God give to Nebuchadnezzar the first prophetic vision sweeping earth's history to its conclusion? Why not to Daniel, His beloved prophet of the time? Daniel was not the reigning potentate and had no ambition to build an eternal dynasty. God's plans were diametrically opposed to those of King Nebuchadnezzar, and what was not recognized by either the ancient king or by scholars who have examined these things, the diadem of divine authority had passed from *Israel to Babylon* (Ezek. 21:26–27). God was now prepared to enlist the king as His anointed agent in protecting Israel during its exile. Two references in this chapter respond to these questions. Daniel 2, verses 34 and 35, describe an event that impacts all the great kingdoms of the earth within the framework of history: a rock strikes the statue *on the feet* in the last days of time and "brake them to pieces" (Dan. 2:34), whereupon they "became like chaff of the summer threshingfloors; and the wind carried them away" (verse 35). This last phrase prevents the specious interpretation that they fade away or merge through natural attrition, or that man's ambition is sufficient to sustain political power by his own volition. Verses 44 and 45 connect this idea with an identifiable timing of the predicted destruction, "in the days of these kings" (verse 44). That is, while these nations are still recognizable and viable as independent powers.

The stone of Daniel 2 does not represent the second coming of Christ.[226] An explanation is found in verse 44 which says, "And in the days of these kings shall the God of heaven set up a kingdom, which shall never be destroyed." The kingdoms of today are represented by

---

225 "Interesting Facts about Nebuchadnezzar & the Babylonian Empire," biblecharts.org, https://1ref.us/1k2 (accessed February 8, 2021).
226 See Appendix 2, p. 212, "The Mystery Stone of Daniel 2."

the feet and toes of Nebuchadnezzar's great image. The stone was cut out of something, or separated from something, and then used to destroy whatever it is that defines a nation. To be formed without "hands" implies an agent other than human, and to destroy the viability of earthly politics expresses a power beyond anything that earth has known since it adopted the concept of nations. The God of heaven will Himself *form an entity* that He will use to accomplish His end-time purpose: harvest the earth of its "wheat and barley," the multitude of faithful, His sheep not of this fold.

Jeremiah 51:19–23 describes God's intent for Israel that was never realized. However, God's ultimate will is never frustrated, and He will accomplish through spiritual Israel what He was unable to accomplish through national Israel.

> The *portion of Jacob* [God] is not like them; for he is the former of all things: and Israel is the rod of his inheritance: the LORD of hosts is his name. Thou art my battle axe and weapons of war ... And *with thee* will I break in pieces the horse and his rider; and *with thee* will I break in pieces the chariot and his rider; *with thee* also will I break in pieces man and woman; and *with thee* will I break in pieces old and young; and *with thee* will I break in pieces young man and the maid; I will also break in pieces *with thee* the shepherd and his flock; and *with thee* will I break in pieces the husbandman and his yoke of oxen; and *with thee* will I break in pieces captains and rulers. (Jer. 51:19–23, emphasis mine)

God's pre-advent judgment, when it passes to the living, begins with the house of God, and it is at this point that we must tread carefully, because our understanding of probation and its closing is somewhat murky. Some principles governing free moral agency might be of help. Even though born in sin, "knit me together in my mother's womb" (Ps 139:13, ESV), God has held sacrosanct my will by which I am to work out my own salvation with fear and trembling. By my daily choices I either move closer to or am distanced from God until my soul is fixed one way or the other. Those who have found their way into the inner circle of truth and enjoy special blessings and privileges are held to a standard and responsibility not applied to others. Thus, as Paul so eloquently declares, I am indebted to both the Romans and Greeks, the wise and foolish (Rom 1:14). And, as pointed out above in Jeremiah 51:19–23, God forms His people to be a "rod" in His hand, to perform His purpose. It is at this point that the 144,000 are prepared to issue the loud cry and to harvest the faithful outside God's fold. A statement from the Spirit of Prophecy helps to clarify this issue:

> Oh, that the people might know the time of their visitation! There are many who have not yet heard the testing truth for this time. There are many with whom the Spirit of God is striving. *The time of God's destructive judgments is the time of mercy for those who have had no opportunity to learn what is truth.* Tenderly will the Lord look upon them. His heart of mercy is touched; His hand is still stretched out to save, *while the door is closed to those who would not enter.*[227]

God's purpose in these two scenes is to emphasize *His* utter management in the affairs of men.

> The Lord God omnipotent reigneth. All kings, all nations, are His, under His rule and government. His resources are infinite.

The wise man declares, "The king's heart is in the hand of the Lord, as the rivers of water: he turneth it whithersoever he will." Those upon whose actions hang the destinies of nations, are watched over with a vigilance that knows no relaxation by Him who "giveth salvation unto kings," to whom belong "the shields of the earth."[228]

Examples in Scripture of great leaders who rallied to the service of God include Joseph, Moses, Joshua, David and his son, Solomon. It is true today in God's work that humble men are preferred, not the self-exalted who move from political expediency.

Examples in Scripture of great leaders who rallied to the service of God include Joseph, Moses, Joshua, David and his

---

227 Ellen G. White, *Testimonies for the Church*, vol. 9 (Mountain View, CA: Pacific Press, 1909), p. 97, emphasis mine.
228 Ellen G. White, *SDA Bible Commentary*, vol. 4 (Washington, DC: Review and Herald, 1955), p. 1170.

son, Solomon. It is true today in God's work that humble men are preferred, not the self-exalted who move from political expediency.

> It was not the scholarly theologians who had an understanding of this truth, and engaged in its proclamation. Had these been faithful watchmen, diligently and prayerfully searching the Scriptures, they would have known the time of night; the prophecies would have opened to them the events about to take place. But they did not occupy this position, and the message was given by humbler men.[229]

Daniel 3

King Nebuchadnezzar was himself a man of immense power (with a core of honesty), although beset by an ego of large proportion. Countering God's effort to command his heart, Satan attempted to entrap him and at once destroy the influence of the Hebrews in Babylon. This is the subject of chapter 3, *the image of gold and the fiery furnace*. It also prefigures with remarkable clarity the primary end-time issue, that which is the theme of the three angels' messages: worship! Choose you this day whom you will serve (Josh. 24:15)!

As the image in the dream passed from precious metal to baser metals, so the nations represented by each degenerated in moral strength. "Wickedness, blasphemy, and corruption prevailed. The kingdoms that followed were even more base and corrupt; and these sank lower and still lower in the scale of moral worth."[230] Still resisting, Nebuchadnezzar was persuaded to exalt himself before the nations and, in defiance of God, build an image of continuous glory to his own majesty. God pressed upon him the folly of his thinking.

Daniel 4

God pursued Nebuchadnezzar by a second dream in which he was warned of his dangerous course of action. Becoming more and more elevated in his own eyes and recognizing less and less God's place in his life, Nebuchadnezzar was given the divine perspective in vision. He dreamed of a tree bearing the unmistakable imprimatur of Daniel's God, and once more faced a moral decision. His respected prime minister, Daniel, provided not only understanding of the dream but the

---

229 Ellen G. White, *The Great Controversy* (Mountain View, CA: Pacific Press, 1911), p. 312.
230 Ellen G. White, *Prophets and Kings* (Mountain View, CA: Pacific Press, 1917), p. 502.

encouragement of a caring friend. Yet within a year Nebuchadnezzar succumbed to his pride and was reduced to an ox-like mentality. Seven years passed over him while his pride ebbed away. Chapter 4 ends with victory, and the king praises God with new-found humility.

Daniel 5

The narrative leaps from Nebuchadnezzar's closing years past several monarchs who succeeded him. The leap, however, is relatively brief since Nebuchadnezzar may have died within a year upon regaining his sanity, and his successors enjoyed short terms in office. Evil-Merodach, his son, reigned but two years, 561–560 BC, and was put to death. He was followed by his brother-in-law, Neriglissar who, after four years, was slain in battle. His son, Laborosoarchod, succeeded him for a period of nine months, after which he, too, was slain for "vile and flagitious things."[231] Nabonidus, a man of rank and the son-in-law of Nebuchadnezzar, attained the throne next. Within two years of his seventeen-year reign, he appointed his son, Belshazzar, co-regent in Babylon.[232] Fifteen years later, Cyrus the Mede conquered the empire.

Chapter 5 is a record of the closing day in Babylon's history. Redolent with symbolism and pregnant with lessons, especially for the final generation, the narrative now passes, with chapter 6, to apocalyptic prophecy. Daniel has been inactive in matters of government and is approaching his most senior years.

Daniel 6

"And Darius the Median took the kingdom, being about threescore and two years old" (Dan. 5:31) and reigned two years—538–536 BC. During the conquest of the city, Daniel was discovered in a royal robe, bearing the insignia of the third highest office. When asked about the affairs of the kingdom, they found him to be so thoroughly informed that he was given chief place in the reorganization. In chapter 6 human nature asserts itself yet again, placing Daniel in jeopardy for his life. Pride and jealously conspire to put him in a den of lions, providing God the opportunity to reveal His majesty to a new nation.

---

231 Humphrey Prideaux, *The Old and New Testament Connected, in the History of the Jews and Neighbouring Nations* (1836), https://1ref.us/1oo (accessed April 8, 2021).
232 "Who was King Nebuchadnezzar's son?" Bible Q, https://1ref.us/1k3 (accessed February 9, 2021).

This experience of Daniel prefigures the death decree that will confront God's people at the end of time.

Daniel 7

It is important at this point, perhaps, to recognize the relationship between chapters 7, 8, and 9 of Daniel. Chapter 7 presents Jesus as *king,* chapter 8 presents Him as *priest,* and chapter 9 presents Jesus as *sacrifice,* and the visions were given to Daniel in that order. Notice that this order is the reverse of that in which reality occurred: Jesus was first our sacrifice, then our High Priest, and finally our king. Why are the portrayals not presented in the sequence of their actual occurrence?

> *It is important at this point, perhaps, to recognize the relationship between chapters 7, 8, and 9 of Daniel. Chapter 7 presents Jesus as king, chapter 8 presents Him as priest, and chapter 9 presents Jesus as sacrifice.*

Modern western European thinking reasons from *cause to effect*; ancient Semitic people commonly reasoned from *effect back to cause*. Instead of saying, 'You are a sinful, wicked, and rebellious people, therefore your land will be destroyed,' the biblical prophets could also put the matter the other way around: 'Your land will be destroyed.' Why? 'Because you are a sinful, wicked, and rebellious people.' A good biblical example of this kind of thought order can be found in Micah 1:10–15 where the cities that mourn for the exiles are listed first, followed by the list of the cities from which the exiles came. We would put the matter the other way around …. The sacrifice of chapter 9 enabled the priest of chapter 8 to become priest, and the priesthood of the Prince enabled the Prince of chapter 8 to become the king of chapter 7. There is a logical, consistent, and interrelated sequence here that is quite direct and reasonable when we understand that the sequence begins at the end and works backward as far as the literary order of the book is concerned.[233]

---

[233] William H. Shea, *The Abundant Life Amplifier,* Daniel 7–12 (Boise, ID: Pacific Press, 1996), pp.160–161.

The scenes of Daniel chapter 7 were presented in the first year of Belshazzar, king of Babylon in 553 BC. Daniel, the beloved of God, is honored to receive an animated version of Nebuchadnezzar's dream of the metal man, a recapitulation of earth's closing history in prophecy. The issues and principles are identical, only the symbols are changed. This time the issue with Babylon is brief since its fate is fixed and will soon pass from the scene of prophecy into history.[234] The winged lion transmogrifies into mere man and is dismissed, being replaced by a bear of peculiar proportion: it is lopsided and voracious. Medo-Persia absorbs Lydia, Babylon, and Egypt. The bear of Darius and Cyrus passes to the leopard of Alexander the Great. His swift and terrifying appearance leaves the world agog with wonder and admiration. The leopard transforms into a beast with four heads, yet with authority to rule.

At this point in the narrative brevity gives place to vivid detail, and Daniel is astonished by the emergence of a fourth beast, terrifying, frightening, and very powerful. It is nondescript, having no comparative likeness anywhere in nature. But that which arrested Daniel's attention most forcibly was *ten horns*. While still in shock, he witnessed as the ten horns were reduced to seven by the emergence of one having eyes of a man and a mouth that spoke boastfully (Dan. 7:8). On the heels of this phenomenon the scene changes dramatically to a heavenly tribunal where the Personages assembled are divine. Thrones are cast down, judgment is set, and books are opened.

Now is resumed the earthly scene of the troubling beast. Tumultuous events follow each other down through a long history until the beast is slain and its body destroyed. Other beasts, political entities also stripped of their authority, were allowed to live (verse 12) until one like the Son of Man laid claim to the nations of earth and established an everlasting dominion (verse 14). What was Daniel to make of this? He approached one standing near and asked him the true meaning (verse 16). The rest of the chapter interprets the symbols of this astonishing vision.

---

[234] These beasts are modified in the vision to accommodate the effects of the history they reflect. A beautiful word descriptive of this phenomenon is the word "transmogrify/transmogrification" and its variants.

Daniel 8

"In the third year of the reign of king Belshazzar [550 BC] a vision appeared unto me ... which appeared unto me at the first" (Dan. 8:1). Two years later, the prophetic theme that has persisted throughout his life is repeated a third time: powers of nations to the end of time.

In this vision a ram and a he-goat (both sacrificially clean animals) typify worldly powers that dominate the political landscape of his future. A ram with two long horns was seen standing beside the Ulai Canal. The longer of the two horns had grown up later. The ram charged in three compass directions with great freedom until an adversary with one prominent horn challenged it. A goat appeared from the west, crossing the earth with such furious swiftness that it knocked the ram to the ground, breaking both of its horns. The greatness of the goat was interrupted briefly by the breaking of its own curious horn, which immediately transmogrified into four prominent horns dominating the four winds of heaven. These two animals caricature the histories of Medo-Persia and Greece.

The four horns of the goat continued to morph, and a fifth horn appeared, small at first, but grew in specific directions, exercising great power and doing astonishing deeds of blasphemy. Daniel himself was agog and speechless at the audacity and endurance of this horn power. A companion, perceiving his astonishment, asked for him a pointed question: "When will the activity of this dreadful power end?" (Dan. 8:13–14, paraphrase). Upon receiving the information, his companion turned to Daniel and said, "It will take 2,300 prophetic days, and then the sanctuary will be cleansed" (Dan. 8:14, paraphrase). From verse 19 to verse 27 (the end of the chapter) the vision is explained in cryptic terms. The last verse describes the physical effect this revelation has had upon Daniel. He was exhausted and ill for several days, not only because the vision was beyond his understanding, but in his misapprehension, he tended to misapply the time factor.

Daniel 9

In the first year of Darius (539 BC), Daniel's concern for the well-being of Israel persists. From reading the prophecies of Jeremiah he had calculated that the term of Israel's captivity was nearly ended. Understanding the nature of divine commerce, he was compelled to intercede for his people and for God's honor. Verses 4 to 19 record his petition, and the remainder of the chapter focuses on that part of the ram-goat vision that had so perplexed him twelve years earlier. The "seventy sevens" mark off a probation during which the nation Israel would respond to the glorious duties defining the very purpose of her existence or else suffer eternal ignominy. A further riddle is posed when the Anointed One is prophesied to be cut off in the middle of the last seven, and all ritual sacrifice and offering ceases (verses 26 and 27).

Daniel 10

In the third year of Cyrus (536 BC), Daniel received a vision delineating that which had been earlier revealed. Chapter 10 provides the prequel to that delineation. It is remarkable for the heavenly attention given to the affairs of men and the respect for man's thoughtful involvement. Heaven is certainly nearer than we supposed! The solicitation of heaven's mightiest angel is revealed in verse 20 when He poses the question, "Do you know why I have come to you?" And then the rest of Daniel's book is dedicated to the answer of that question.

Daniel 11 and 12

The scenes of Daniel chapters 11 and 12 were presented in the first year of Darius (539 BC). Four notable kings of Medo-Persia were predicted there: Cambyses, Smerdis, Darius Hystaspes, and Xerxes (the rich one). Xerxes, the fourth king after Cyrus, was the son of Darius Hystaspes. Determined to conquer Greece, he mustered an army 5,250,000 strong, but his human arm was overruled, and he suffered defeat in 480 BC, sixty years after the "first year of Darius."[235]

Daniel 11:1–22 carries the action down from the time of Daniel himself to the coming of the Messiah, at which point verse 23 marks a transition in the prophecy. Daniel 11:23–30 is dealing with the activities of Rome's second phase, papal Rome, which now becomes the "king of the north."[236]

(Dan. 11:3) Alexander the Great rose to power in 331 BC and died of pneumonia 323 BC after a drunken celebration. He reigned but eight years, after which his kingdom was divided among his four generals. Greek dominance is measured between 323 BC and 168

---

235 "Battle of Thermopylae," Britannica, https://1ref.us/1k4 (accessed February 9, 2021).
236 William H. Shea, *The Abundant Life Amplifier*, Daniel 7–12 (Boise, ID: Pacific Press, 1996), pp. 193–196.

BC—155 years. Infighting among the generals resulted in a polarizing of the kingdom into a "North" and a "South."

(Dan. 11:14) Pagan Rome enters prophecy in verse 14 (200 BC) and becomes the King of the North, dominating discussion in verses 14 to 31. Verse 14 contains a thought that is pithy indeed: "And in those times there shall many stand up against the king of the south: also the robbers of thy people shall exalt themselves to establish [to circumvent] the vision; but they shall fall." To develop the sense of this thought it must be connected with the divine fiat expressed in Ezekiel 21:26–27. There, God pronounces sentence upon the last king of Israel, who culminates a long line of disobedient kings. God commands, "Remove the diadem, and take off the crown ... exalt him that is low, and abase him that is high. *I will overturn, overturn, overturn, it ... and I will give it him*" (Ezek. 21:26–27, emphasis mine). "The crown removed from Israel passed successively to the kingdoms of Babylon, Medo-Persia, Greece, and Rome."[237] Daniel's vision developed this prophecy in detail. To connect these two texts, it must be recognized that the *diadem* Babylon inherited from Israel was *overturned* to Medo-Persia, who *overturned* it to Greece, who *overturned* it to Rome. Verse 14 of Daniel 11 exposes a strategic interception attempted by Satan to thwart the prophetic plan of God. The robbers of verse 14 are Antiochus Magnus of Greece and Philip of Macedon (not the Philip who was Alexander's father). These two formed an alliance to overrun Egypt and her satellites and divide the spoils. The success of this scheme would have robbed the people of Rome of their prophetic turn at the diadem. The young Rome asserted herself for the first time, rescuing the infant Ptolemy from defeat and preserving the prophecy of Daniel.[238]

Between 200 BC and 168 BC, Rome developed into a world power. It was in 161 BC that she connected with the Jews by an alliance, mutual help pact.

In verse 19, Julius Caesar dies, and verse 20 introduces Augustus Caesar, the raiser of taxes. He made a decree in 4 BC, the year Jesus Christ was born, and died in AD 14. In verse 21, a vile person, Tiberius Caesar, reigns. It was during his reign that Jesus was crucified, the Prince of the Covenant cut off. Tiberius died AD 37.

---

237 Ellen G. White, *Education* (Mountain View, CA: Pacific Press, 1903), p. 179.
238 Uriah Smith, *The Prophecies of Daniel and the Revelation* (Mountain View, CA: Pacific Press, 1944), pp. 242–243.

Daniel 1–12: The Book of Daniel

(Dan. 11:23–30) According to Shea, these verses are not arranged in *chronological* order but rather in *topical* order:[239]

1. Verses 23–30: actual military campaigning.
2. Verse 30: subversion of the system of salvation.
3. Verses 32–34: persecution.
4. Verses 35–39: self-exaltation.

The military campaigning of verses 23–30 depict the crusades of the eleventh century AD. The translation of a preposition in verse 30 interjects some confusion, in which the Hebrew *be* or *beth* is wrongly said to be *"against"* rather than *"by, in, at,* or *with."* Thus, the ships of the Chittim, or western coastlands, did not come *against* the King of the North; they came *with* him. They were *his* ships. The final crusade attempted to invade Egypt, led by King Louis IX of France.[240] It was a disaster, resulting in defeat and surrender to the Egyptians, and Louis IX was taken prisoner and held for ransom.

(Dan. 11:36–39) These verses cover the span of time indicated in the 1,260-day prophecy. "He shall do wickedly" (verse 32) refers to the French Revolution, which was the sure result of more than 1,000 years of suppression by the Catholic Church, during which it prevented access to Scripture by the masses for fear of losing control of nations.[241] The 1,260 years ended in AD 1798 and ushered in the "time of the end." The 2,300-day prophecy ended in 1844, as well as the principle that ties prophecy to calendar dates. Daniel, intensely interested in when this event would occur, asked the question, "How long will be the time that the sanctuary and the host be trodden under foot?" (Dan. 8:13, paraphrase). The answer came swiftly in the very next verse (Daniel 8:14): Until 2,300 days—

> *The 1,260 years ended in AD 1798 and ushered in the "time of the end." The 2,300-day prophecy ended in 1844, as well as the principle that ties prophecy to calendar dates.*

---

239 Shea, *The Abundant Life Bible Amplifier, Daniel 7–12* (Boise, ID: Pacific Press, 1996), p. 196.
240 "Battle of Fariskur," Wikipedia, https://1ref.us/1k5 (accessed February 9, 2021).
241 Ellen G. White, *The Great Controversy* (Mountain View, CA: Pacific Press, 1911), pp. 265–288.

1844. Daniel 7:26 says that at that time the judgment shall sit, and they shall take away his dominion and destroy it unto the end.

Between verses 39 and 40 of chapter 11, there appears to be a lapse of at least 200 years. Verse 40 reads: "And *at the time of the end* shall the king of the south push at him" (emphasis mine). Another expression used in discussing apocalyptic matters is "at the end of time." A distinction should be noted between these two phrases. "The time of the end" denotes a position along a particular continuum, while "the end of time" denotes the last remnant of an issue. For example, "the time of the end" addresses a period beyond the middle half before expiration, and the "end of time" addresses the very last ticks of the clock before the final curtain falls. In the case mentioned above, Daniel uses, in the Hebrew tongue, the word "*quets*," translated "end." *Quets* (pronounced "kates") indicated the utmost end, extreme end, to chop off.[242] As translated, the context appears to favor the period of time between 1798 and 1844, but the context of verse 40 is better understood as referring to events yet future.

Daniel wrote the prophecies in both the Hebrew and the Chaldean languages. In *Strong's Concordance*, the original words for the phrases, "time of the end" and "the end of time" is explained.[243] As inferred above, tradition applies these passages to the period between 1798 and 1844. Ellen White used the context, "the end of time."[244] However, Bible translators have evidently taken it to mean "the time of the end." In *Strong's*, the Chaldean (Aramaic) meaning of the phrase is consistent with Ellen White's understanding: "utmost end of time" or "the final end of time." This is a solid basis for understanding Daniel 11:40–45. "The time of the end" always refers to the end of appointed time, *which is the end of the 2,300 days.*

The prophetic time period marked out for Daniel's prophecies began in 457 BC and ended in AD 1844. Seven weeks, or forty-nine years exactly, and the walls were built; sixty-nine weeks, or 483 years exactly, and Jesus was baptized in AD 27; seventy weeks, or 490 years exactly, and the Jews' probation ended in AD 34. In the midst of that

---

242 *Strong's Exhaustive Concordance of the Bible* (Peabody, MA: Hendrickson Publishers), p. 7093.
243 Strong's lists the texts in which these two phrases occur (p. 304), and refers one to "7093,"which is the Hebrew/Chaldee Dictionary in the back of the concordance (p. 104), which translates the word definition from Hebrew to English: after, (utmost) border, end, [in-] finite).
244 Ellen G. White, *Testimonies to Ministers and Gospel Workers* (Mountain View, CA: Pacific Press, 1923), pp. 115–116.

week, Messiah was cut off (crucified)—exactly! Until AD 538 (504 years), another probation would prevail within which the apostolic church would prove itself. The little horn power would then tread down the sanctuary in heaven for the balance of the 2,300 days. Then, beginning with 1844, the sanctuary would be cleansed. Thus, *calendar time ended*. No longer would any event hang from an exact date of calendar time. From 1844 onward all prophetic time is to be understood literally within the context of an identifiable event. *God has given His people events that, when identified, establish with certainty where we are in the march of history.*

In *Testimonies to the Church* is a passage important for all of us to read often. It says that we who are watchmen should show the people where we are in *prophetic history*. That place is located at the point of each fulfillment.[245] I heard a program on 3ABN the other day in which the speaker was commenting on Christ's soon coming. He said, "Christ can come at any moment!" He is tragically wrong! Christ Himself spoke of the event so that His people can know when His coming is *near*. "When you *see* ... you [can] *know*" (Matt 24:33, NLT, emphasis mine). Daniel prophesies, "From the time that the daily is taken away and the abomination set up, there will be 1,290 days. Blessed and holy are those that wait and come to the 1,335 days" (Dan. 12:11–12, paraphrase). This is significant because at the end of the 1,335 days the elect will be delivered by the voice of God Himself. The end-time event that is closed to man's calculation is the *close of probation*.

As portrayed in Ezekiel 8:16, the greatest abomination against God was for the twenty-five priests to turn their backs to the temple and worship the sun toward the east. And when the papal power came into existence in AD 538, they were identified in prophecy as "the abomination of desolation." Daniel 11:31 says that the initiation of a false liturgy was the placing of the abomination that makes desolate, and in Daniel 12:11 he is told by the angel that an abomination that makes desolate shall again be set up. This, in the context of confessed ignorance by Daniel himself. He does not understand the application of this part of the vision, which we take to be part of the end of time that is yet future.

When Protestantism in America passes the Sunday law, they will make God's law void and will make God's work in the earth desolate. This will be the last act in the drama.

---

245 Ellen G. White, *Testimonies for the Church*, vol. 5 (Mountain View, CA: Pacific Press, 1889), pp. 711–718.

Other terms used throughout Daniel 11 are "The King of the North" and "The King of the South." The King of the North was the conquering power threatening from the north of Israel. The King of the South was the dominant power south of Israel. Neither of these terms was used in prophecy prior to the time that Alexander the Great died and his kingdom was divided among his four generals. For many years Seleucus was the "King of the North." He conquered Lacimicas and Cassandra, thus ruling Greece, Macedonia, Turkey, and Assyria. Ptolemy became the "King of the South" in Egypt. Since that time, Islam is a candidate for the King of the South. The King of the North passed to pagan Rome and then to papal Rome.[246] In 1798, papal Rome lost power when the pope was taken prisoner and died an exile in France the following year.

Revelation 13:11–18 speaks of another power arising *at that time*— the two-horned beast. It would speak like a dragon; it would unite with the papal power and make an image to the beast. In our time, the superpower of the world is the United States of America. It is obvious that we are fast forming a likeness of power to the persecuting power of papal Rome and will receive the same number as the beast—666.[247]

It will be the United States, in union with the papal power, that treads down the saints. Their number (666), the number of man, indicates dominance completely separate from God, thus making the United States of America, the superpower in our time, a prime candidate for "King of the North." A cautious application of Daniel 11:40 might be: And at the time of the end shall the King of the South (Islam) push at him (the King of the North—USA). And the King of the North (USA) shall come against him (the King of the South—Islam, Afghanistan, Iraq) like a whirlwind, with chariots, and with horsemen, and with many ships; and he (USA) shall enter into the countries, and shall overflow and pass over.

Verse 43 of Daniel 11 states that "he [USA] shall have power over the treasures of gold and of silver." But verse 45 says, "[Y]et he [USA] shall come to his end, and none shall help him." The *SDA Bible Commentary*, identifying the ten horns of Revelation 17:12, states that *all*

---

246 *Andrews Study Bible* (Berrien Springs, MI: Andrews University Press, 2010), pp. 1132–1135. For excellent information, the map on page 1132 gives present-day info for ancient locations of "Kings of North and South," and the chart on page 1134 gives a great comparison of Daniel 11 to Daniel 8 and 9.

247 Ellen G. White, *A Word to the Little Flock* (Washington, DC: Review and Herald, 1847), pp. 9, 18–19 and *Andrews Study Bible* (Berrien Springs, MI: Andrews University Press, 2010), pp. 1675–1676.

Daniel 1–12: The Book of Daniel

of Satan's forces will be destroyed.[248] This is described in Revelation 18, and in Revelation 19:20 the beast and the false prophet are cast alive into the lake of fire. And all this is *before* the thousand years. Revelation 20:10 says that the devil is cast into the lake of fire (after the thousand years) where the beast and the false prophet *are*.

The foregoing scenario is an appropriate fit of the prophecy of Daniel 11:40–45. The only key events yet to occur are the purification and the sanctification of God's 144,000, and the passing of the Sunday law in America by apostate Protestantism.

Note the account of a remarkable scene given in vision to Ellen White while she was on the East Coast:

> On one occasion, when in New York City, I was in the night season called upon to behold buildings rising story after story toward heaven. These buildings were warranted to be fire-proof, and they were erected to glorify their owners and builders. Higher and still higher these buildings rose, and in them the most costly material was used. Those to whom these buildings belonged were not asking themselves: "How can we best glorify God?" The Lord was not in their thoughts .... As these lofty buildings went up, the owners rejoiced with ambitious pride that they had money to use in gratifying self and provoking the envy of their neighbors. Much of the money that they thus invested had been obtained through exaction, through grinding down the poor .... The scene that next passed before me was an alarm of fire. Men looked at the lofty and supposedly fire-proof buildings and said: "They are perfectly safe." But these buildings were consumed as if made of pitch. The fire engines could do nothing to stay the destruction. The firemen were unable to operate the engines.[249]

On September 11, 2001, two of the largest buildings in New York City met with destruction hauntingly similar to that depicted in her vision. From this event there continues to flow around the globe influences and power calculated to fulfill prophecy.

"But who reads the warnings given by the fast-fulfilling signs of the times? What impression is made upon worldlings? What change

---

248 Ellen G. White, *SDA Bible Commentary*, vol. 7 (Washington, DC: Review and Herald, 1957), p. 882.
249 Ellen G. White, *Testimonies for the Church*, vol. 9 (Mountain View, CA: Pacific Press, 1909), pp. 12–13.

is seen in their attitude? No more than was seen in the attitude of the inhabitants of the Noachian world .... [T]oday the world, utterly regardless of the warning voice of God, is hurrying on to eternal ruin."[250]

On page 129 of *Last Day Events* is a statement which says that when calamities are filling the earth, Satan will put his interpretation on them and his people will think, as he wants them to think, that they are the result of Sunday breaking. They then rush to pass a Sunday law, thinking to bring an end to the calamities. When this takes place, "Her sins reach to heaven" (Rev. 18:5, paraphrase).[251]

Natural calamities, spoken of in the Spirit of Prophecy, have increased sharply just in the past several years, and are to increase until Jesus comes. Specific mention is made of the signs (events) that will take place at the deliverance of the saints.[252] We should know what to expect when we see these signs (events). God expects His watchmen to know what signs to look for when probation closes so that our faith will not fail, and our anguish will not be more than we can bear. *These events will be different from the calamities of nature* and are not intended to prefigure probation's close, but to assure His true worshipers that He has not abandoned them in their distress. Daniel 12:10 says that the wise shall understand, but the wicked shall not understand. Read 1 Thessalonians 5 very carefully: That day does not come as a thief to those who are watching. We are children of *light* (verses 1 through 5).

The prophecies of both Daniel and Revelation show plainly that for us the very next events to take place are the cleansing of God's church and the passing of the Sunday law. Then the closing events will occur in rapid *succession*.

So just what are these events that are to come immediately after the close of probation? *They are the first four trumpets!* Notice in Revelation 8:5 that which marks the closing up of the judgment: the casting down of the censer. The very next verse says that the angels prepare to sound the trumpets. And they do! The first four are of a different description than the calamities of nature. God's people who are

---

250 Ibid., p. 14.
251 Ellen G. White, *Last Day Events* (Boise, ID: Pacific Press, 1992), p. 198.
252 Ellen G. White, *The Great Controversy* (Mountain View, CA: Pacific Press, 1911), pp. 589–590, 635–636.

watching will know when they see these four plagues that probation has closed, and that God will sustain them.[253]

A primary anchor point in understanding the prophecies of Daniel 11 (and subsequently Daniel 12) is the discussion found in verses 11 to 21. There, unmistakable profiles of three dominant emperors of Rome are recorded: Julius Caesar, Augustus Caesar, and Tiberius Caesar. Julius shall *stumble* (verse 19); Augustus shall be a *raiser of taxes* (verse 20); and Tiberius shall be a *vile person* (verse 21). These verses fix the reader firmly in the streams of history and prophecy. We can then follow them both down to our present time with unerring accuracy.

A fuller look at an event described in Daniel 11:20 fixes prophecy and history together in exact time. There is predicted to arise "a raiser of taxes." History has affirmed him to be Augustus Caesar. Luke 2:1–7 verifies that indeed Caesar Augustus made a decree for all the world to be taxed. It also affirms that Cyrenius was governor of Assyria. Jesus would be born that very year.

Daniel 11:21, the very next verse, predicts that a "vile person" would follow Augustus on the throne of Rome. And history affirms that his nephew, Tiberius, ascended the throne and holds the dubious honor of cutting off the Prince of the Covenant—the crucifixion of Jesus on the cross in the midst of the last week of prophecy, AD 27 to AD 34. These events are the unequivocal glue holding together the twin lines of history and prophecy.

Taking this point back to verses 14, 15, and 16 in Daniel chapter 11, we find the mysterious "King of the North." At this time in history Rome held all the qualifications for the title, replacing Seleucus as the dominant power in the Mediterranean region. Verse 16 and onward describes an irresistible power that shall prevail for many years. Pagan Rome retained the title "King of the North" until Daniel 11:31. In AD 538 the little horn placed the abomination of desolation that maketh desolate in the holy place, an act repugnant to God. By this effrontery, papal Rome claimed the title, "King of the North." She, in turn, lost the title at the utter end of her reign in AD 1798. At the same time that the little horn was losing its power, another power was emerging that would speak as a dragon and become the greatest superpower the world has ever known. Today the entire world knows that the United

---

253 Ellen G. White, *Early Writings* (Washington, DC: Review and Herald, 1882), pp. 279–285 and Ellen G. White, *Last Day Events* (Boise, ID: Pacific Press, 1992), pp. 242–246.

States of America is the undisputed monarch of nations. She is speaking like a dragon and will soon exercise despotic power over individual conscience. When she does, the United States will become the final King of the North. Ellen White refers to the United States as the one who should come to his end and none shall help him (Dan. 11:45).[254] His number, along with the beast, is 666—the number of man.

The last six verses of chapter 11 segues into the subject matter of chapter 12. Shea suggests that these verses relate a literal event in the life of Cambyses, the Persian king, in order to explain a dynamic significant to *the time of the end.*[255] The literal Persian king and the literal king of Egypt have become symbols for powers at the end of time. These powers are the papacy/apostate Protestantism (the King of the North) and atheism (the King of the South). In the clash of powers yet future, the papal-Protestant alliance will gain some sort of victory over the forces of atheism, but while the papal-Protestant powers are enjoying a short-lived victory, more serious challenges will arise in the east (verses 43 and 44).

Cambyses had conquered Egypt and intended to pursue the submission of Libya to the west and Nubia to the south, when he received dire news from his rear—the east and north. Cambyses, being upset greatly, decamped with much fury to rectify the situation. Retracing his steps north, he came again to Judah and, while passing through, he encamped between the seas and the beautiful holy mountain (Dan. 11:45). He did not come up to Mount Zion but only pitched his tents toward it. His actual campsite was down on the coastal plain of Sharon, between the seas and the beautiful holy mountain. His target was not Jerusalem, as he was intent on returning to the north whence his bad news had originated. However, while encamped in Judea he was overtaken by his end. Whether it was a suicide attempt or an accident, Cambyses stabbed himself in the thigh with his sword and died after twenty days. He was viewed as a madman by the people of his time who saw his demise as punishment from God. One of his more insane acts had been to kill the sacred Apis bull when he entered Egypt by stabbing it in the thigh. This all ties in with the ancient contest between God and Baal that took place just above the plain of Sharon in Mount Carmel (1 Kings 18:20–40), which of course prefigures the spiritual

---

254 Ellen G. White, *A Word to the Little Flock* (Washington, DC: Review and Herald, 1847), pp. 8, 9, 18, 19.
255 Shea, *The Abundant Life Bible Amplifier, Daniel 7–12* (Boise, ID: Pacific Press, 1996), p. 212.

struggle that will be worldwide just before the return of Jesus. The modern Cambyses will fail too, and the powers of earth and their kingdoms will become the kingdoms of our God and of His Christ. Thus is introduced chapter 12 of the book of Daniel.

(Daniel 12:1-4) "And at that time ...." connects the events of chapter 12 with the verses of chapter 11 immediately preceding. That is, at the time of the end, Michael will stand up, that Great Prince. One who is prince is heir apparent, not yet crowned king. The judgment is finished, the kingdom is determined, and Christ is soon to receive from His Father full authority to rule forever and ever. The "standing up" of verse 1 closes probation and introduces a time of trouble such as never was since there was a nation. It is then that the saints are delivered, everyone found written in the book. Prophecy has moved to the future in verse 40 of chapter 11, so we can expect to remain in the future tense until the end of the book. Again, Daniel is tormented by a question of time: how long will these fearful wonders last? What is the antecedent to "these wonders?" Does it go back to verse 40 of chapter 11, or does it ripple further back, even to the year AD 538?

If the antecedent is AD 538, then everything beyond is epilogue, and the vision ends with verse 4. The three mysterious numbers of Chapter 12 are then moot, having review value only. If, however, the antecedent begins with the events in verse 40 of Chapter 11, we must pursue their application in a future context. The first of the three numbers appears in verse 7: "a time, times, and an half," after which the power of the people will be scattered. The second time period mentioned in Daniel 12 is found in verse 11: From the time that the daily sacrifice is abolished and the abomination that causes desolation is set up, there will be 1,290 days. The last time period of Daniel 12 appears in verse 12: "Blessed is he that waiteth, and cometh to the thousand three hundred and five and thirty days." What prophetic/historic events bind these days?

They are without doubt cast in terms of the *time of the end*, which began in 1798. This would rule out AD 538 and leave little option for alternate considerations. If the SOP (Spirit of Prophecy) hermeneutic is followed—the scenes of Revelation occur in their order,[256] then perhaps the same principle applies to Daniel 12 as well.

---

256 Ellen G. White, *Testimonies for the Church*, vol. 8 (Mountain View, CA: Pacific Press, 1904), p. 302.

Jesus Walks the Earth

It has been widely taught for many years (without citation) that Jesus would not physically present Himself on earth between His ascension and His second coming. However, events yet to transpire during the unfolding of earth's closing scenes suggest otherwise. Events that pertain to the final scenes leading up to the second coming are presented in their order. Raising His hands, Jesus proclaims a loud voice, "It is done!"[257] Every case had been decided for life or death. There was now no mediator—nor need of one—between guilty man and an offended God. "Jesus lay off His priestly attire and clothe Himself with His most kingly robes. Upon His head were many crowns, a crown within a crown."[258] "[Jesus] leaves the sanctuary, [and] darkness covers the inhabitants of the earth."[259] "Surrounded by the angelic host, He left heaven. The plagues were falling upon the inhabitants of the earth."[260]

The question naturally arises, "Where does He go?" The first few pages of *The Great Controversy* chapter, "The Time of Trouble," describe exactly that—events that require a certain amount of time.[261] And in the book, *Maranatha,* Ellen White compares the inhabitants of the earth to the antediluvians of Noah's time who for seven days knew not that their doom was fixed, and who continued their careless, pleasure-loving life. So now "[t]he people are fast being lulled to a fatal security, to be awakened only by the outpouring of the wrath of God. The Lord in judgment will at the close of time walk through the earth, the fearful plagues will begin to fall."[262] The assurance of Psalm 91 will be fulfilled at this time in a most graphic manner.

> When the protection of human laws shall be withdrawn from those who honor the law of God, there will be, in different lands, a simultaneous movement for their destruction .... The people of God—some in prison cells, some hidden in solitary retreats in the forests and the mountains—still plead for divine protection, while in every quarter companies of armed men, urged on by hosts of evil angels, are preparing for the work of

---

257 Ellen G. White, *Early Writings* (Washington, DC: Review and Herald, 1882), p. 279.
258 Ibid., p. 281.
259 Ellen G. White, *The Great Controversy* (Mountain View, CA: Pacific Press, 1911), p. 614.
260 Ellen G. White, *Early Writings* (Washington, DC: Review and Herald, 1882), p. 281.
261 Ellen G. White, *The Great Controversy* (Mountain View, CA: Pacific Press, 1911), pp. 613–634.
262 Ellen G. White, *Maranatha* (Washington, DC: Review and Herald, 1976), p. 264.

death. It is now, in the hour of utmost extremity, that the God of Israel will interpose for the deliverance of His chosen. Saith the Lord; "Ye shall have a song, as in the night when a holy solemnity is kept; and gladness of heart, as when one goeth ... to come into the mountain of the Lord, to the Mighty One of Israel. And the Lord shall cause His glorious voice to be heard, and shall show the lighting down of His arm, with the indignation of His anger, and with the flame of a devouring fire, with scattering, and tempest, and hailstones."[263]

Thus, perhaps it would be more accurate to say that Jesus will not *visibly* present Himself on earth between His ascension and His second coming. Surely, of all periods in earth's history of the great controversy, God's presence should be at this time most likely! Then, when He *comes visibly* the second time, the journey will be a short one for Him since His presence is already reality, requiring only the *emergence* of His visible glory.

---

[263] Ellen G. White, *The Great Controversy* (Mountain View, CA: Pacific Press, 1911), p. 635.

Appendix 2

Daniel 2: The Mystery Stone of Daniel 2

Bernard E. Seaton, author of the 1981 fall quarter *Sabbath School Bible Study Guides*, observed percipiently, "[Christ] came so His kingdom could come .... The central ambition (in the purest possible sense) of the Son of Man's existence *was the establishment of that kingdom on earth.*"[264] Ellen White affirms:

"[The student] should gain a knowledge of [the Bible's] grand *central theme*, of God's *original purpose* for the world."[265]

> *God's original purpose for the world was to incubate a population to replace the rebel angels, but the virus of sin thwarted that purpose until God intervened with the ingenious plan of salvation, which makes viable His original purpose.*

God's original purpose for the world was to incubate a population to replace the rebel angels, but the virus of sin thwarted that purpose until God intervened with the ingenious plan of salvation, which makes viable His original purpose.

"[T]he saints of the most High shall *take the kingdom, and possess the kingdom* for ever, even for ever and ever" (Dan. 7:18, emphasis mine).

Satan has sought every occasion to interrupt this purpose and has, for the most part, been quite successful:

---

264 Bernard E. Seaton, "Thy Kingdom Come," Adult Sabbath School Lessons, October 25, 1981.
265 Ellen G. White, *Education* (Mountain View, CA: Pacific Press, 1903), p. 190, emphasis mine.

Daniel 2: The Mystery Stone of Daniel 2

1. The highest created being in heaven declared war.
2. The first created couple defected soon after receiving life.
3. The firstborn of the new race became a murderer.
4. A flood of water destroyed the seventh generation from Adam.
5. The new nation, Israel, apostatized continually.
6. God-with-us—the Son of man—was despised and crucified.
7. Within three centuries of its founding, His new church adopted paganism and tradition as its creed.

A divine strategy of persuasion ever since Eden has been to showcase our sinful preference. We have an innate fascination for sin and a short memory for its consequences. Experiences and examples of the consequences of sin are only used to get our attention, then God showers us with BLESSING. And so it goes.

However, God has ever had His *remnant*, even though it has been a paltry remnant. When Judah (what was left of His remnant nation) apostatized so completely that the only way to preserve the Davidic line was to engineer a captivity, God selected Babylon, Satan's stronghold. Can you just see God smile at His own audacity? He dared to go beyond sustaining His own people; He sought to convert the pagan king and make a prophet of him. God gave *the dream* to Nebuchadnezzar rather than to Daniel, His resident prophet, so that he, and every king who followed him, might know that earthly kingdoms are all temporal at best, and must pass away, and that the only eternal kingdom, which shall never pass away, is the kingdom of Christ.

Babylonia, *the great and golden*, passed away

under weaker rulers.[266] In 539 BC, Nabonidus and his son, Belshazzar (the next generation after the dream was given), were succeeded by Medo-Persia under Cyrus *the Great* at the battle of Opis. Greece ruled until 190 BC, losing to the new upstart power, Rome. Rome unified its imperial holdings in 168 BC, and controlled the Mediterranean region for the next 600 years.[267] Through the incursions of barbarians from northern and eastern Europe, the Roman Empire experienced division that has been understood by many as the *mixture of iron and clay*. Efforts have been put forth to weld the nations of Europe into one homogeneous whole: (1) intermarriage, referred to in the prophecy as mingling themselves with the seed of men; (2) force of arms—Charlemagne, Napoleon, Kaiser Wilhelm, and Hitler; (3) diplomacy that failed many times; and (4) monetary unity, the most recent effort. Ellen White tells us that the *iron and the clay* are *statecraft and churchcraft,* which will not mingle until after probation closes and the nations are gathered for the Battle of Armageddon.[268] God has clearly reserved unification to Himself. By His own methods and in His own time God will bring unity to the universe because man can only compromise within himself in the sole interests of greed and power.

> [S]tatesmen will uphold the spurious Sabbath, and will mingle their religious faith with the observance of this child of the papacy, placing it above the Sabbath which the Lord has sanctified and blessed, setting it apart for man to keep holy, as a sign between Him and His people to a thousand generations. *The mingling of churchcraft and statecraft is represented by the iron and the clay.* This union is weakening all the power of the churches. This investing the church with the power of the state will bring evil results.[269]

In explaining the vision, Daniel told the king:

"Thou sawest till [watched until] that *a stone was cut out without hands,* which smote the image upon his feet that were of iron and clay, and brake them to pieces" (Dan. 2:34, emphasis mine).

"Smote the image upon his *feet*." There were ten Germanic tribes that were involved in the breakup of the pagan Roman Empire, and

---

266 Ellen G. White, *SDA Bible Commentary*, vol. 4 (Washington, DC: Review and Herald, 1955), p. 774.
267 Ibid., pp. 774–775.
268 Ibid., pp. 1168–1169.
269 Ibid., emphasis mine.

when the smoke of battle cleared, only seven remained. Three had been uprooted, never to be heard of thereafter.

"Cut out" supernaturally, but cut out of what? Verse 34 does not identify what. We must look to verse 45:

"Forasmuch as thou sawest that the stone was cut out of *the mountain* without hands" (Dan. 2:45).

The stone was cut out of the mountain. Notice the definite article "the" (singular, just one of its kind). "Without hands" implies a supernatural effort, one not involving mankind. Let's finish the thought from verses 34 and 35.

> [T]hou sawest till that a stone was cut out without hands, which smote the image upon his feet that were of iron and clay [*statecraft and churchcraft*], and brake them to pieces. Then was the iron, the clay, the brass, the silver, and the gold, broken to pieces together, and became like the chaff of the summer threshingfloors; and the *wind* carried them away, that no place was found for them: and the stone that smote the image became a great mountain, and filled the whole earth. (Dan. 2:34–35)

"Whereas you saw the feet and *toes*, partly of potter's clay and partly of iron, the kingdom shall ... be in it, just as you saw the iron mixed with ceramic clay. And *as* the *toes* of the feet *were* partly of iron and partly of clay, *so* the kingdom shall be partly strong and partly fragile" (Dan. 2:41–42, emphasis mine).

Expositors have made much of the toes by adding significance to the number of them (10), i.e., the earth will be divided into ten territories under one despotic ruler. This is unwarranted as Daniel makes no mention of *ten*, nor does he infer anything regarding territories or rulers.

Notice that Daniel, in looking back, presents the symbols in their reverse order. Let's look again at verse 44:

"And in the *days of these kings* shall the God of heaven set up a kingdom, which shall never be destroyed" (Dan. 2:44, emphasis mine).

In the days of *what* kings? In the days of the kingdoms represented by the feet and toes—the kingdoms that come after pagan Rome. Thus, the kingdom of God is set up *not after*, but rather *in* the days of these kings. Can we infer from the discussion so far that the kingdom of God on earth is represented by that stone, and that it supersedes all other kingdoms, all other nations represented by the feet and toes? Do you see that the most important aspect of Nebuchadnezzar's dream has to do with the stone and its origin—the mountain? We must next ascertain the meaning of "the mountain," since the stone is a part of it. We have learned from previous studies that heads, kings, hills (mountains) are synonymous terms. The mountain of Daniel 2 is manifestly not a literal mountain but, like the image, the stone, the chaff, and the summer threshing floors, is figurative in Joel 3:17, as well as in several other places, God speaks of His Church as "Zion, *my holy mountain*." Let's take a look:

"So shall ye know that I am the LORD your God dwelling in Zion, *my holy mountain*" (Joel 3:17, emphasis mine).

"Even them [strangers and sons of strangers in Judah] will I bring to *my holy mountain,* and make them joyful in my house of prayer" (Isa. 56:7, emphasis mine).

"But in the last days it shall come to pass, that the *mountain of the house of the LORD* shall be established in the top of [or above all] the mountains" (Mic. 4:1, emphasis mine).

The mountain of Daniel 2 symbolizes God's church today, and embodies the nucleus of God's kingdom, represented by the *stone*. The *stone* is to be made up of a portion of the membership of God's church today, *cut out of the mountain,* separated from the body by some means. "[M]any be called, but few chosen" (Matt. 20:16). And in *Testimonies to the Church* there's this: "[T]he great proportion of those who now appear to be genuine and true will prove to be *base metal.*"[270]

By now it should be clear that the stone does not represent *Christ coming in person in the clouds of heaven at His second appearing* because, in the first place, Christ is not in any sense *cut out* of His church. Also, at His second coming the wicked are destroyed, and the righteous, both living and the resurrected, are caught *up to Him in the air,* the opposite of what the stone is to do. Whereas, at His coming He *empties* the earth; the stone *fills the earth.*

To say it another way, the stone smiting the image on its feet, breaking it in pieces, is the equivalent of *Christ, in His people, breaking the nations in pieces.* Zechariah prophesied just that in addressing Judah:

---

[270] Ellen G. White, *Testimonies for the Church*, vol. 5 (Mountain View, CA: Pacific Press, 1889), p. 136, emphasis mine.

"Behold, I will make Jerusalem a cup of trembling unto all the people round about .... And in that day [the great day of the Lord—one among many in the Old Testament] will I make Jerusalem a *burdensome stone* for all people: all that burden themselves with it *shall be cut in pieces*" (Zech. 12:2–3, emphasis mine).

In the Old Testament there were many *days of the Lord,* and they all prefigured the *great* day of the Lord. When looking at the small days of the Lord, when justice was being visited upon different groups of people addressed by the prophet, both Israel and Judah were visited several times; God was very patient with them. In each of the accounts preserved for our edification we can learn a lesson to be applied to that great day of the Lord. We are not so different from apostatizing Israel, are we?

In Chapter 51, Jeremiah projects Israel, God's people, as an instrument by which He will vindicate His name on earth:

"The portion of Jacob [Jesus] is not like them; for he is the former [one who forms] all things: and Israel is the rod of his inheritance: the LORD of hosts is his name. [He says,] *Thou art my battle axe and weapons of war*" (Jer. 51:19–20, emphasis mine).

Now notice how the passage continues:

And *with thee* will I break in pieces the horse and his rider; and *with thee* will I break in pieces the chariot and his rider; *with thee* also will I break in pieces man and woman; and *with thee* will I break in pieces old and young; and *with thee* will I break in pieces the young man and the maid; I will also break in pieces *with thee* the shepherd and his flock; and *with thee* will I break in pieces the husbandman and his yoke of oxen; and *with thee* will I break in pieces captains and rulers. (Jer. 51:21–23, emphasis mine)

The anomalous (unique) fact that the stone *is cut out of the mountain without hands* exhibits a separation of the one class from the other—a supernatural act. After the stone is cut out of the mountain, it smites the image upon its feet and thus breaks it in pieces. And as it continues to break the nations in pieces, *polarizing to itself the righteous out* of "every nation, and kindred, and tongue, and people" (Rev. 14:6), it grows, filling the whole earth, and is itself in turn symbolized by a *great* mountain, a kingdom. First, representing but the nucleus of

God's kingdom, the 144,000, it grows into a great multitude. Does that make sense?

We have already studied the phenomenon of the shaking, the coalescing of the 144,000, and their duty to give the loud cry, calling God's faithful out of Babylon, and we know that that group is an unnumbered throng. Many of God's faithful are there. A question uppermost in many minds when discussing this topic is this: which church affiliations are in the sealed group, and which church affiliations are in the called-out group? The *brand that we wear on our hip* often impedes the discussion of spiritual things with people. *No one* will ever be saved by church membership. There is but one way for anyone to be saved—that way is a personal confrontation with Jesus Himself. Once that salvation contract is made (and you are not a thief on a cross having just moments to live), you must now equip yourself in some way to survive and to serve. Armor is necessary in order to survive this wicked world—the best that money can buy. So, the shopping begins: the Baptist shop, the Episcopalian shop, the Jehovah's Witness shop, the Catholic shop. All of them have armor—some of it good, some of it not so good. The shopper must be astute, not only reading Scripture but being in consultation with the Holy Spirit who will guide them to the best shop, furnishing the best armor, to give the best possible chance to survive this wicked world until their day comes.

When I was seven, my folks shopped around and settled on the Seventh-day Adventist shop—it seemed to have superior equipment for survival. Then I took my own little journey, and when it was time for me to shop I, too, thought that the Seventh-day Adventist shop afforded the best spiritual armor. That's why I am a Seventh-day Adventist. I don't believe my little SDA tattoo is a passport to heaven. When crunch time comes, by far, the majority of us will be purged out, and those most prominent among us will lead the way to become our bitterest enemies. The church will then appear as about to fall, but it *will not!* It will go through. What is it that constitutes the appearance of falling? Do you think it might be the dissolution of our institutions? Our schools, medical institutions, and publishing houses closing, and even our church properties going down, and a majority of our membership being purged out, leaving only a noninstitutionalized few? The physical identity of Seventh-day Adventists as we know it would be gone. But those who radiate identity with God will survive—with-

Daniel 2: The Mystery Stone of Daniel 2

out buildings and without institutions. So, to focus largely on brand names might be distracting.

Read the prophet Joel. You will recognize the language as clearly referring to the great harvest work of the 144,000. This remarkable passage describes vividly the great harvest to be powered by the Holy Spirit between the closing Sunday law and the close of probation.

> Blow ye the trumpet in Zion, and sound an alarm in my holy mountain: let all the inhabitants of the land tremble: for the day of the LORD cometh, for it is nigh at hand; a day of darkness and of gloominess, a day of clouds and of thick darkness, as the morning spread upon the mountains: a great people and a strong; there hath not been ever the like, neither shall be any more after it, even to the years of many generations. A fire devoureth before them; and behind them a flame burneth: the land is as the garden of Eden before them [the promise], and behind them a desolate wilderness [the rejection]; yea, and nothing shall escape them. The appearance of them is as the appearance of horses; and as horsemen, so shall they run. Like the noise of chariots on the tops of mountains shall they leap, like the noise of a flame of fire that devoureth the stubble, as a strong people set in battle array [describes the orderliness with which God will finish His work]. Before their face the people shall be much pained: all faces shall gather blackness. They shall run like mighty men; they shall climb the wall like men of war; and they shall march every one on his ways, and they shall not break their ranks: neither shall one thrust another; they shall walk every one in his path; and when they fall upon the sword, they shall not be wounded. They shall run to and fro in the city; they shall run upon the wall, they shall climb up upon the houses; they shall enter in at the windows like a thief. The earth shall quake before them; the heavens shall tremble: the sun and the moon shall be dark, and the stars shall withdraw their shining: and the LORD shall utter his voice before his army: for his camp is very great: for he is strong that executeth his word: for the day of the LORD is great and very terrible; and who can abide it? (Joel 2:1–11)

Both Micah and Isaiah prophesy the same great-and-dreadful event in virtually the same words:

"But *in the last days* it shall come to pass, that the mountain of the house of the LORD shall be established in the top of the mountains, and it [the house of the Lord] shall be exalted above the hills; and *people shall flow unto it* (Mic. 4:1, emphasis mine)."

"And it shall come to pass in the last days, that the mountain of the LORD's house shall be established in the top of the mountains, and [the house of the Lord] shall be exalted above the hills; and *all nations shall flow unto it*" (Isa. 2:2, emphasis mine).

> *"And it shall come to pass in the last days, that the mountain of the LORD's house shall be established in the top of the mountains, and [the house of the Lord] shall be exalted above the hills; and all nations shall flow unto it" (Isa. 2:2, emphasis mine).*

The two references to mountains are symbolic of two churches: the first to God's purged few, the last to those remaining of the apostatized Babel. The stone and its *two mountains* are the *denouement* of the prophecy of Daniel 2. "[I]n the days of these kings [not *before* or *after*]" (Dan. 2:44, emphasis mine), will "many nations shall come, and say, Come, and let us go up to the *mountain of the LORD*, and to the house of the God of Jacob; and he will teach us of his ways, and we will walk in his paths: for the law shall *go forth of Zion,* and the word of the LORD from Jerusalem" (Micah 4:2, emphasis mine).

These verses describe the loud cry, the great harvest, the third angel's message, the latter rain effect, and the finishing of the gospel. Daniel knew it, and John affirmed it on Patmos. And now it is our turn to be told of these things that we may go forth and tell others before it is forever too late. Are we to concern ourselves with the credibility of our message? It is enough to tell it, and to tell it well. God, Himself, will bring conviction.

"Look unto me, and be ye saved, all the ends of the earth: for I am God, and there is none else. I have sworn by myself, the word is gone out of my mouth in righteousness, and shall not return, That unto me every knee shall bow, every tongue shall swear" (Isa. 45:22–23).

Who, with eyes to see and ears to hear, can fail to understand that heaven's great plan of redemption is of *such scope and magnitude* as to dwarf the ill-defined, constricted concepts held by earthlings, even by Christians in general? Many times, our understanding, our sight of this last gospel, is so small. We must enlarge our view of God's presence and management of the great controversy. Here He has traced the twin streams of power that will clash in the Battle of Armageddon. God selected Babylon to do a work for Him, which it did. But Satan perverted it, and Babylon became a cage for every hateful bird. He selected Medo-Persia to do a work for Him, but Satan perverted the service of Medo-Persia, preserving through them ancient Mithraism. And God selected Greece and pagan Rome, the last to wear the diadem. All of them stood in the light of God's commission. Even early papal Rome was God's church, though Satan's invasion turned it inside out. God has worked mightily within and through the Catholic Church, to the extent that He is allowed to work. He hasn't forsaken the Christians there. God does not pout or abandon human beings. He is long suffering, not willing that any should perish.

When we entered the Papal Wilderness, the "is not—yet" is part of prophetic history (1798), there is where God deliberately disabled the papal power—their power to persecute. And He did it to create a time of peace so that His tender shoot, the latter church, would have a congenial atmosphere in which to grow in preparation for the great final difficulties. William Miller came on the scene shortly after Napoleon took the pope captive. The pope was taken captive in 1798, and Miller began his studies in the early 1820s. A great religious awakening ensued, Bibles were printed, missionary societies were formed, and some of the most powerful hymns were written during this time. We are still in a time of peace and open borders that will continue until a national Sunday law will again kindle the fires of persecution. This will usher in the seventh, and final, persecuting power whose object will be to exterminate God's saints on the earth, the *Neo-Papal* period.

> So the heathen shall fear the name of the LORD, and all the kings of the earth thy glory [authority]. When the LORD shall build up Zion [the loud cry], he shall appear in his glory [authority]. He will regard the prayer of the destitute, and not despise their prayer. This shall be written for the generation to come: and the people which shall be created [of the stone] shall praise the LORD" (Ps. 102:15–18).

Appendix 3

Ezekiel 9: Countdown to Harvest— The Sealing of the 144,000

The last campaign before the long probation of sinful history plays itself out will be a divinely orchestrated harvest of souls in two stages. God, not willing that any should perish, has prepared for a grand slam finish. Already the faint sound of trumpets can be heard in the prophetic distance, calling God's people to the fields, white and ready for harvest. Who will go and work for Me today? Our response to that call will come from the heart, not the head. *Now* is the time to think, to decide, for then the action will be too swift to ponder and weigh such portentous issues.

> *The last campaign before the long probation of sinful human history plays itself out will be a divinely orchestrated harvest of souls in two stages. God, not willing that any should perish, has prepared for a grand slam finish.*

Has inspiration provided an agenda for those times such as never were since there was a nation (Dan. 12:1)? God has promised to do nothing except He reveals it to His servants, the prophets (Amos 3:7). We have only to look in the Holy Writ for what will prepare us to stand in the ranks then. The general order of things might proceed as follows:

1. ??? (This event will become clear as we proceed through this chapter.)

2. Time of trouble (little).
3. Calamities (shaking).
4. Latter rain.
5. Loud cry.
6. Harvest (eleventh hour).
7. Probation closes.
8. Time of trouble (Jacob's).
9. Battle of Armageddon.
10. Seventh plague.
11. The second coming of Jesus.

God's motive in arranging this sequence/collection of events is to call out a people, a work force, to:

- Demonstrate God's mercy and justice.
- Fit them for their mission.
- Send them on their way.
- Give the loud cry.
- Gather in the loyal from Babylon.
- Demonstrate the power of salvation.

Prior examples of this modus operandi are presented in Scripture.

Judges 7: Gideon gathered 32,000 warriors to challenge the Midianites. "And the LORD said unto Gideon, The people that are with thee are too many for me to give the Midianites into their hands, lest Israel vaunt themselves against me" (Judges 7:2). In the first cut, 22,000 left the ranks in fear. Of the second cut, only 300 remained with whom God accomplished a great work.

Genesis 14: Abraham was inspired to confront four kings and their combined forces with only 318 armed servants. He returned to Salem with all the hostages and much plunder, of which he gladly returned a tithe to Melchizedek.

1 Samuel 14: The army of King Saul had cowardly defected to the Philistine enemy or had retreated into caves out of fear. Jonathan, Saul's noble son, with his armor bearer, proposed to confront the Philistine garrison single-handedly. In the confidence of God, they initiated a defeat of the entire Philistine nation, breaking seven years of servile bondage.

2 Kings 1: Elijah, threatened by 100 armed soldiers, appealed to God, who promptly dispatched them and their captains with fire from heaven.

The question before God today is how to select a people to fitly represent Him in this, the final clash between good and evil. His number He declares to be 144,000 (Rev. 7:4, and how He will select them is described in Ezekiel 9). Until the fullness of time for that event, He has commanded the angels in charge to hold back the four (universal) winds of strife.

> And after these things I saw four angels standing on the four corners of the earth, holding the four winds of the earth, that the wind should not blow on the earth, nor on the sea, nor on any tree. And I saw another angel ascending from the east, having the seal of the living God: and he cried with a loud voice to the four angels, to whom it was given to hurt the earth and the sea, saying, Hurt not the earth, neither the sea, nor the trees, *till we have sealed the servants of our God in their foreheads.* (Rev. 7:1–3, emphasis mine)

After *what* things? After the judgment is set, the books are opened, and the seven seals have been introduced. After the opening of the first six seals, more particularly the opening of the sixth seal that reveals the visible manifestations of God's approaching presence into man's final affairs. Those signs are presented in two groups: first signs and last signs. Between these appearances the body of chapter 7 becomes viable. Angels hold back winds until a certain group has been sealed, sealed for a divine purpose explained in the final verses of the chapter. At this time God prepares for His final harvest. Remember the parable of the sower.

> The kingdom of heaven is [formed in this way] like a man [Jesus] who sowed good seed in his field [church]; but while men slept [were not alert], his enemy [Satan] came and sowed tares [apostates] among the wheat and went his way …. the grain had sprouted and … the tares also appeared …. So, the servants said to him, "Do you want us then to go and gather them up [the tares]?" But he said, "No …. [l]et both grow

together [in the church] until the harvest, and at the time of harvest I will say to the reapers [six angels], 'First gather together the tares and bind them in bundles to burn them, but gather the wheat into my barn.'" (Matt. 13:24–30, NKJV)

This parable is descriptive of a fullness of time right upon us when God will purify the church. He will go among the fields and select first fruits as a pledge of the full harvest. The application of these thoughts is significant to our times because it addresses an event that must precede the turmoil of full harvest activity. The separation of wheat and tares is represented as preceding the *winds of strife*. Follow the logic in the next four frames.

> John sees the elements of nature—earthquake, tempest, and political strife—represented as being held by four angels. These winds are under control until God gives the word to let them go. There is the safety of God's church. The angels of God do His bidding, holding back the winds of the earth, that the winds should not blow on the earth, nor on the sea, nor on any tree, *until the servants of God should be sealed in their foreheads.* The mighty angel is seen ascending from the east [or God's throne] (or sunrising). This mightiest of angels has in his hand the seal of the living God, or of Him who alone can give life, who can inscribe upon the foreheads the mark or inscription, to whom shall be granted immortality, eternal life. It is the voice of this highest angel that had authority to command the four angels to keep in check the four winds until this work was performed, and until he should give the summons to let them loose.[271]

> Even now he [Satan] is at work. In accidents and calamities by sea and by land, in great conflagrations, in fierce tornadoes and terrific hailstorms, in tempests, floods, cyclones, tidal waves, and earthquakes, in every place and in a thousand forms, Satan is exercising his power. He sweeps away the ripening harvest, and famine and distress follow. He imparts to the air a deadly taint, and thousands perish by the pestilence.

---

271 Ellen G. White, *Testimonies to Ministers and Gospel Workers* (Mountain View, CA: Pacific Press, 1923), pp. 444–445, emphasis mine.

These visitations are to become more and more frequent and disastrous.[272]

> And after these things I saw four angels standing on the four corners of the earth, holding the four winds of the earth, that the wind should not blow on the earth, nor on the sea, nor on any tree. And I saw another angel ascending from the east, having the seal of the living God: and he cried with a loud voice to the four angels, to whom it was given to hurt the earth and the sea, saying, Hurt not the earth, neither the sea, nor the trees, *till we have sealed the servants of our God in their foreheads.* (Rev. 7:1–3, emphasis mine)

The four angels are to hold back the four winds until the 144,000 are sealed. *Winds* here will be manifested in two notable events: (1) a universal Sunday closing law, and (2) a universal death decree. *Winds* are typical of war, bloodshed, and strife. *Four* is typical of the universal nature of the event. *First fruits* are a sample, a token number of the final yield. The apostle John and Ellen White were shown the group that is to make up the first fruits of those translated.

"And I heard the number of them which were sealed: and there were sealed an hundred and forty and four thousand of all the tribes of the children of Israel" (Rev. 7:4).

> I have tried in the fear of God to set before His people their danger and their sins, and have endeavored, to the best of my feeble powers, to arouse them. I have stated startling things, which, if they had believed, would have caused them distress and terror, and led them to zeal in repenting of their sins and iniquities. I have stated before them that, from what was shown me, *but a small number of those now professing to believe the truth would eventually be saved*—not because they could not be saved, but because they would not be saved in God's own appointed way.[273]

What will that small number allow the Holy Spirit to do for them?

---

272 Ellen G. White, *The Great Controversy* (Mountain View, CA: Pacific Press, 1911), pp. 589–590.
273 Ellen G. White, *Testimonies for the Church*, vol. 2 (Mountain View, CA: Pacific Press, 1871), p. 445, emphasis mine.

"And in their mouth was found *no guile*: for they are without fault before the *throne of God*" (Rev. 14:5, emphasis mine).

It looks simple enough! Just two conditions qualify them for membership in this elite group: (1) in their mouth is found no guile. When I was teaching school, one rule for entrance into my classroom was *no gum in the mouth.* Moving from the ridiculous to the sublime, what was found in Eve's mouth when she was beguiled by the serpent? A misstatement respecting God's instruction for life in the garden. The serpent had inquired, "Is it true that you cannot eat of any tree in the garden?" Eve replied, "They are *all* ours! Of every tree of the garden we may freely eat: but of the tree of the knowledge of good and evil we shall not eat of it *neither shall we touch it lest we die*" (Gen. 3:1–3, paraphrase).

> Eve had *overstated* the words of God's command. He had said to Adam and Eve, "But of the tree of the knowledge of good and evil, thou shalt not eat of it: for in the day that thou eatest thereof thou shalt surely die." In Eve's controversy with the serpent, she added, *"Neither shall ye touch it."* Here the subtlety of the serpent appeared. This statement of Eve gave him advantage; he plucked the fruit and placed it in her hand, using her own words, He hath said, If ye touch it, ye shall die.[274]

This experience illustrates clearly the nature of guile. From Eve's own mouth sprang the fatal trap. Guile is the ancient word for fish bait. The fish that allows guile in its mouth is caught thereby. The 144,000 are not so naïve. They are able to parse truth and error amid the most guileful of generations.

The second condition to qualify the small number for membership among the 144,000 is not only is no guile found in their mouths, but (2) they are without fault *before the throne of God.* Why before the throne? Because it is the judgment throne, and they have sent their faults before them in confession, asking forgiveness. Cannot any humble soul find membership here?

"Those who come up to every point, and stand every test, and overcome, be the price what it may, have heeded the counsel of the

---

[274] Ellen G. White, *Confrontation* (Washington, DC: Review and Herald, 1971), p. 14, emphasis mine.

True Witness, and they will receive the latter rain, and thus be fitted for translation."[275]

Is not God's grace sufficient for all His requirements? The sincere candidate need only submit his will to the loving desire of One who was tempted in all points like as we are *yet without sin*. But what is the testimony concerning the general response of the house of God?

> *God has made ample provision for even the frailest among us. Those who would be sealed to stand as first fruits need only avail themselves of His generosity.*

"It is a solemn statement that I make to the church, that *not one in twenty* whose names are registered upon the church books are prepared to close their earthly history, and would be as verily without God and without hope in the world as the common sinner."[276]

God has made ample provision for even the frailest among us. Those who would be sealed to stand as first fruits need only avail themselves of His generosity.

> It is not enough to have good intentions; it is not enough to do what a man thinks is right or what the minister tells him is right. His soul's salvation is at stake, *and he should search the Scriptures for himself.* However strong may be his convictions, however confident he may be that the minister knows what is truth, this is not his foundation. *He has a chart pointing out every waymark* on the heavenward journey, and *he ought not to guess at anything.*
>
> It is the first and highest duty of every rational being to learn from the Scriptures what is truth, and then to walk in the light and encourage others to follow his example. We should day by day *study the Bible diligently,* weighing every thought and comparing scripture with scripture. With divine help we are to *form our opinions for ourselves* as we are to answer for ourselves before God.

---

275 Ellen G. White, *Testimonies for the Church*, vol. 1 (Mountain View, CA: Pacific Press, 1868), p. 187.
276 Ellen G. White, *Christian Service* (Hagerstown, MD: Review and Herald, 1925), p. 41, emphasis mine.

The truths most plainly revealed in the Bible have been involved in doubt and darkness *by learned men*, who, with a pretense of great wisdom, teach that the Scriptures have a mystical, a secret, spiritual meaning not apparent in the language employed. These men are false teachers. It was to such a class that Jesus declared: "Ye know not the Scriptures, neither the power of God" Mark 12:24. *The language of the Bible should be explained according to its obvious meaning, unless a symbol or figure is employed.* Christ has given the promise: "If any man will do His will, he shall know of the doctrine" John 7:17. If men would but take the Bible as it reads, if there were no false teachers to mislead and confuse their minds, a work would be accomplished that would make angels glad and that would bring into the fold of Christ thousands upon thousands who are now wandering in error.[277]

"These [144,000] are they which were not defiled with women; for they are virgins. These are they which follow the Lamb whithersoever He goeth. These were redeemed from among men, being the firstfruits unto God and to the Lamb" (Rev. 14:4).

The first fruits are not defiled with women. That is, they are not called out of Babylon since they have diligently capitalized their blessings, having received knowledge of sanctifying truth ahead of the time of trouble. The parallel to this notion is that *they are virgins*. As a result, they have followed (and will continue to follow) the Lamb in every respect, a prime example of meekness. No doubting, no questions asked, perfect confidence in God. That they are redeemed among men is significant to first fruits. "First" implies more of the same yet to come. The Landlord went Himself among His orchards, fields, and flocks, selecting prime examples to show to the merchants—and this before commanding the reapers to gather in the bulk of the harvest.

What is the antitype of this allegory? How will God select His own first fruits from among those members of His remnant church?

"All the world will be on one side or the other of the question. The battle of Armageddon will be fought. And that day must find none of us sleeping. Wide awake we must be, as wise virgins having oil in our vessels with our lamps. The power of the Holy Ghost must be upon us

---

[277] Ellen G. White, *The Great Controversy* (Mountain View, CA: Pacific Press, 1911), pp. 598–599, emphasis mine.

and the Captain of the Lord's host will stand at the head of the angels of heaven to direct the battle."[278]

The context of this statement includes that event just prior to the Sunday closing crisis and does not apply to general Christendom.

"The time of the judgment is a most solemn period, when the Lord gathers His own from among the tares. Those who have been members of the same family are separated. *A mark is placed upon the righteous.* 'They shall be Mine, saith the Lord of hosts, in that day when I make up My jewels; and I will spare them, as a man spareth his own son that serveth him.'"[279]

God gathers His own *from among the tares*. Where had the enemy sowed tare seed? *In the Master's field*—not in the public domain. What is symbolized by "the Master's field"? His *church!* Therefore, the Lord must begin there. Why are the righteous to be distinguished by a *mark*? Something subsequent to the mark must be in the offing! As a consequence of the mark, the Lord of hosts declares, *I will spare them.*

> The same *angel who visited Sodom* is sounding the note of warning, "Escape for thy life." The bottles of God's wrath cannot be poured out to destroy the wicked and their works until all the people of God have been judged, and the cases of the living as well as the dead are decided. And even after the saints are sealed with the seal of the living God, His elect will have trials *individually*. Personal afflictions will come; but the furnace is closely watched by an eye that will not suffer the gold to be consumed. The indelible mark of God is upon them. God can plead that His own name is written there.[280]

We will discover that the bottles of God's wrath will be poured out in two distinct phases of end-time justice. Agents of divine destruction in these cases are clearly defined as heavenly angels.

> He who presides over His church and the destinies of nations is carrying forward the last work to be accomplished for this world. *To His angels He gives the commission to execute His judgments.* Let the ministers awake, let them take in the situation. The work of judgment begins *at the sanctuary*. "And,

---

278 Ellen G. White, *Last Day Events* (Boise, ID: Pacific Press, 1992), pp. 250–251.
279 Ellen G. White, *Testimonies to Ministers and Gospel Workers* (Mountain View, CA: Pacific Press, 1923), p. 234, emphasis mine.
280 Ibid., p. 446, emphasis mine.

behold, six men came from the way of the higher gate, which lieth *toward the north,* and every man a slaughter weapon in his hand; and one man among them was clothed with linen, with a writer's inkhorn by his side: and they went in, and stood beside the brazen altar." Read Ezekiel 9:2–7. The command is, "Slay utterly old and young, both maids, and little children, and women: but come not near any man upon whom is the mark; and *begin at My sanctuary.*"[281]

Here the focus narrows dramatically. He who presides over His church is carrying forward the last divine work. Notice the commencing point: *ministers* first, and then the *sanctuary.* It will not be a work of mercy; it will be a work of judgment. And then we are admonished to read the Scripture passage, Ezekiel 9:2–7, clearly implying that it must be understood in the context of this judgment. Let us look at Ezekiel 9 to discover the divine methodology in selecting His first fruits.

He cried also *in mine ears with a loud voice,* saying, Cause them that have charge over the city to draw near, even every man with his destroying weapon in his hand. And, behold, six men came from the way of the higher gate, which lieth toward the north, and every man a slaughter weapon in his hand; and one man among them was clothed with linen, with a writer's inkhorn by his side: and they went in, and stood beside the brasen altar. (Ezek. 9:1–2, emphasis mine)

The message must be of the utmost importance to have God shouting with a loud voice directly into the prophet's ears. God is not addressing Ezekiel directly—He is speaking to those who have charge over the city (Zion/church). They are to assemble themselves beside the brazen altar, fully equipped for some grisly task. Those in charge consist of six men whose point of origin is from the *north.* This is significant, because *north* is a divine location.

"For thou hast said in thine heart, I will ascend into heaven, I will exalt my throne above the stars of God: I will sit also upon the mount of the congregation, *in the sides of the north*: I will ascend above the heights of the clouds; I will be like the most High" (Isa. 14:13–14, emphasis mine).

---

281 Ibid., pp. 431–432, emphasis mine.

Here, *north* is situated first in heaven, above the stars, or station of angels. The station of angels is further described as upon the mount of congregation, or the great meeting hall of heaven, which is located in the sides of the *north*, the place where God personally resides.

During my own spiritual crisis when I was a young man of thirty, I experienced an epiphany. Struggling with the thoughts of my head, I was out in the front yard examining a new growth of shade tree when I was *taken off,* or I was *visited,* or I experienced a confrontation with God. I seemed to be arrested, possessed of a voiceless messenger *from the north direction*. At the time I sensed coldness, emptiness, a void—imminent abandonment. I *knew* it was the voice of God. I sensed that my probation was to be shortly terminated, and that God's patience with me was nearly exhausted. For a long time, I puzzled over the *north* element in this terrifying experience. I have since associated it with God's address.

The six angels who have charge of the city (Zion/church) are aware of their commission and its purpose. They are equipped with garments of authority, a code of discrimination, marking instruments, and weapons of execution. They await the command to proceed. What are we to make of this? It is most certainly apocryphal, but is it literal, or is it figurative?

"The time of the harvest will fully determine the character of the two classes specified under the figure of the tares and the wheat. The work of separation is given to the angels of God [six of them?], and not committed into the hands of any man."[282]

"I then saw the third angel. Said my accompanying angel, 'Fearful is his work. Awful is his mission. He is the angel that is to select the wheat from the tares, and seal, or bind, the wheat for the heavenly garner [the one with the writer's inkhorn?]. These things should engross the whole mind, the whole attention.'"[283]

We will pursue the question of figurative or literal application shortly, but first let us look at Ezekiel's further testimony.

And the glory [authority] of the God of Israel rose from between the Guardian Angels where it had rested and stood above the entrance to the Temple. And the Lord called to the man with the writer's case and said to him, "Walk through the streets of Jerusalem [Zion/church] and put a mark on the foreheads of the men who weep and sigh

---
[282] Ibid., p. 47.
[283] Ellen G. White, *Early Writings* (Washington, DC: Review and Herald, 1882), p. 118.

because of all the sins they see around them [in the church]. (Ezek. 9:3, TLB)

A process of great import is being launched upon the institution of God's favor in the earth: One who has had charge of the church is to sort through the membership, placing a mark upon those who grieve over Laodicean carelessness. The criterion of discrimination to be used by the marking angel is *not* one of doctrine but of heart: have they developed the capacity to mourn insult directed at God?

> And to the others he said in mine hearing, Go ye after him through the city, and smite: let not your eye spare, neither have ye pity: Slay utterly old and young, both maids, and little children, and women: but come not near any man upon whom is the mark; and begin at my sanctuary. Then they began at the ancient men which were before the house. And he said unto them, Defile the house, and fill the courts with the slain: go ye forth. And they went forth, and slew in the city. (Ezek. 9:5–7)

The playing out of the vision was for Ezekiel's benefit—and thus, for ours. We must understand God's work in finishing sin and rebellion. The time of mercy passes, making way for final justice, which not only begins at God's house but commences in the very sanctuary of God's house. The work is to be a complete work, one in which probation is utterly absent. All categories of membership have voted and are now fixed in their opinions. Beginning with the ancient men (leadership/General Conference), and without regard to erstwhile protocol (rules of purification), the very priesthood is to be sorted out on the spot, and those found wanting executed summarily. While Ezekiel watched, they went forth to carry out their grisly commission.

> And it came to pass, while they were slaying them, and I was left, that I fell upon my face, and cried, and said, Ah Lord GOD! wilt thou destroy all the residue of Israel in thy pouring out of thy fury upon Jerusalem? Then said he unto me, The iniquity of the house of Israel and Judah is exceeding great, and the land is full of blood, and the city full of perverseness: for they say, The LORD hath forsaken the earth, and the LORD seeth not. And as for me also, mine eye shall not spare, neither will I have pity, but I will recompense their way upon their head. (Ezek. 9:8–10)

Ezekiel is horrified. Unlike Elijah who was certain that in all Israel he only had not bent the knee, Ezekiel sensed a larger body of faithfulness than were marked by the angel. In astonishment he cried out, "Ah, Lord God! Will your fury against Jerusalem wipe out everyone left in Israel?" God replies, "The iniquity of the house is *very great*. The land is full of murder and injustice. They insist that God is on vacation, that He is not concerned. Therefore, they have been weighed in the balance and will not be spared."

"With unerring accuracy the Infinite One still keeps an account with all nations. While His mercy is tendered with calls to repentance, this account will remain open; but when the figures reach a certain amount which God has fixed, the ministry of His wrath commences. The account is closed. Divine patience ceases. There is no more pleading of mercy in their behalf."[284]

"I would say that we are living in a most solemn time. In the last vision given me, I was shown the startling fact that but *a small portion of those who now profess the truth will be sanctified by it and be saved*. Many will get above the simplicity of the work. They will conform to the world, cherish idols, and become spiritually dead."[285]

The prophet of our time confirms what was shown to Ezekiel. The highly touted numbers of increased membership will be shown to be greatly inflated. What will be the end of the matter?

"And, behold, the man clothed with linen, which had the inkhorn by his side, reported the matter, saying, I have done as thou has commanded me" (Ezek. 9:11).

> I saw angels hurrying to and fro in heaven. An angel with a writer's inkhorn by his side returned from the earth and reported to Jesus that his work was done, and the saints were numbered and sealed. Then I saw Jesus, who had been ministering before the ark containing the ten commandments, throw down the censer. He raised His hands, and with a loud voice said, *"It is done."*[286]

In Ezekiel 9, Ezekiel was shown what the 144,000 must do to receive the seal. John was shown in Revelation 7 how many, and from

---

[284] Ellen G. White, *Testimonies for the Church*, vol. 5 (Mountain View, CA: Pacific Press, 1889), p. 208.

[285] Ellen G. White, *Testimonies for the Church*, vol. 1 (Mountain View, CA: Pacific Press, 1868), pp. 608–609, emphasis mine.

[286] Ellen G. White, *Early Writings* (Washington, DC: Review and Herald, 1882), p. 280.

where they came. Let us now pursue the question: is Ezekiel 9 to be understood literally?

> Satan will work his miracles to deceive; he will set up his power as supreme. The church may appear as about to fall, but it does not fall. *It remains, while the sinners in Zion will be sifted out*—the chaff separated from the precious wheat. *This is a terrible ordeal*, but nevertheless it must take place. None but those who have been overcoming by the blood of the Lamb and the word of their testimony will be found with the loyal and true, without spot or stain of sin, without guile in their mouths.[287]

Scriptural examples of separation theory abound. Consider four examples:

- Matthew 13:30   wheat/tares
- Malachi 3:3   gold/dross
- Matthew 13:47   good fish/bad fish
- Matthew 25:32   sheep/goats

Now let's examine an Old Testament event that connects with that of our present concern.

> When God was about to smite the firstborn of Egypt, He commanded the Israelites to gather their children from among the Egyptians into their own dwellings and strike their door posts with blood, *that the destroying angel might see it and pass over their homes.* It was the work of parents to gather in their children. This is your work, this is my work, and the work of every mother who believes the truth. The angel is to place a mark upon the forehead of all who are separated from sin and sinners, and *the destroying angel will follow, to slay utterly both old and young.*[288]

Study the ninth chapter of Ezekiel. *These words will be literally fulfilled*; yet the time is passing, and the people are asleep. They refuse to humble their souls and to be converted. Not a great while longer will the Lord bear with the people who

---

[287] Ellen G. White, *Maranatha* (Washington, DC: Review and Herald, 1976), p. 32, emphasis mine.
[288] Ellen G. White, *Testimonies for the Church*, vol. 5 (Mountain View, CA: Pacific Press, 1889), p. 505, emphasis mine.

have such great and important truths revealed to them, but who refuse to bring these truths into their individual experience. The time is short. God is calling. Will you hear? Will you receive His message? Will you be converted before it is too late? Soon, very soon, every case will be decided for eternity.[289]

"It is not His [God's] will that they shall get into controversy over questions which will not help them spiritually, such as, Who is to compose the hundred and forty-four thousand? Those who are the elect of God will in a short time know without question."[290]

"We are amid the perils of the last days, the time will soon come when the prophecy of *Ezekiel 9* will be fulfilled; that prophecy should be carefully studied, for it will *be fulfilled to the very letter.*"[291]

The dominos of final events, then, have been identified for us and appear in their order:

1. Purification of the church.
2. Time of trouble (little).
3. Calamities (shaking).
4. Latter rain.
5. Loud cry.
6. Harvest (eleventh hour).
7. Probation closes.
8. Time of trouble (Jacob's).
9. Battle of Armageddon.
10. Seventh plague.
11. The second coming of Jesus.

The day of God's vengeance is just upon us. *The seal of God will be placed upon the foreheads of those only who sigh and cry for the abominations done in the land.* Those who link in sympathy with the world are eating and drinking with the drunken, and will surely be destroyed with the workers of iniquity. "The

---

[289] Ellen G. White, *Manuscript Releases*, vol. 18 (Silver Spring, MD: Ellen G. White Estate, 1990), p. 236, emphasis mine.
[290] Ellen G. White, *Selected Messages*, book 1 (Washington, DC: Review and Herald, 1958), p. 174.
[291] Ellen G. White, *The Ellen G. White 1888 Materials* (Washington, DC: Ellen G. White Estate, 1987), p. 1303, emphasis mine.

eyes of the Lord are upon the righteous, and His ears are open unto their cry;" but "the face of the Lord is against them that do evil." Psalm 34:15, 16.

Our own course of action will determine whether we shall receive the seal of the living God, or be cut down by the destroying weapons. Already a few drops of God's wrath have fallen upon the earth; but when the seven last plagues shall be poured out without mixture into the cup of His indignation, then it will be forever too late to repent, and find shelter. No atoning blood will then wash away the stains of sin.

"And at that time shall Michael stand up, the great prince which standeth for the children of thy people; and there shall be a time of trouble, such as never was since there was a nation even to that same time: and at that time thy people shall be delivered, everyone that shall be found written in the book." Daniel 12:1. When this time of trouble comes, every case is decided; there is no longer probation, no longer mercy for the impenitent. The seal of the living God is upon His people.

This small remnant, unable to defend themselves in the deadly conflict with the powers of earth that are marshaled by the dragon host, make God their defense.[292]

---

[292] Ellen G. White, *Christian Experience and Teachings of Ellen G. White* (Mountain View, CA: Pacific Press, 1922), pp. 187–188, emphasis mine.

Appendix 4

Daniel 11: The King of the North vs. the King of the South

The "King of the North" and his counterpart, the "King of the South," have been much discussed within Adventist circles since the very early days—who they were, and the place of each in the scheme of prophetic fulfillment. For the most part, a systematic study with careful attention to hermeneutic rules has been haphazard. For example, the term "king" implies a kingdom, or an anointed political figure. The terms "north" and "south" imply opposition, tension, or strife.

Such a study would have traced the origin of the terms and the various contexts that sustain them. It would identify the connection, if any, to the people of God. It is axiomatic that *all* things scriptural are applicable in some way to final events in the great controversy, and that Scripture itself will explain the mysteries presented.

The symbol "King of the North" begins in Scripture as one of the divisions of the Grecian Empire, then is used to symbolize the pagan Roman Empire, and emerges finally as the great apostasy that controls the church of the Dark Ages. In each of these transmogrifications a series of heads has sustained the philosophy and goal represented by the term. Careless exegetes have seized on notable historic figures and events and have fabricated spurious doctrine leading astray multitudes.

The archetypal "King of the North" is God Himself. In fact, God is the only true King of the North. Throughout the Old Testament, north was the point of the compass assigned to God, the place from which God ruled.

Daniel 11: The King of the North vs. the King of the South

"And he shall kill it on the side of the altar *northward*, before the LORD: and the priests, Aaron's sons, shall sprinkle his blood round about upon the altar" (Lev. 1:11, emphasis mine).

"Great is the LORD, and greatly to be praised in the city of our God, in the mountain of his holiness. Beautiful for situation, the joy of the whole earth, is Mount Zion, on the *sides of the north*, the city of the great King" (Ps. 48:1–2, emphasis mine).

> Mount Zion, the city of God, the place from which God ruled ancient Israel, was said to be on the *side of the north*. Ancient Jerusalem contained two hills; the northernmost one was Zion. It is the place where Solomon later built the temple. In the temple was the Shekinah glory, the literal presence of God on earth. Ezekiel the prophet was taken to the north gate of the temple, where the rebellious Israelites had erected an image of jealousy. There Ezekiel saw the glory of God at the *north gate* (Ezekiel 8:3, 4). Thus, it would be logical for the ancient Jews to look to the north as the place where God's presence was—the place from which He ruled.[293]

Isaiah declared that God would raise up a deliverer for His people from the Babylonian captivity who would come from the north and from the east (Isa. 41:25). While referring to Cyrus, who rescued God's people from Babylon, other Scripture employs it as a type of the final deliverance of God's people. Daniel appears to echo this sentiment.

"[T]idings out of the east and out of the north shall trouble him" (Dan. 11:44).

Satan is the original usurper of the King of the North. He aspired to God's throne in heaven and continues his effort more than 6,000 years later. The warfare that ensued in heaven was followed by a notable success in Eden. Satan immediately claimed to be prince of this world—the King of the North, ruler of planet earth.

> *The warfare that ensued in heaven was followed by a notable success in Eden. Satan immediately claimed to be prince of this world—the King of the North, ruler of planet earth.*

---

293 Russell Burrill, "The New World Order," Seminars Unlimited, p. 72, emphasis mine.

"For thou hast said in thine heart, I will ascend into heaven, I will exalt my throne above the stars of God: I will sit also upon the mount of the congregation, *in the sides of the north*" (Isa. 14:13, emphasis mine).

In the New Testament, Mount Zion refers to the church of Jesus Christ.

"But ye are come unto mount Sion, and unto the city of the living God, the heavenly Jerusalem, and to an innumerable company of angels, to the general assembly and church of the firstborn, which are written in heaven, and to God the Judge of all, and to the spirits of just men made perfect" (Heb. 12:22–23).

> *Control of Mount Zion is Satan's final attempt to dominate the church of the last days.*

And so the battle rages. Control of Mount Zion is Satan's final attempt to dominate the church of the last days. A synopsis of the King of the North would proceed from Seleucus, one of the four generals who divided the kingdom of Greece upon the death of Alexander the Great. Seleucus absorbed the portions of Cassander and Lysimachus, except for Macedonia. Ptolemy retained control of Egypt and North Africa on the south shore of the Mediterranean Sea. The relationships were fierce, and the issues settled by warfare. These events are an important part of scriptural history because they directly impinged God's chosen people caught between them, as well as for other notable reasons which will be developed later.

Various kings arose in succession to sustain the rivalry between Syria on the north and Egypt on the south. When the Roman power emerged to conquer them both, Rome assumed the northern mantle. This mantle passed smoothly from pagan Rome to papal Rome (AD 538), guaranteeing unbroken hostility toward God's people. The King of the South was overshadowed until AD 1798, when in figure the philosophy of Egypt rises again to dominance, garbed in atheism, humanism, and spiritualism which have sustained a prevailing influence in science, religion, and politics throughout the nineteenth and twentieth centuries. Soon, however, the King of the North (papacy), who has been steadily gaining in strength, will again dominate in world affairs, poised for the final clash between Christ and Satan.

The King of the South

The King of the South emerges as one of the divisions of the Grecian Empire, much as did the King of the North. The initial title referred particularly to the Egyptian division under the Ptolemies. From verse 25 onward, the King of the South appears to be losing power to the King of the North until the King of the South virtually disappears. Egypt ceased to be a major power in 31 BC in the battle of Actium, when Octavius defeated the forces of Marcus Antonius and Cleopatra.[294]

The Daniel 11 narrative from verses 31 through 39 describe a time when the King of the North is dominant, symbolizing the church of the Dark Ages. During this time (the 1,260 years of papal supremacy), there is no reference to the King of the South. However, suddenly in verse 40 the King of the South reappears, entering the prophetic arena with great fury. Daniel introduces the biblical time of the end, AD 1798, the conclusion of the 1,260 year prophecy.

"And at the time of the end shall the king of the south push at him: and the king of the north shall come against him like a whirlwind, with chariots, and with horsemen, and with many ships; and he shall enter into the countries, and shall overflow and pass over" (Dan. 11:40).

This passage can be confusing because of a convention in modern writing. Where pronouns abound, the present rule is the antecedent of last mention. However, in ancient writing the rule is the antecedent of *first mention*. In the verse above, which of them, the King of the North or the King of the South, "shall enter into the countries and shall overflow and pass over"? Consistent with the context of Daniel's time, it must be the King of the South. In what guise does the King of the South now reappear? What power attacks the King of the North around 1798? Whatever the power, it must be consistent with the characteristics evinced by ancient Egypt. How did Egypt relate to the covenant people? Is there a spiritual connecting link in Scripture to the power that brings an end to the papal supremacy?

> Of all nations presented in Bible history, Egypt most boldly denied the existence of the living God and resisted His commands. No monarch ever ventured upon more open and highhanded rebellion against the authority of Heaven than did the king of Egypt. When the message was brought him by Moses, in the name of the Lord, Pharaoh proudly answered: "Who

---

[294] "The Battle of Actium," History, https://1ref.us/1k6 (accessed February 9, 2021).

is Jehovah, that I should hearken unto His voice to let Israel go? I know not Jehovah, and moreover I will not let Israel go." Exodus 5:2, A.R.V. This is atheism, and the nation represented by Egypt would give voice to a similar denial of the claims of the living God and would manifest a like spirit of unbelief and defiance. "The great city" is also compared, "spiritually," to Sodom. The corruption of Sodom in breaking the law of God was especially manifested in licentiousness. And this sin was also to be a pre-eminent characteristic of the nation that should fulfill the specifications of this scripture.

According to the words of the prophet, then, a little before the year 1798 some power of satanic origin and character would rise to make war upon the Bible. And in the land where the testimony of God's two witnesses should thus be silenced, there would be manifest the atheism of the Pharaoh and the licentiousness of Sodom. This prophecy received a most exact and striking fulfillment in the history of France [during the Revolution in 1798.][295]

The context of Revelation 11 is set in chapter 10, which describes the appearance of the little scroll that later was so bitter in John's stomach, rehearsing the disappointment of 1844. Chapter 11 introduces the time of the judgment and the events leading up to it. The beginning verses review the suppression and abuse of Scripture practiced by papal Rome. Verses 7 and 10 describe the French Revolution and the rise of the Age of Reason. For three and a half years atheism dominated the politics of France. Catch the reflection as history repeats itself.

> *In Egypt's notable confrontation with God, Moses stood before Pharaoh and demanded that Egypt let God's people go. Pharaoh's reply is indicative of the power and mindset of atheism*

In Egypt's notable confrontation with God, Moses stood before Pharaoh and demanded that Egypt let God's people go. Pharaoh's reply is indicative of the power and mindset of atheism ("Who is the LORD, that I should ... let Israel

---

295 Ellen G. White, *The Great Controversy* (Mountain View, CA: Pacific Press, 1911), p. 269.

go?" [Exod. 5:2]), denial and defiance of God's eternal authority. Thus, throughout biblical history Egypt has become a symbol of defiant atheism.

> The power which arises around 1798, at the very time the king of the south is reactivated in Daniel 11:40, is also a power that is linked to Egypt in Revelation 11:18. This is an unmistakable reference to the French Revolution at the end of the eighteenth century. During this time, France totally rebelled against medieval Catholicism, against the papacy, and against all religion, and tried to institute atheism. This revolution began in 1798 and continued to 1801. It was one of the most trying times in the history of France and Europe. Its implications continue well beyond the scope of the actual Revolution, as we shall shortly see.
>
> Atheism reached its height in France from November 26, 1793, when the decree abolishing religion was issued in Paris, to June 17, 1797, when the restriction against religion was removed. Amazingly, this terrible period lasted for exactly three and a half years, just as predicted in Revelation 11:9.[296]

The book of Revelation equates this revolution to Egypt, Sodom, and Jerusalem: Egypt for its atheism, Sodom for its immorality, and Jerusalem for its attacks against Christ (Rev. 11:8). The result of the French Revolution was the smashing of the medieval papacy foretold in Daniel 11:40, but the ideas then promulgated did not die. Even today this period is recognized as the beginning of the modern atheistic movement. In the aftermath of the French Revolution, attacks by the French against the papacy increased. Berthier, under Napoleon, took the pope captive; George Hegel became the father of modern atheism in philosophy and religion; Charles Darwin heralded the ascendancy of evolution in the field of science; Karl Marx spawned godless communism, and eventually the entire eastern bloc of Europe, China, and many developing nations of the earth adopted the communist belief system. Western society abandoned their divine philosophies of government and education and imbibed instead a secular humanism that has dominated thought and practice for the past several decades. Thus, during most of the twentieth century the King of the South has become the dominant philosophy of the world.

---
296 Russell Burrill, "The New World Order," Seminars Unlimited, p. 72, pp. 86–87.

Appendix 5
From Laodicea to the 144,000

E. G. White

I was shown that *love of the world* has to a great extent shut Jesus from the church. God calls for a change, a surrender of all to Him. *Unless the mind is educated to dwell upon religious themes* [and is trained to be exercised in these things], it will be weak and feeble in this direction. But while dwelling upon worldly enterprises, it will be strong; for in this direction it has been cultivated, and has strengthened with exercise. The reason it is so difficult for men and women to live religious lives is because they do not exercise the mind unto godliness. It is trained to run in an opposite direction. Unless the mind is constantly exercised in obtaining spiritual knowledge and in seeking to understand the mystery of godliness, it is *incapable* of appreciating eternal things because it has no experience in that direction. This is the reason why nearly all consider it uphill business to serve the Lord.

When the heart is divided, dwelling principally upon the things of the world, and but little upon the things of God, there can be no special increase of spiritual strength. Worldly enterprises claim the larger share of the mind, calling into exercise its powers; therefore in this direction there is strength and power to claim more and more of the interest and affections, while less and less is reserved to devote to God. It is impossible for the soul to flourish while prayer is not a special exercise of the mind. Family or public prayer alone is not sufficient. Secret prayer is very important; in solitude the soul is laid bare to the inspecting eye of God, and every motive is scrutinized. Secret prayer! How precious! The soul communing with God! Secret prayer is to be heard only by the prayer-hearing God. No curious ear is to receive the burden of such petitions. In secret prayer the soul is free from surrounding influences, free from excitement. Calmly, yet fervently, will it reach out after God. Secret prayer is frequently perverted, and its sweet designs lost, by loud vocal prayer. Instead of the calm, quiet trust and faith in God, the soul drawn out in low, humble tones, the voice is raised to a loud pitch, and excitement is encouraged, and secret prayer loses its softening, sacred influence. There is a storm of feeling, a storm of words, making it impossible to discern the still, small voice that speaks to the soul while engaged in its secret, true, heartfelt devotion. Secret prayer, properly carried out, is productive of great good. But prayer [thought to be secret] which is made public to the entire family and neighborhood is not secret prayer, even though thought to be, and divine strength is not received from it. Sweet and abiding will be the influence emanating from Him who seeth in secret, whose ear is open to answer the prayer arising from the heart. By calm, simple faith the soul holds communion with God and gathers to itself divine rays of light to strengthen and sustain it to endure the conflicts of Satan. God is our tower of strength.

Jesus has left us word: "Watch ye therefore: for ye know not when the Master of the house cometh, at even, or at midnight, or at the cockcrowing, or in the morning: lest coming suddenly He find you sleeping. And what I say unto you I say unto all, Watch." We are waiting and watching for the return of the Master, who is to bring the morning, lest coming suddenly He find us sleeping. What time is here referred to? Not the revelation of Christ in the clouds of heaven to find a people asleep. No; but to His return from His ministration in the most holy place of the heavenly sanctuary, when He lays off His priestly attire and clothes Himself with garments of vengeance, and when the mandate goes forth: "He that is unjust, let him be unjust still: and he which is filthy, let him be filthy still: and he that is righteous, let him be righteous still; and he that is holy, let him be holy still."

When Jesus ceases to plead for man, the cases of all are forever decided. This is the time of reckoning with His servants. To those who have neglected the preparation of purity and holiness, which fits them to be waiting ones to welcome their Lord, the sun sets in gloom and darkness, and rises not again. Probation closes; Christ's intercessions cease in heaven. This time finally comes suddenly upon all, and those who have neglected to purify their souls by obeying the truth are found sleeping. They became weary of waiting and watching; they became indifferent in regard to the coming of their Master. They longed not for His appearing, and thought there was no need of such continued, persevering watching. They had been disappointed in their expectations and might be again. They concluded there was time enough yet to arouse. They would be sure not to lose the opportunity of securing an earthly treasure. It would be safe to get all of this world they could. And in securing this object, they lost all anxiety and interest in the appearing of the Master. They became indifferent and careless, as though His coming was yet in the distance. But while their interest was buried up in their worldly gains, the work closed in the heavenly sanctuary, and they were unprepared. *If such had only known that the work of Christ in the heavenly sanctuary would close so soon,* how differently would they have conducted! How earnestly would they have watched! The Master anticipated all this, and gave them timely warning in the command to watch. He distinctly states the suddenness of His coming. He does not measure the time, lest we shall neglect a momentary preparation, and in our indolence look ahead to the time when we think He will come, and defer the preparation. "Watch ye therefore: for ye know not." Yet this foretold uncertainty, and suddenness at last, fails to rouse us from stupidity to earnest wakefulness, and to quicken our watchfulness for our expected Master. Those not found waiting and watching are finally surprised in their unfaithfulness. The Master comes, and instead of their being ready to open unto Him immediately, they are locked in worldly slumber, and are lost at last.

A company was presented before me in contrast to the one described. They were waiting and watching. Their eyes were directed heavenward, and the words of their Master were upon their lips: "What I say unto you I say unto all, Watch." "Watch ye therefore: for ye know not when the Master of the house cometh, at even, or at midnight, or at the cockcrowing, or in the morning: lest coming suddenly He find you sleeping." The Lord intimates a delay before the morning finally dawns. But He would not have them give way to weariness, nor relax their earnest watchfulness, because the morning does not open upon them as soon as they expected. The waiting ones were represented to me as looking upward. They were encouraging one another by repeating these words: *"The first and second watches are past. We are in the third watch,* waiting and watching for the Master's return. There remains but a little period of watching now." I saw some becoming weary; their eyes were directed downward, and they were engrossed with earthly things, and were unfaithful in watching. They were saying: "In the first watch we expected our Master, but were disappointed. We thought surely He would come in the second watch, but that passed, and He came not. We may be again disappointed. We need not be so particular. He may not come in the following watch. We are in the third watch, and now we think it best to lay up our treasure on the earth, that we may be secure against want." Many were sleeping, stupefied with the cares of this life and allured by the deceitfulness of riches from their waiting, watching position.

Angels were represented to me as looking on with intense interest to mark the appearance of the weary yet faithful watchers, lest they be too sorely tried, and sink under the toil and hardships made doubly severe because their brethren had been diverted from their watch, and become drunk with worldly cares and beguiled by worldly prosperity. These heavenly angels grieved that those who were once watching should, by their indolence and unfaithfulness, increase the trial and burdens of those who were earnestly and perseveringly endeavoring to maintain their waiting, watching position.

I saw that it was impossible to have the affections and interests engrossed in worldly cares, to be increasing earthly possessions, and yet be in a waiting, watching position, as our Saviour has commanded. Said the angel: "They can secure but one world. In order to acquire the heavenly treasure, they must sacrifice the earthly. They cannot have both worlds." I saw how necessary a continuance of faithfulness in watching was in order to escape the delusive snares of Satan. He leads those who should be waiting and watching, to take an advance step toward the world; they have no intention of going further, but that one step removed them that much further from Jesus, and made it easier to take the next; and thus step after step is taken toward the world, *until all the difference between them and the world is a profession, a name only.* They have lost their peculiar, holy character, and there is nothing except their profession to distinguish them from the lovers of the world around them. I saw that watch after watch was in the past. Because of this, should there be a lack of vigilance? Oh, no! There is the greater necessity of unceasing watchfulness, for now the moments are fewer than before the passing of the first watch. Now the period of waiting is necessarily shorter than at first. If we watched with unabated vigilance then, how much more need of double watchfulness in the second watch. The passing of the second watch has brought us to the third, and now it is inexcusable to abate our watchfulness. The third watch calls for threefold earnestness. To become impatient now would be to lose all our earnest, persevering watching heretofore. *The long night of gloom is trying;* but the morning is deferred in mercy, because if the Master should come, so many would be found unready. God's unwillingness to have His people perish has been the reason for so long delay. But the coming of the morning to the faithful, and of the night to the unfaithful, is right upon us. By waiting and watching, God's people are to manifest their peculiar character, their separation from the world. By our watching position we are to show that we are truly strangers and pilgrims upon the earth. The difference between those who love the world and those who love Christ is so plain as to be unmistakable. While worldlings are all earnestness and ambition to secure earthly treasure, God's people are not conformed to the world, but show by their earnest, watching, waiting position that they are transformed; that their home is not in this world, but that they are seeking a better country, even a heavenly.

I hope, my dear brethren and sisters, that you will not pass your eye over these words without thoroughly considering their import. As the men of Galilee stood looking steadfastly toward heaven, to catch, if possible, a glimpse of their ascending Saviour, two men in white apparel, heavenly angels commissioned to comfort them for the loss of the presence of their Saviour, stood by them and inquired: "Ye men of Galilee, why stand ye gazing up into heaven? this same Jesus, which is taken up from you into heaven, shall so come in like manner as ye have seen Him go into heaven."

God designs that His people shall fix their eyes heavenward, looking for the glorious appearing of our Lord and Saviour Jesus Christ. While the attention of worldlings is turned to the various enterprises, ours should be to the heavens; our faith should reach further and further into the glorious mysteries of the heavenly treasure, drawing the precious, divine rays of light from the heavenly sanctuary, to shine in our hearts, as they shine upon the face of Jesus. The scoffers mock the waiting, watching ones, and inquire: "Where is the promise of His coming? You have been disappointed. Engage now with us, and you will prosper in worldly things. Get gain, get money, and be honored of the world." The waiting ones look upward and answer: "We are watching." And by turning from earthly pleasure and worldly fame, and from the deceitfulness of riches, they show themselves to be in that position. By watching they become strong; they overcome sloth and selfishness and love of ease. Affliction's fire kindles upon them, and the waiting time seems long. They sometimes grieve, and faith falters; but they rally again, overcome their fears and doubts, and while their eyes are directed heavenward, say to their adversaries: "I am watching, I am waiting the return of my Lord. I will glory in tribulation, in affliction, in necessities."

We are hurrying about, engaging with zeal and earnestness in different enterprises, but God is forgotten, and

The desire of our Lord is that we should be so watching, that when He cometh and knocketh we may open to Him immediately. A blessing is pronounced upon those servants whom He finds watching [1,335 days, Dan. 12]. "He shall gird Himself, and make them to sit down to meat, and will come forth and serve them." Who among us in these last days will be thus especially honored by the Master of assemblies? Are we prepared without delay to open to Him immediately and welcome Him in? Watch, watch, watch. Nearly all have ceased their watching and waiting; we are not ready to open to Him immediately. The love of the world has so occupied our thoughts that our eyes are not turned upward, but downward to the earth. We are hurrying about, engaging with zeal and earnestness in different enterprises, but God is forgotten, and the heavenly treasure is not valued. We are not in a waiting, watching position. The love of the world and the deceitfulness of riches eclipse our faith, and we do not long for, and love, the appearing of our Saviour. We try too hard to take care of self ourselves. We are uneasy and greatly lack a firm trust in God. Many worry and work, contrive and plan, fearing they may suffer need. They cannot afford time to pray or to attend religious meetings and, in their care for themselves, leave no chance for God to care for them. And the Lord does not do much for them, for they give Him no opportunity. The do too much for themselves, and believe and trust in God too little.

The love of the world has a terrible hold upon the people whom the Lord has commanded to watch and pray always, lest coming suddenly He find them sleeping. "Love not the world, neither the things that are in the world. If any man love the world, the love of the Father is not in him. For all that is in the world, the lust of the flesh, and the lust of the eyes, and the pride of life, is not of the Father, but is of the world. And the world passeth away, and the lust thereof: but he that doeth the will of God abideth forever."

I have been shown that God's people who profess to believe present truth are not in a waiting, watching position. *They are increasing in riches* and are laying up their treasures upon the earth. *They are becoming rich in worldly things*, but not rich toward God. *They do not believe in the shortness of time; they do not believe* that the end of all things is at hand, that Christ is at the door. *They may profess* much faith; but they deceive their own souls, for *they will act out* all the faith that they really possess. *Their works show* the character of their faith and testify to those around them that the coming of Christ is not to be in this generation. According to their faith will be their works. *Their preparations are being made* to remain in this world. *They are adding house to house*, and land to land, and are citizens of this world. The condition of poor Lazarus feeding upon the crumbs from the rich man's table is preferable to that of these professors. If they possessed genuine faith, instead of increasing their treasures upon the earth they would be selling off, freeing themselves from the cumbersome things of earth and transferring their treasure before them to heaven. Then their interest and hearts will be there, for the heart of man will be where his greatest treasure is. Most of those who profess to believe the truth testify that that which they value the most is in this world. For this they have care, wearing anxiety, and labor. To preserve and add to their treasure is the study of their lives. They have transferred so little to heaven, have taken so little stock in the heavenly treasure, that their minds are not specially attracted to that better country. They have taken large stock in the enterprises of this earth, and these investments, like the magnet, draw down their minds from the heavenly and imperishable to the earthly and corruptible. "Where your treasure is, there will your heart be also." Selfishness girds many about as with iron bands. It is "my farm," "my goods," "my trade," "my merchandise." Even the claims of common humanity are disregarded by them. Men and women professing to be waiting and loving the appearing of their Lord are shut up to self. The noble, the godlike, they have parted with. The love of the world, the lust of the flesh, the lust of the eyes, the pride of life, have so fastened upon them that they are blinded. They are corrupted by the world and discern it not. They talk of love to God, but their fruits show not the love they express. They rob Him in tithes and offerings, and the withering curse of God is upon them. The truth has been illuminating their pathway on every side. God has wrought wonderfully in the salvation of souls in their own households, but where are their offerings, presented to Him in grateful thanks for all His tokens of mercy to them? Many of them are as unthankful as the brute creation. The sacrifice for man was infinite, beyond the comprehension of the strongest intellect, yet men who claim to be partakers of these heavenly benefits, which were brought to them at so great a cost, are too thoroughly selfish to make any real sacrifice for God. Their minds are upon the world, the world, the world. In the forty-ninth psalm we read: "They that trust in their wealth, and boast themselves in the multitude of their riches; none of them can by any means redeem his brother, nor give to God a ransom for him (for the redemption of their soul is precious, and it ceaseth forever)." If all would bear in mind, and could in a small degree appreciate, the immense sacrifice made by Christ, they would feel rebuked for their fearfulness and their supreme selfishness. "Our God shall come, and shall not keep silence: a fire shall devour before Him, and it shall be very tempestuous round about Him. He shall call to the heavens from above, and to the earth, that He may judge His people. Gather My saints together unto Me; those that have made a covenant with Me by sacrifice." Because of selfishness and love of the world, God is forgotten, and many have barrenness of soul, and cry: "My leanness, my leanness." The Lord has lent means to His people to prove them, to test the depth of their professed love for Him. Some would let go of Him and give up their heavenly treasure rather than to decrease their earthly possessions and make a covenant with Him by sacrifice. He calls for them to sacrifice; but the love of the world closes their ears, and they will not hear.

I looked to see who of those who professed to be looking for Christ's coming possessed a willingness to sacrifice offerings to God of their abundance. I could see a few humble poor ones who, like the poor widow, were stinting themselves and casting in their mite. Every such offering is accounted of God as precious treasure. But those who are acquiring means, and adding to their possessions, are far behind. They do comparatively nothing to what they might. They are withholding, and robbing God, for they are fearful they shall come to want. They dare not trust God. This is one of the reasons that, as a people, we are so sickly, and so many are falling into their graves. The covetous are among us. Lovers of the world, also those who have stinted the laborer in his hire, are among us. Men who had none of this world, who were poor and dependent on their labor, have been dealt with closely and unjustly. The lover of the world, with a hard face and harder heart, has grudgingly paid over the small sum earned by hard toil. Just so they are dealing with their Master, whose servants they profess to be. Just in this grudging manner do they put into the treasury of God. The man in the parable had not where to bestow his goods, and the Lord cut short his unprofitable life. So will He deal with many. How difficult, in this corrupt age, to keep from growing worldly and selfish. How easy to become ungrateful to the Giver of all our mercies. Great watchfulness is needed, and much prayer, to keep the soul with all diligence. "Take ye heed, watch and pray: for ye know not when the time is."[297]

---

[297] Ellen G. White, *Testimonies for the Church*, vol. 2 (Mountain View, CA: Pacific Press, 1871), pp. 189–199, emphasis mine.

Bibliography

Andrews Study Bible. Berrien Springs, MI: Andrews University Press, 2010.

"Battle of Fariskur." Wikipedia. https://1ref.us/1k5 (accessed February 9, 2021).

"Battle of Thermopylae." Britannica. https://1ref.us/1k4 (accessed February 9, 2021).

"Bible translations into Arabic." Wikipedia. https://1ref.us/1jk (accessed February 8, 2021).

"Bible translations into Armenian." Wikipedia. https://1ref.us/1ji (accessed February 8, 2021).

"Bible translations into Persian." Wikipedia. https://1ref.us/1jj (accessed February 8, 2021).

Boettner, Loraine. *Roman Catholicism.* Philadelphia, PA: Presbyterian and Reformed, 1962.

Burrill, Russell. "The New World Order." *Seminars Unlimited.*

"Council of Ephesus." Wikipedia. https://1ref.us/1jf (accessed February 8, 2021).

de Souza, Elias Brasil. *Adult Sabbath School Bible Study Guide.* 1st Quarter 2020.

Finley, Mark. *Understanding Daniel and Revelation.* Nampa, ID: Pacific Press Publishing Association, 2020.

"First Council of Nicaea." Britannica. https://1ref.us/1jn (accessed February 8, 2021).

Foxe, John. *Foxe's Book of Martyrs.* England: John Day, 1563.

Froom, Leroy Edwin. *The Prophetic Faith of our Fathers.* Vol. 4. Hagerstown, MD: Review and Herald Publishing Association, 1954.

Gill, N.S. "Nabopolassar." ThoughtCo. https://1ref.us/1k1 (accessed February 9, 2021).

It Is Written Bible Study Lessons, Unsealing Daniel's Mysteries. Lesson 1. "Prophetic Symbols Revealed." Chattanooga, TN, 2004–2020.

"John the Apostle." Wikipedia. https://1ref.us/1jd (accessed February 8, 2021).

"Laodicea on the Lycus." Wikipedia. https://1ref.us/1jo (accessed February 8, 2021).

"Lateran Treaty." Britannica. https://1ref.us/1jv (accessed February 8, 2021).

"Leonids." Wikipedia. https://1ref.us/1jr (accessed February 8, 2021).

"1755 Lisbon earthquake." Wikipedia. https://1ref.us/1jq (accessed February 8, 2021).

Marrapodi, Eric. "Why Ralph Reed matters." CNN Belief Blog. https://1ref.us/1jy (accessed February 8, 2021).

Maxwell, C. Mervyn. *God Cares*. Vol. 2. Boise, ID: Pacific Press Publishing Association, 1985.

Morey, Robert A. *The Encyclopedia of Religion*. Edited by Paul Meagher. *Islam Unveiled: The True Desert Storm*. Shermans Dale, PA: The Scholars Press, 1991.

"Mormons at a glance." BBC. https://1ref.us/1ju (accessed February 8, 2021).

Neuhaus, Richard. *The Catholic Moment*. San Francisco, CA: Harper & Row Publishers, 1987.

"New England's Dark Day." Wikipedia. https://1ref.us/163 (accessed February 8, 2021).

New Living Translation, Life Application Study Bible. Carol Stream, IL: Tyndale House Publishers, Inc., 2004.

Parrinder, Geoffrey, ed. *World Religions From Ancient History to the Present*. New York, NY: Facts on File Publications, 1983.

"Patmos the Island of the Apocalypse (Revelation)." Patmos Island. https://1ref.us/1je (accessed February 8, 2021).

Pietersma, Albert and Benjamin G. Wright, III. *A new English translation of the Septuagint*. New York, NY: Oxford University Press, 2007.

"Roman Catholicism." EUROPEAN-AMERICAN EVANGELISTIC CRUSADES. https://www.eaec.org/cults/romancatholic.htm.

Seaton, Bernard E. "Thy Kingdom Come." *Adult Sabbath School Lessons,* October 25, 1981.

Shea, William H. *The Abundant Life Bible Amplifier, Daniel 1–7.* Nampa, ID: Pacific Press Publishing Association, 1996.

———. *The Abundant Life Bible Amplifier, Daniel 7–12.* Nampa, ID: Pacific Press Publishing Association, 1996.

Smith, Uriah. *The Prophecies of Daniel and the Revelation.* Mountain View, CA: Pacific Press Publishing Association, 1944.

Stefanovic, Ranko. "The Seven Heads of the Beast in Revelation 17." Ministry Magazine. https://1ref.us/1jz (accessed February 9, 2021).

Strong's Exhaustive Concordance of the Bible. Peabody, MA: Hendrickson Publishers.

"Terror experts see a new kind of war on the horizon." Walla Walla Union Bulletin. July 10, 2005.

"The Battle of Actium." History. https://1ref.us/1k6 (accessed February 9, 2021).

"The beliefs of Jehovah's Witnesses and how they differ from mainstream Christianity." BBC. https://1ref.us/1jt (accessed February 8, 2021).

"The Communist Manifesto." Wikipedia. https://1ref.us/1jw (accessed February 8, 2021).

"The Daughters of Allah." Muslim Hope. https://1ref.us/1js (accessed February 8, 2021).

The Seventh-day Adventist Bible Commentary. Vol. 8. Dictionary. Washington, DC: Review and Herald Publishing Association, 1960.

"The Tenth Persecution, Under Diocletian, A.D. 303." Bible Study Tools. https://1ref.us/1jh (accessed February 8, 2021).

"THE ROMAN EMPIRE FROM 313–538 AD." Lineage Journey. https://1ref.us/1jx (accessed February 8, 2021).

Thompsen, Alden. *Probe Study Guide.* Lesson 1, July 1, 2006.

Valente, Francesca Romana. "7 PAGAN FESTIVALS WE STILL CELEBRATE TODAY." THROUGH ETERNITY. https://1ref.us/1jl (accessed February 8, 2021).

White, Ellen G. "A Missionary Appeal." *The Review and Herald Publishing Association,* December 15, 1885.

———. *Acts of the Apostles, The.* Mountain View, CA: Pacific Press Publishing Association, 1911.

———. *Adventist Home, The.* Hagerstown, MD: Pacific Press Publishing Association, 1952.

———. *A Word to the Little Flock.* Washington, DC: Review and Herald Publishing Association, 1847.

———. *Christian Experience and Teachings of Ellen G. White.* Mountain View, CA: Pacific Press Publishing Association, 1922.

———. *Christ's Object Lessons.* Washington, DC: Review and Herald Publishing Association, 1900.

———. *Christian Service.* Hagerstown, MD: Review and Herald Publishing Association, 1925.

———. *Christ Triumphant.* Hagerstown, MD: Review and Herald Publishing Association, 1999.

———. *Confrontation.* Washington, DC: Review and Herald Publishing Association, 1971.

———. *Counsels to Writers and Editors.* Nashville, TN: Southern Publishing Association, 1946.

———. *Desire of Ages, The.* Mountain View, CA: Pacific Press Publishing Association, 1898.

———. *Early Writings.* Washington, DC: Review and Herald Publishing Association, 1882.

———. *Education.* Mountain View, CA: Pacific Press Publishing Association, 1903.

———. *Ellen G. White 1888 Materials, The.* Washington, DC: Ellen G. White Estate, 1987.

———. *Faith I Live By, The.* Washington, DC: Review and Herald Publishing Association, 1958.

———. *Fundamentals of Christian Education.* Nashville, TN: Southern Publishing Association, 1923.

———. *Great Controversy, The.* Mountain View, CA: Pacific Press Publishing Association, 1911.

———. *Last Day Events.* Boise, ID: Pacific Press Publishing Association, 1992.

———. *Manuscript Releases.* Vol. 12. Silver Spring, MD: Ellen G. White Estate, 1990.

———. *Manuscript Releases.* Vol. 18. Silver Spring, MD: Ellen G. White Estate, 1990.

———. *Maranatha.* Washington, DC: Review and Herald Publishing Association, 1976.

———. "Our Great Treasure-House." *The Signs of the Times,* July 4, 1906.

———. "Patmos." *The Review and Herald,* September 5, 1912.

———. *Patriarchs and Prophets.* Mountain View, CA: Pacific Press Publishing Association, 1890.

———. "Personal Responsibility and Work." *The Home Missionary,* November 1, 1897.

———. *Prophets and Kings.* Mountain View, CA: Pacific Press Publishing Association, 1917.

———. *Publishing Ministry, The.* Hagerstown, MD: Review and Herald Publishing Association, 1983.

———. *SDA Bible Commentary.* Vol. 4. Washington, DC: Review and Herald Publishing Association, 1955.

———. *SDA Bible Commentary.* Vol. 5. Washington, DC: Review and Herald Publishing Association, 1956.

———. *SDA Bible Commentary.* Vol. 6. Washington, DC: Review and Herald Publishing Association, 1956.

———. *SDA Bible Commentary.* Vol. 7. Washington, DC: Review and Herald Publishing Association, 1957.

———. *SDA Bible Commentary.* Vol. 7A. Washington, DC: Review and Herald Publishing Association, 1970.

———. *Selected Messages.* book 1. Washington, DC: Review and Herald Publishing Association, 1958.

———. *Selected Messages.* book 2. Washington, DC: Review and Herald Publishing Association, 1958.

———. *Selected Messages.* book 3. Washington, DC: Review and Herald Publishing Association, 1980.

———. *Testimonies for the Church.* Vol. 1. Mountain View, CA: Pacific Press Publishing Association, 1868.

———. *Testimonies for the Church.* Vol. 2. Mountain View, CA: Pacific Press Publishing Association, 1871.

———. *Testimonies for the Church.* Vol. 5. Mountain View, CA: Pacific Press Publishing Association, 1889.

———. *Testimonies for the Church.* Vol. 6. Mountain View, CA: Pacific Press Publishing Association, 1901.

———. *Testimonies for the Church.* Vol. 8. Mountain View, CA: Pacific Press Publishing Association, 1904.

———. *Testimonies for the Church.* Vol. 9. Mountain View, CA: Pacific Press Publishing Association, 1909.

———. *Testimonies to Ministers and Gospel Workers.* Mountain View, CA: Pacific Press Publishing Association, 1923.

———. "The Rebellion of Korah." *The Review and Herald,* November 12, 1903.

White, Gavin. "Babylonian Star-lore." Sky Script. https://1ref.us/1k0 (accessed February 9, 2021).

"Who was King Nebuchadnezzar's son?" Bible Q. https://1ref.us/1k3 (accessed February 9, 2021).

TEACH Services, Inc.
P U B L I S H I N G

We invite you to view the complete
selection of titles we publish at:
www.TEACHServices.com

We encourage you to write us
with your thoughts about this,
or any other book we publish at:
info@TEACHServices.com

TEACH Services' titles may be purchased in
bulk quantities for educational, fund-raising,
business, or promotional use.
bulksales@TEACHServices.com

Finally, if you are interested in seeing
your own book in print, please contact us at:
publishing@TEACHServices.com

We are happy to review your manuscript at no charge.

www.ingramcontent.com/pod-product-compliance
Lightning Source LLC
Chambersburg PA
CBHW071151160426
43196CB00011B/2056